Anything Dale Ralph Davis touches
say that about the Scriptures since
thus I should say that Davis reveals
there. His commentary on Luke is cl~
insightful exposition along with theo
commentaries, I find it quite easy to set them aside, but Davis's
exposition of Luke is so winsome, wise, and illuminating that I
found it hard to put down. His pastoral application with stories
and illustrations is nothing short of brilliant. Read the exposition,
meditate and pray on what you read, and encounter Jesus Christ.

Thomas R. Schreiner

James Buchanan Harrison Professor of New Testament Interpretation
Associate Dean, The Southern Baptist Theological Seminary,
Louisville, Kentucky

This pithy and well-informed exposition is a delight to dig through.
It concisely and creatively opens up Luke's Gospel section by section.
The footnotes show that the author has read widely and done his
homework. Illustrations are numerous, some humorous, some
harrowing (like contemporary accounts of tortured Christians).
Most significantly, the character and brilliance of Jesus shine forth.
Readers at all levels will deepen in their knowledge and devotion
to Him through the wisdom that abounds in these pages.

Robert W. Yarbrough

Professor of New Testament, Covenant Theological Seminary,
St. Louis, Missouri, USA

Brimming with insightful exegesis, theological depth, vivid illustration and pastoral application, these two volumes are vintage
Dale Ralph Davis. Whether you use them in personal devotion, or
a small group, or as a preacher seeking to teach your congregation,
this engaging journey through Luke's gospel will be a very useful
and edifying guide.

Reuben Hunter

Pastor, Trinity West Church, West London

A remarkable, crisply written, practical expository commentary.
As always, Dale Ralph Davis does what any skilled chef does. With
due diligence, Davis raids the exegetical pantry stocked with Bible
dictionaries, Bible translations, exegetical-critical commentaries,
theological wordbooks, scholarly articles, and other written works
on Luke. Using the ingredients gathered, he insightfully engages

the text of Scripture with a solid understanding of the original language and the perspective of an Old Testament Scholar. Then, in his characteristically plain-spoken and often witty style of writing, Ralph serves up a straightforward, theocentric, finger-on-the Text, applicable, engaging, and incredibly tasty two-volume commentary on the Gospel of Luke. Davis not only informs your mind (helpful technical footnotes are included on the bottom of the pages); he feeds your soul, fills your heart, and moves you to praise and thank God for the one who came to seek and to save the lost (Luke 19:10).

Steve Jussely
Senior Pastor, Lakeland Presbyterian Church (PCA),
Flowood, Mississippi,
Former Adjunct Professor of Homiletics,
Reformed Theological Seminary

Written with Dale Ralph Davis' usual clarity, humour and warmth, these volumes will not only serve as a sure guide to help readers understand Luke's Gospel but will strengthen them in their faith in the Jesus about whom Luke writes.

Peter Orr
Lecturer in New Testament,
Moore Theological College, Sydney

Dr Davis is one of the most hospitable commentators you'll ever know. His books, like his preaching, have an unusual ability to combine theological precision with a warm and pleasant style. You'll be glad you opened the cover and settled in. You won't find the drudgery and technicality that are common in other commentators. But you will find helpful and engaging footnotes. You also won't find even a hint of the dry, doubting, soul-sucking unbelief that resides in many academic commentaries. But here is a scholar (he is a ninja in the original languages) and a convicted pastor and a winsome believer. In Dr Davis' Luke exposition, your eye is drawn to authorial intent and your heart is drawn to the matchlessness of Christ. Dr Davis continually reminds me to preach with the agenda of the text at the forefront and the wise pastor's effort to speak to the people where they are and bring them into the world of the text. This masterful Old Testament preacher knows his way around the New Testament as well!

Austin T. Duncan
Professor of Pastoral Ministries, Director of D.Min Studies, Director,
The MacArthur Center for Expository Preaching,
The Master's Seminary, Los Angeles, California

LUKE

On the Road to Jerusalem

LUKE

On the Road to Jerusalem

Dale Ralph Davis

CHRISTIAN
FOCUS

Dale Ralph Davis lives in Tennessee with his wife. He was formerly Minister in Residence of First Presbyterian Church, Columbia, South Carolina. Prior to that he was pastor of Woodland Presbyterian Church, Hattiesburg, Mississippi and Professor of Old Testament at Reformed Theological Seminary, Jackson, Mississippi.

Copyright © 2021 Dale Ralph Davis

ISBN 978-1-5271-0642-0

10 9 8 7 6 5 4 3 2 1

Printed in 2021
by
Christian Focus Publications Ltd.,
Geanies House, Fearn, Ross-shire,
IV20 1TW, Scotland, U.K.

www.christianfocus.com

Cover design by Moose77

Printed and bound by
Bell & Bain, Glasgow

Contents

Abbreviations

AB	Anchor Bible
ABD	*Anchor Bible Dictionary*
AV	Authorized Version
BECN	Baker Exegetical Commentary on the New Testament
BST	The Bible Speaks Today
CSB	Christian Standard Bible
DJG	*Dictionary of Jesus and the Gospels*
EBC	*Expositor's Bible Commentary*
EGGNT	Exegetical Guide to the Greek New Testament
ESV	English Standard Version
HCSB	Holman Christian Standard Bible
ICC	International Critical Commentary
ISBE	*International Standard Bible Encyclopedia*
KJV	King James Version
LXX	The Septuagint
NAC	New American Commentary
NASB	New American Standard Bible (updated ed.)
NDB	*New Bible Dictionary*
NCB	New Century Bible
NET	New English Translation
NICNT	New International Commentary on the New Testament

NICOT	New International Commentary on the Old Testament
NIDB	*New Interpreter's Dictionary of the Bible*
NIDNTTE	*New International Dictionary of New Testament Theology and Exegesis*
NIGTC	New International Greek Testament Commentary
NIV	New International Version
NKJV	New King James Version
PNTC	Pillar New Testament Commentary
RSV	Revised Standard Version
TDNT	*Theological Dictionary of the New Testament*
TEV	Today's English Version
TNTC	Tyndale New Testament Commentaries
TOTC	Tyndale Old Testament Commentaries
TWOT	*Theological Wordbook of the Old Testament*
ZECNT	Zondervan Exegetical Commentary on the New Testament
ZIBBC	*Zondervan Illustrated Bible Backgrounds Commentary*

Preface

I have a personality disorder that has controlled my life. I am always driven to pull for the underdog. Which explains why I have spent most of my academic and pastoral days preaching, teaching, and writing on what we usually call the Old Testament. It has always been, it seems, the 'under-testament,' shamefully neglected in the church. One dreams, then, of redressing that wrong. Still, one dare not ignore the New Testament. One dare not want to right a wrong by committing another wrong; hence I've probably spent forty per cent of my time in NT studies, though, for myself, I tend to find the New Testament more difficult than the Old Testament. One day, while in a New Testament orbit, I had noticed that the 'Focus on the Bible' series seemed to have no 'Luke' volume. One should not be curious about such things, but, upon inquiry, I was told I could submit one if I liked. Which nicely occupied four years.

I should alert you to certain matters. This commentary is exegetically based but is cast in an expository form and is not allergic to application (though I do not major on this last). I try at least to keep a proper balance between 'forest' and 'trees.' Translations of biblical texts are my own unless noted otherwise. And I've provided no 'proper' introduction to Luke (see the first chapter). As our forbears might say, there are 'sundry and divers' places where a reader can find that material.

This book is the work of an unprofitable servant (17:10) but is nevertheless dedicated to the One who came to seek and to save the lost (19:10)—even though He had to come into a Presbyterian manse to find him.

DALE RALPH DAVIS

June 2020

11

A Working Outline for Luke

[The commentary does not religiously follow this outline; it is provided as a 'reader's map' for Luke's gospel]

Preface, 1:1-4

I. **A New Chapter in World History, 1:5-4:13**
   Remnant church, 1:5-2:52
   Faithful forerunner, 3:1-20
   Triumphant Savior, 3:21-4:13

II. **The Year of the Lord's Favor, 4:14-9:50**
   An introduction to Jesus' ministry, 4:14-5:16
      Negative, 4:14-30
      Positive, 4:31-5:16
   Jesus and His critics, 5:17-6:11
   An introduction to Jesus' teaching, 6:12-49
   Jesus and His friends, 7:1-50 (centurion, widow, John, sinner)
   The problem of the word of God, 8:1-21
   Jesus and His triumphs, 8:22-56
   An introduction to Jesus' discipleship, 9:1-50

III. **The Turn in the Road (or: The Shadow of the Cross), 9:51-19:10**
   Preparing the Lord's way, 9:51-10:24
   A critique of Judaism, 10:25-37
   Proper devotion, 10:38-11:13

The problem with 'this generation,'
11:14-12:12

The priorities of the kingdom, 12:13-53

The kingdom of God and the Jewish people,
12:54-14:24

The cost of discipleship—again, 14:25-35

Answer to critics: the hilarity of grace, 15:1-32

Instruction of disciples: the use of riches,
16:1-31

Kingdom servants, 17:1-10

The kingdom: scope, coming, and justice,
17:11-18:8

Humility and kingdom, 18:9-30

The shadow of the cross and Jericho grace,
18:31-19:10

IV. The Time of Jerusalem's Visitation, 19:11-24:53

Perspective, 19:11-27

Triumph and tragedy, 19:28-48

Conflict with the leaders of Israel, 20:1-21:4

The destiny of Jerusalem, 21:5-38

The Lord's supper and teaching, 22:1-38

The Lord's prayer and arrest, 22:39-53

The Lord's disciple—and failure, 22:54-65

The Lord's trial and innocence, 22:66-23:25

The Lord's death—and victory, 23:26-49

The Lord's resurrection—and perplexity,
23:50-24:12

The Lord's appearance—and joy, 24:13-35

Epilogue as prologue, 24:36-53

1

Having Jesus for Lunch
(Luke 14:1-24)

Here we meet with four scenes around the lunch table. A prominent Pharisee invited Jesus to Sabbath lunch (v. 1). We don't know where this occurs—Luke is sparse on such detail. But all 24 verses take place around the table. The underlying theme is still 'the kingdom of God and the Jewish people'.[1] I think we can divide up the text by considering certain *questions* Jesus seems to be posing to His hearers. I say 'seems to' because Jesus does not overtly or explicitly ask these questions, but they seem to be implied in and catch the thrust of what He is saying.

In verses 1-6, then, He seems to ask, **Can you see your bondage?** The Pharisees there were 'watching him closely' (v. 1). And—what do you know—there's a man with dropsy (edema)[2] right in front of Him (v. 2). Was this fellow a 'plant'? Commentators debate the matter, but I think he was. Quite likely he himself did not know he was being 'used'. So Jesus 'answers' the unexpressed attitude of the legal experts and Pharisees with, 'Is it lawful to heal on the Sabbath or not?' (v. 3). But they are silent (v. 4a). It's a non-cooperative silence, a challenging silence, a silence

---

1. See our introductory comments to 12:54-13:21 in *Luke 1-13: The Year of the Lord's Favor* (Ross-shire: Christian Focus Publications, 2021), p. 235.

2. A condition in which there's an excessive accumulation of fluid in tissues or in a body cavity that causes swelling.

that says, 'Step into the trap and then see what we think.' So Jesus does. He takes hold of the fellow, heals him, and lets him go, then poses His second question: 'Should one of you have a son or an ox that falls into a well—wouldn't he immediately haul him out on the Sabbath day?' (v. 5).[3] He wouldn't holler down, would he, with 'Son, just hang on a few more hours till the Sabbath's over; you can do it—other people have had broken legs from such falls and lived to tell about it.' No—out of simple compassion any one of these fellows would pull out a son or an ox on the Sabbath day. The claim of compassion would overrule the stricture of tradition. Again, they are silent (v. 6), but this time it is the silence of defeat.

Is it too much to think Jesus is making an appeal to these Pharisees? As if to say, Can't you see that your tenacious commitment to your extra-biblical Sabbath traditions can keep you from living out a proper piety? Isn't there something wrong if you would have a man suffer dropsy for another day [cf. 13:14] rather than seeing him get relief on the Sabbath? Haven't you tied yourselves up into a contorted box when the Sabbath gets so associated with tying knots or untying knots, with lighting or extinguishing fires, with whether a tailor walks out with his needle—and dozens of such picky details you've added to biblical commandments?[4] Don't you feel the misery of being slaves to man-made requirements?[5] There is something terribly wrong when Jesus even has to ask the question of verse 3. But, of course, these men suffer from an even deeper bondage, for the problem is not merely that they are sticklers for legalistic rectitude as that they hate and

---

3. The Dead Sea Scrolls (Qumran) sect had stricter provisions (see I. H. Marshall, *The Gospel of Luke*, NIGTC [Grand Rapids: Eerdmans, 1978], p. 580), but Jesus is not dealing with them.

4. On Jewish Sabbath observance reflected in the Mishnah, see Emil Schürer, *The History of the Jewish People in the Age of Jesus Christ*, new rev. ed. (Edinburgh: T. & T. Clark, 1979), vol. 2:467-75.

5. The problem is not limited to first century Judaism. One can meet an array of such strictures in contemporary Christian circles, such as: you toy with apostasy if you allow your children to go to public (as in the US) school; Christian young people must not 'date,' but follow a 'courting' procedure; Christian women must not wear make-up; Christian married couples must never use contraceptives. Such matters may be held more tenaciously in some circles than the Apostles' Creed.

despise Him—so entrenched is their anti-Jesus-ism. And that is a bondage only the Father can break (John 6:44).

In verses 7-11 Jesus seems to ask, **Can you see your pride?** He was noting how the Pharisee's guests were trying to choose the prime positions at table. Your place at table reflected your social status, and this was so not only in a Jewish context but throughout the Greco-Roman world.[6] So Jesus told a parable, a sort of application of Proverbs 25:6-7. Imagine, Jesus says, the scramble for seats at a marriage banquet where this passion for reputation would be so obvious. It seems, however, that the most honorable guests tended to come a bit late.[7] That would accord with current practice in the American south where guests are said to be 'fashionably late'. This, of course, could put someone in a real pickle. If one had already nailed down a 'high class' position, the host might come along with a more prominent late arrival and ask the occupant to vacate his coveted place in favor of the newcomer. 'Give place to this fellow' (v. 9). Public demotion—pure, shame-faced embarrassment. Better to start out low than end up there. So Jesus advises, 'Settle down in the lowest place' (v. 10) and the host will come by and make a most welcome correction. And how admired (or envied) one would be then!

Someone may say, however, that Jesus' advice appeals to the crassest form of self-interest and is scarcely worthy of Him. I don't think I'd worry about that; Jesus will make His own point in verse 11. In verses 7-10, is it too much to assume Jesus may have spoken then with a twinkle in His eye? Or better perhaps, that He said these words tongue-in-cheek? As if He were telling the guests, 'Let me give you a little practical tip in order to avoid huge public embarrassment in situations like this.' Is there also an unspoken undertow: 'Can't you see how ludicrous your mad game of "musical chairs" is, as you demonstrate what slaves you are to the idol of recognition?' In short, Can't you see your pride?

Naturally, we can see *their* pride; often ours is not so obvious. J. B. Phillips, the New Testament translator of

---

6. See, e.g., Mark Strauss, 'Luke,' ZIBBC, 1:440-41.

7. Marshall, p. 581.

the mid-twentieth century, was in consultation with a psychiatrist, Dr Leonard Browne. Browne knew that one of Phillips' problems was 'shame at the unacceptable conceit revealed by his inner thoughts'. Phillips was told he should jot down these thoughts. One of his entries in May 1945 read: 'I want to be colossal or soon die. Christianity is a bore unless it can help me to demonstrate my uniqueness. I really haven't any interest in others—unless they are connected with building up my reputation. *My reputation*—that's the thing! The best vicar ever!'[8] That is stark and perhaps shocking. We try to evade such candor. But I have to say I understand that perfectly. Pardon the grammar, but it is both mad and me. It is well with my soul to see how unwell my soul is.

Jesus draws His own application in verse 11: 'Because everyone who exalts himself will be humbled, and the one who humbles himself will be exalted.' The main verbs are 'divine passives', i.e., will be humbled or exalted *by God*. We run on to language like this in Jesus elsewhere (13:30; 18:14), and therefore we may regard it as a sort of commonplace. It's nothing of the sort. It's a reference to the last judgment and to God's action at that time, and so this matter of nailing down prominent seats is not a bit of trivia—it is a symptom of that self-centered arrogance and self-idolatry that will be damned. 'If self-admiration and exaltation can lead to disastrous consequences in human social settings, it will lead to even more disastrous results in the final judgment.'[9]

Thirdly, Jesus' words to His host ask, **Can you see your insulation?** (vv. 12-14). Some may be aghast that Jesus would dare to instruct His host about his hospitality. But we must beware of making assumptions about what folks must not do. I remember my next older brother, who was about fourteen at the time, sitting in the back pew in a Sunday evening service. My father who was preaching thought he saw him whispering to his friend and called him out on it: 'Jim should sit up and listen to his father's sermon!' Now that's the sort of thing one saves for later; one doesn't give a personal rebuke right

---

8. Vera Phillips and Edwin Robertson, *The Wounded Healer* (Grand Rapids: Eerdmans, 1985), p. 12 (emphasis in original).

9. David E. Garland, *Luke*, ZECNT (Grand Rapids: Zondervan, 2011), p. 576.

in a church service. But my father did. He wasn't necessarily conventional. And neither is Jesus—so He takes the liberty to correct His host's hospitality, blunt and ungracious as that may seem.

It's common for expositors to assure us that Jesus does *not* mean that we can *never* invite friends or relatives for dinner, and that's fine. But Jesus wants to press His host to see hospitality as an opportunity for generosity and to use it as such. There is such a danger of getting caught in a pay-back routine. 'When you make a lunch or dinner, don't summon your friends nor your brothers nor your relatives nor rich neighbors, lest they also invite you back and "pay-back" occurs' (v. 12). Instead, when throwing a reception, Jesus says to invite the poor, disabled, lame, blind, who 'do not have the resources to pay you back, for you will be paid back at the resurrection of the righteous' (v. 14).

Jesus' counsel fits nicely with the directions Yahweh gave Israel in Deuteronomy. For example, when they celebrated the 'Feast of Weeks,' they were to be glad 'before Yahweh your God, you and your son and your daughter and your male servant and your female servant, and the Levite within your gates, and the sojourner, the orphan and the widow who are among you, at the place which Yahweh your God will choose to make his name dwell there' (Deut. 16:11; cf. 14:29; 16:14; 26:11). There were others beyond the family circle, ones with a touch-and-go livelihood, who were to be included in their festive meals at the sanctuary. It is interesting how Jesus links 'last things' with here-and-now needs, as if the 'resurrection of the righteous' should supply motive enough for inclusion of poor, disabled, lame, and blind. Eschatology should drive present-time service. But Jesus' host and his ilk will have to break out of their cocoon of simply receiving pay-back invitations and enjoying adulation from their peers.

Bishop John Hooper (d. 1555, martyred by 'Bloody Mary') exemplified what Jesus had in mind. John Foxe describes something he discovered when Hooper was Bishop of Worcester:

> Twice I was, as I remember, in his house in Worcester, where, in his common hall, I saw a table spread with a good store of

meat, and beset full of beggars and poor folk. And I asking his servants what this meant, they told me that every day their lord and master's manner was to have customably to dinner a certain number of the poor folk of the said city, by course, who were served by four at a mess, with whole and wholesome meats. And when they were served (being before examined by him or his deputies, of the Lord's prayer, the Articles of their faith, and the Ten Commandments), then he himself sat down to dinner, and not before.[10]

We ourselves, however, must take care not to throw stones at Pharisees, for we can so easily slide into the mode of only consorting with congenial Christian friends. And sometimes Jesus must push us out of *our* insulation. Perhaps we live in a university town and some university students (not necessarily professing Christians) show up at our church. What an opportunity to invite them home for lunch and conversation. Or, you may be part of a large and fairly affluent church, but if people come there because there is faithful biblical teaching, you will find plenty of folk who are not 'upper crust.' Here's a head of house, for example, who is currently unemployed, or a couple who work part-time jobs to make ends meet— ones you can make welcome by having them into your house and forming a bond with them. Or we might think of our neighborhoods. I live in what is thought to be the friendly American south. But move in and hardly any neighbors will come by to welcome you or introduce themselves. I usually have to go and greet my neighbors who had arrived long before I did. But no matter. It gives an opportunity to invite several of them over for dessert. Are they Christians? Not usually. Mostly pagans. But who knows what opportunity may arise over peach cobbler? Maybe we're wandering from Jesus' concern, but I don't think so. We have to watch out that we don't imprison ourselves in our own Christian hothouse. Can you see your insulation?

Finally, Jesus so much as asks His fellow diners, **Can you see your danger?** (vv. 15-24). Jesus' use of 'blessed' and His

---

10. Cited in J. C. Ryle, *Light from Old Times* (1890; reprint ed., Welwyn: Evangelical Press, 1980), pp. 92-93.

allusion to 'the resurrection of the righteous' in verse 14 sparked one of the guests to exclaim, 'How blessed whoever eats bread in the kingdom of God!' (v. 15; cf. 22:18, 29-30; Isa. 25:6-9). In response Jesus tells what we may call a parable with the sense: 'Well, yes, but there will be no such final blessedness if you despise the offer of grace to enter and enjoy the kingdom of God now.'

First, a bit of general background for the parable. Such major social affairs always involved a 'double' invitation. There was an initial one that gave the details and secured a commitment of the invitee to attend. Then, at the actual time of the dinner, another all's-ready-come-now invitation would be issued. Verses 16-17 reflect this practice; the host 'invited many' (v. 16), but then at a later time, at 'the hour of the supper,' he told those 'who *had been* invited' to come (v. 17). The initial invitation (and commitment to come) is essential, for the host needs to calculate how much meat to butcher and provide for the number of guests.[11] The initial acceptance obligates one to respond at the hour of the banquet (the 'second' invitation).

Now we can move on to details. Once we understand the initial commitment that was secured, we can appreciate the outrageous development Jesus depicts in verses 18-20. It's enough to snap the straps on your sandals.

Would you believe? 'One and all they began to beg off' (v. 18a). The first fellow says, 'I have bought a field and I really must go out and see it' (v. 18b). This is a smoke screen. No one would buy land without having already inspected it. One would want to know about springs and wells, trees, rainfall, position vis-à-vis the sun—all that before ever discussing a purchase.[12] Moreover, the dinner would begin in the late afternoon—there is so little time for such 'business' left in the day. This is a pure affront to the host.

Then there's the livestock dealer: 'I have bought five yoke of oxen and I am going to test them out' (v. 19). Five yoke of oxen. That is a humongous investment, which tells us he is

---

11. Kenneth E. Bailey, *Poet & Peasant* and *Through Peasant Eyes*, combined ed. (Grand Rapids: Eerdmans, 1983), p. 94.

12. Bailey, pp. 95-97.

both rich and likely lying. No one would buy oxen like that. One would test them *before* purchase, to see if they pulled well together, for example. Bailey likens this to a man calling his wife and telling her he has just purchased five used cars over the phone and he's going by the dealer's place to see what they're like and if they start.[13] One is tempted to ask, How do you spell 'dope'? This man simply doesn't want any part of the banquet he had agreed to attend.

Then there is lover boy, who says, 'I have married a wife and for that reason I am not able to come' (v. 20). He had recently married, and, though he had originally agreed to come to the supper, he seems to say that he and his new Mrs plan to do some love-making that afternoon and evening—and he would prefer that.

There's nothing wrong with real estate or livestock or wives in themselves; but these are not merely flimsy excuses, they are *hostile* ones. These men *despise* their host's invitation and regard him and his banquet with *disdain.* Here you see Jesus' method in this parable—He uses what would be regarded as a wild picture of things to depict an extreme danger. In normal Jewish circles, no one would dream of treating a host with such shoddiness and contempt. It would be on the level of Queen Elizabeth II showing up for a BBC interview wearing cut-offs and an old sweatshirt and in her bare feet. By such exaggeration Jesus holds up as in a mirror what the Jewish leadership is doing—how they are bending over backwards to reject God's offer of the kingdom through Jesus.

Well, there's a bit more in verses 21-23. But skip to verse 24 for Jesus' response: 'For I tell you that not one of those men who had been invited will taste of my supper.' Jesus is not simply rehearsing the words of the master of the house to his servant in the parable. If that were so, the 'you' in 24a would be singular. But that is not the case—it is plural (Gr. *humin*). These words are Jesus' own pronouncement to *all those* at the Pharisee's table that day and He refers to the banquet as 'my supper.' It is His declaration of rejection to all those who share the attitude of the invitees in the parable. Jesus could hardly say more clearly, 'Can you see your danger?'

---

13. Bailey, pp. 97-98.

Readers of Luke's gospel, however, must realize that arrogant rejection of Jesus is not something restricted to first-century Israel. It is always extant. I think of Benjamin Franklin, who was a close and cordial friend of evangelist George Whitefield. Whitefield did not fail in his most gracious way to press the gospel on Franklin. After Whitefield's death Franklin wrote, 'Mr Whitefield used to pray for my conversion, but never had the satisfaction of believing that his prayers were heard.'[14] Can you not hear the strain of arrogance in Franklin's statement, almost an air of smug superiority? That's what will keep any of us from Jesus' supper.

I have tried to stress the main thrust of Jesus' parable. However, in His parable Jesus includes two 'footnotes' and we should note those. The first footnote tells us that *grace is invincible*. No sooner does the master hear of his original guests' contempt (v. 21a) than he sends his slave out to rummage other guests (v. 21b; cf. v. 13!) from the streets and alleys. The idea may be that the leadership of Israel may reject Jesus' kingdom offer but the outcasts and no-counts in Israel may enjoy it. But let us stick to the main point: the rejection of the kingdom invitation did not cancel the banquet. The master went on to have his house filled (v. 23b). You simply cannot frustrate or defeat the grace of God. He is determined to have a people and He is going to get them, even if He must get them out of the riff-raff. Here, if I may twist a quote, it's as if Jesus says, 'I will build my church and the disdain and unbelief of men will never be able to stop it.'

The second footnote tells us that *grace is incredible*. I hesitate to use that adjective because 'incredible' is such an incredibly misused and overused word. Sportscasters can be some of the worst offenders. They will tout some athlete's achievements as 'incredible.' They may be impressive or amazing or dramatic or remarkable but for all that quite credible. It is almost incredibly disgusting to hear very credible matters billed as 'incredible.' Still, here in this text, grace is incredible.

---

14. A. A. Dallimore, *George Whitefield*, 2 vols. (Westchester, IL: Crossway, 1979), 2:453.

The slave is to go after the next batch of guests beyond the city limits into the country and 'compel (them) to come in' (v. 23).[15] Why 'compel'? Kenneth Bailey may be of help here with Middle Eastern background. Bailey says that should a nobleman issue an invitation to someone of a much lower class, that person feels duty-bound to spend the first fifteen minutes refusing the invitation, and he does so because he is convinced that the invitation cannot possibly be serious. Hence at some point in the extended conversation, the emissary must take him by the hand and gently urge him along. It seems too good to be true.[16]

When Ronald Reagan was governor of California he received a letter from one of the state's GIs stationed in Vietnam. The soldier was a resident of nearby Orangevale and he wrote the governor telling him about life in southeast Asia and of how much he missed his wife. In a word, he was miserable and wanted to tell his wife how much he loved her and longed for her. And this particular day was their anniversary and though he had sent her a card, he wondered, in case the card had not arrived, if the governor could take time to phone her to see if she was okay and then pass along his love for her. On 'anniversary day,' Reagan left his office early. He picked up a dozen red roses and delivered them to the soldier's wife in Orangevale. And then spent an unrushed hour with her, sipping coffee and asking about their children.[17] A phone call from the governor would've been moving, but flowers and a visit—it stretches belief. That's the import of verse 23; you never get over grace. 'Come, because everything is ready.'

---

15. This text must not be hijacked to justify strong-arm tactics and persecution.

16. Bailey, 108; see also his *Jesus Through Middle Eastern Eyes* (Downers Grove, IL: InterVarsity, 2008), pp. 317-18.

17. Michael K. Deaver, *A Different Drummer* (New York: Harper Collins, 2001), p. 177.

2

Jesus Goes on Disrupting
(Luke 14:25-35)

I may be overstating when I compare Jesus' pathway in Luke 14 to a tornado. But He has been terribly disrupting— blatantly healing on the Sabbath (vv. 1-6), billboarding the pride of the other guests (vv. 7-11), handing His host a revised guest list (vv. 12-14), and, with apparent arrogance, speaking of 'eating bread in the kingdom of God' (v. 15) as 'my banquet' (v. 24). And though the scene changes (v. 25), He doesn't stop—He goes right on disrupting. There are 'huge crowds' (v. 25) going along with Him but He attempts to destroy the 'Jesus bandwagon' by repeatedly declaring who 'cannot be my disciple' (vv. 26, 27, 33). It's as if Jesus is determined to upset not only His severe critics (vv. 1-24) but His potential friends (vv. 25-35). So let us try to follow Him—at least in the text.

First, notice **the claim the would-be disciple hears** (vv. 25-26). Verse 26 is stark: 'If anyone comes to me and does not hate his father and mother and wife and children and brothers and sisters, and, yes, even his own life—he cannot be my disciple.' In my opinion expositions and commentaries often get us off in the wrong direction here. They will start saying things like: Now Jesus doesn't literally mean 'hate'; we can run to Matthew 10:37-38 and see what He really meant; we must understand Semitic ways of speaking. Or someone will allude to hyperbole and so on. Everything is qualified and toned down and—what's worse—off on entirely the wrong track. Maybe it's because many assume verse 26 is about discipleship and they focus on that. And it is—but not preeminently. Verse 26 is not first of all a matter of discipleship but of *Christology*. Look at the text. Who gave Jesus the right to talk that way? Who does He think He is? He is saying that He must have the sole and supreme place of affection in your life. What sheer audacity! Don't you see it? Luke 14:26 is simply the first commandment (= Exod. 20:3) in different language. What is Jesus *assuming* in what He says? Luke 14:26 is as blatant a claim to deity as John 8:58. No one but deity has the right to demand such ultimate loyalty from us. And Jesus does so. If I really hear this claim, I will be on my face before Him, and Semitic modes of expression or Matthean parallels won't matter very much.[1]

Secondly, Jesus sets before us **the calculation the would-be disciple must make** (vv. 27-33). Verse 27 illustrates what 'hating even one's own life' (v. 26) might well involve: 'Whoever does not carry his own cross and come after me, cannot be my disciple.' Once more (see on 9:23), carrying one's cross is not a figure that connotes enduring disappointments and reverses. When first-century Jews saw someone carrying the horizontal crossbeam, they knew that person was fodder for a Roman execution. Jesus then implies that the government may execute you in the most cruel and shameful way for being His disciple, and you must be ready for that.[2] Indeed, 9:23 suggests we must renew this realization every day. Hence the need to consider carefully this relation to Jesus.

And so we have the two 'parables' in verses 28-32 about the potential tower-builder and the maybe-fighting king.

---

1. Doesn't verse 26 provide the disciple with the only adequate base for sound human relationships—when we quit deifying others and ourselves?

2. For this view, see Norval Geldenhuys, *Commentary on the Gospel of Luke* (Grand Rapids: Eerdmans, 1951), pp. 398, 400; also W. F. Arndt, *The Gospel According to St. Luke* (St. Louis: Concordia, 1956), p. 344. The form of the cross-bearing may be a bit different in our day. For example, jihadists stop a bus in Kenya, force the passengers out. Two of them are Christians. They are charged to deny their faith; they refuse; they are shot and killed on the spot. Or there's a mainly Christian village in central Mali; almost every resident there was killed in early June 2019; those attempting to escape were shot; those who stayed in their homes were burned to death. Why? They were Christians—and they had counted the cost.

None of Jesus' hearers would likely be in the king's boots but some ('Which one of you') might fancy putting up a tower in their vineyard. In the case of the tower, one must count up the cost from beginning to end; otherwise, both he and a half-erected tower might be the butt of community jokes (vv. 28-30). A king must calculate as well, whether he has sufficient troops to meet a stronger enemy, lest disaster prove to be his lot (vv. 31-32). I don't think, as some, that the emphasis is on the inadequacy of resources; I think Jesus is simply stressing realistic, sober consideration—which, in view of verse 27, is hardly pleasant.

In less than an hour my wife and I are heading to a local funeral home to make 'pre-planning' arrangements for our funerals. One doesn't like to contemplate one's earthly end, but to avoid last-minute chaos, we want to nail down arrangements, lock in the expenses, and pay costs ahead of time. It's not our favorite pastime on a Wednesday morning, but it's wise to face it and relieve one's family of a pile of such details. It's part of life to 'calculate the cost' of the end of it.

In verse 33 Jesus draws it all together. That verse begins with, 'In the same way *therefore* ....' It is summing up what precedes, and I think the 'therefore' goes back and picks up everything including verses 26-27, as well as 28-32. Verse 33 is a kind of re-statement. Whoever 'does not say goodbye to all that he has' cannot be Jesus' disciple. Verses 26-27 sum up or specify what 'all that he has' consists of. In short, nothing must matter more than belonging to Jesus and being His disciple.

Jesus says we must carefully consider this cost of following him. David Garland in his commentary alludes to Joshua's warning to Israel in Joshua 24:19-20. In the covenant renewal Israel has just committed themselves to 'serve Yahweh.' But Joshua, the anti-evangelist, tells them they are not able to serve Yahweh. Do they realize what it is to have a holy and jealous God? Have they thought of their own tendencies to infidelity and of what will happen to them when He consumes them? Joshua doesn't want them to reverse their commitment but to deepen it and think it through. So here in Luke, Jesus' purpose is not to send you packing but to get you thinking. So that you *will* 'come after' Him (v. 27).

Thirdly, Jesus highlights **the crisis the would-be disciple faces** (vv. 34-35). The better Greek texts begin verse 34 with *oun*, 'Therefore,' or 'So,' indicating that verses 34-35 are drawing an inference from what has preceded.[3] And Jesus speaks of salt. But what kind of salt? In Syria and Palestine salt was not obtained by boiling clean salt water or quarried from mines but was obtained from marshes near the seashore or from salt lakes in the interior. The 'salt' might be stored or piled up; in the way it was gathered a lot of earth and other impurities were collected with it; and so contact with the earth, or rain and sun, could render it tasteless and useless, suitable only for street mud (v. 35).[4] Others think Jesus is speaking of 'true' salt, which everyone knew did not lose its seasoning kick. These would hold that Jesus would be suggesting something like: 'We know this can't happen but what if it could? How could it be made salty again?' In either case, whether degenerate salt or genuine salt is in mind, Jesus is underscoring something irreversible. How can you restore saltiness to saltless salt? Think of a balloon with a hole in it: how do you inflate the uninflatable? You don't and you can't.

Jesus is painting the crisis the would-be disciple faces. In this context, does not 'salt' refer to the potential disciple who plunges into a 'Jesus thing' (perhaps because it is popular—see verse 25) without taking account of what such discipleship really demands? Then, when the cost of following Jesus hits home, he or she gradually or abruptly leaves off that discipleship. It's really a re-run of Jesus' parable of the soils in chapter 8: there are those whose emotional enthusiasm oozes away when conflict comes (8:6, 13) and those who in their earthly wisdom realize there is so much more to be preoccupied with than Jesus (8:7, 14). Not much one can do about such folks.

Jesus, then, has spent a whole chapter disrupting both Pharisees and His own would-be friends.

---

3. See Alan J. Thompson, *Luke*, EGGNT (Nashville: Broadman & Holman, 2016), p. 239. ESV and NIV (perhaps too much influenced by English stylists?) do not translate the *oun*.

4. For a very helpful nineteenth-century description, see W. M. Thomson, *The Land and the Book*, 2 vols. (New York: Harper & Brothers, 1873), 2:43-44.

3

Joy in Heaven, Griping on Earth
(Luke 15:1-32)

Sometimes we have the impression that stories in Scripture carry a bit of our own biography. And sometimes we are sure they do not. The latter could be your case with Luke 15. You come to Luke 15, and you read the prodigal story, and it's very beautiful and moving, and yet you may say, 'That's not about me.' You say that because you were never able to sin with such flair or rebel with such rambunctiousness. Take heart then. The whole parable isn't about the 'prodigal' son, nor, in one sense, about the father. It's about the 'Pharisee' son, or, it's as I've sometimes called it in pulpit exposition, 'the parable of the Presbyterian son.' That is, Jesus' parable does not so much address the raunchy sinner as religious ones; it is not calling vile but virtuous sinners to repentance. It may be about you after all.

Verses 1-2 provide the orientation for the whole chapter, and it is here that we meet **the attractive offensiveness of Jesus**. The chapter begins with a change of scene, but Luke does not tell us where this encounter takes place. We are simply to assume it occurs on the way to Jerusalem. And Luke uses a bad word. He says that both the Pharisees and scribes 'were complaining' (or, 'began to complain') about Jesus. The verb is *diagogguzō,* to complain, murmur, grumble. LXX uses this verb along with its base form and related nouns to express the grumbling of Israel in the wilderness, especially in Exodus and Numbers.[1] Something like seventeen times this word group conveys the grumbling, unbelief, and rebellion of Israel in post-exodus time. The 'grumbling' here may be Luke's way of saying the Pharisees & Co. are simply clones of an earlier generation of unbelieving Israel.[2]

Why are they so upset? Well, 'all the tax collectors and sinners were drawing near to hear' Jesus (v. 1). Jesus was teaching these motley low-lifes of Israel. But that wasn't all. The real 'kicker' was that 'this fellow welcomes sinners and eats with them' (v. 2). Jesus not only taught them but spent time with them, even socialized with them. It's simply too much.

Now this complaint provides us with the proper orientation for all of Luke 15. It's in the face of such a complaint that Jesus tells a parable (v. 3), which in its three-fold form is a *defense* of His conduct. All of Luke 15 is Jesus' answer to the griping of the theologians.

But the irony here is delightful. Their grumbling is our gospel. Their dire accusation is our only hope. We become ecstatic over their damning words. Thank heaven for the 'gospel' of the Pharisees: 'This fellow welcomes sinners and eats with them.' What better news could there be? I have called this segment the attractive offensiveness of Jesus, trying to catch this paradox in the text. The offensiveness of Jesus to the Pharisees and scribes and yet His attraction for tax collectors and sinners. I think it was from this text that someone coined the phrase, 'the approachableness of Jesus.'[3] Sinners can't help but revel in the very idea.

There is such an attractive power in this complaining text! David Roper wrote a piece in the 'Daily Bread' devotional booklet. He told of a friend of his whose name was Edith. Edith told him of the day she decided to follow Jesus. Edith, Roper said, cared nothing for religion. But one Sunday morning,

---

1. You can check Exodus 15:24; 16:2, 7, 8, 9, 12; Numbers 11:1; 14:2, 27, 29; and Deuteronomy 1:27 (more than one occurrence in some texts).

2. One might ask if Luke's readers would have caught this point. Quite possibly, if they had some acquaintance with the stories of Exodus 15–17 and Numbers 11–14. Even if they didn't 'get it,' Luke's use of the verb is no compliment to the Pharisees and scribes.

3. It may have been Spurgeon, but I have been unable to verify it.

looking for something to satisfy her inner discontent, she went walking into a church near her apartment. The text that day was Luke 15:1-2, which the pastor read from the King James or Authorized Version (which, on that day, was important!): 'Then drew near unto him all the publicans and sinners for to hear him. And the Pharisees and scribes murmured, saying, This man receiveth sinners, and eateth with them.' That's what was read, but here's what Edith heard: 'This man receiveth sinners and Edith with them.' She sat straight up in that pew. Eventually she figured out her mistake, but the thought that Jesus welcomes sinners (and that that included Edith!) stayed with her. That afternoon was the beginning of her 'drawing near' to Jesus. Never had the archaic ending of a present-tense verb had such a baffling and fruitful effect! But that's how it is with the Pharisees' complaint: it is the playground of the soul.

The second major emphasis in this chapter centers on **the primary attention of Jesus**. This concern appears mostly in the first two parables but is not missing in the third. In defending His ministry (vv. 1-2) Jesus tells stories about what is 'lost.' The Greek verb behind this idea is *apollumi*, which occurs eight times in our chapter (vv. 4 [twice], 6, 8, 9, 17 [translated 'perish' or the like], 24, and 32). Yes, Jesus tells stories about lost things: There are one hundred sheep and one is lost (vv. 4-7); there are ten coins and one is lost (vv. 8-10); there are two sons and *both* are lost (vv. 11-32; more later on this last). And it all makes sense: what could be more sane than the preoccupation of a worried shepherd over a helpless sheep (v. 4) or more understandable than the pains of a diligent housekeeper over a vanished coin (v. 8)? It is right to go after lost stuff and that is the focus of Jesus' work.

There may be more behind Jesus' retort to the Pharisees and scribes than appears on the surface, especially with the shepherd-lost-sheep story. It is hard for a Bible reader to keep Ezekiel 34 from sneaking into his mind when reading verses 4-7. That passage is about the difference a decent shepherd makes. Actually, in Ezekiel 34 Yahweh scourges the leaders ('shepherds') of Israel as those who have mangled rather than cared for the flock of Israel. But in this prophecy Yahweh promises that in the age of restoration He Himself will shepherd His people and He will, among other matters and in contrast to Israel's long line of scurvy leaders, 'seek the lost' (Ezekiel 34:16 versus 34:4). Indeed, the coming Davidic Messiah will be Yahweh's agent in this ministry (vv. 23-24).

Now who knows if the Pharisees and colleagues would conjure up Ezekiel 34 in their minds when they hear verses 4-7 and the constant reference to 'lost' items throughout the chapter. But if Jesus intended an allusion to Ezekiel 34, He could well be claiming to fulfill the very shepherding work Yahweh had promised there, as well as implicitly criticizing the Pharisees and scribes by placing them in the class of Israel's destructive leaders whom Yahweh castigated in that prophecy.

At any rate, the lost receive Jesus' primary attention. But just here there is more. For with Jesus the lost are found (vv. 5, 8-9, 24, 32) and that brings joy (vv. 5, 6, 7, 9, 10, cf. 23-24)—in fact, one could call it the compulsive necessity of joy, for in verse 32 the father tells the older son, 'But we *had* to celebrate and rejoice' (not, 'it was fitting,' as ESV; the Greek *edei* requires *necessity*).

Let's go back to verse 7 to underscore a note or two related to this joy. In concluding the seeking-shepherd, lost-sheep story Jesus said, 'I tell you that in the same way there will be more joy in heaven over one sinner who repents than over ninety-nine righteous folks who have no need of repentance.'[4] That is a very revealing statement. We are liable, if we are not careful, to think that that was just a very sweet thing to say. But I cannot free myself from thinking it is a very serious (though it speaks of joy) Christological claim. Jesus sounds like He is imparting revelation: 'I say to you.' And think of the content. How does Jesus *know* what He tells us? How does He know there is more joy in heaven over one sinner who repents, etc.? How does He know that that math and those numbers are accurate? Does it not lead us to ponder the person of Jesus? Who could possibly know this except 'the one who came down from heaven' (John 3:13; cf. 6:38, 41-42)

---

4. Some find the ninety-nine righteous folks a problem here. I agree with those (e.g., Robert Stein) who take Jesus as speaking ironically, referring to those who think they are righteous.

and who is therefore 'in the know'?[5] Perhaps statements like
verses 7 and 10 do not impress us at first but in them Jesus is
assuming matters like pre-existence and deity. How would
we ever know angels throw parties when a sinner repents
unless Jesus told us so?

A recent phone call with one of our sons found him in
a semi-jocular mood. Whenever we asked him how he was
aware of something, he would reply, 'I know things.' We
might ask details about the situation in the school where
he teaches. His response would be the mantra for the
conversation as he would assure us, 'I know things.' In his
case he was pretending to have some sort of superior access
to esoteric information. It seems to me that something like
that stands behind Jesus' statements in verses 7 and 10. If we
asked Jesus how He can make such statements, might He say,
'I know things, and if you push on to ask how I know, you
will find yourself facing the mystery of my person.'[6]

Thirdly, the bulk of the chapter contains **the sad revelation
of Jesus** (vv. 11-32). I call it a 'sad' revelation because in this
last parable Jesus intends to focus on the older brother's
reactions (vv. 25-32). And it's not pretty. Remember that in
the light of verses 1-2, Jesus, in all the rest of this chapter, is
answering His critics. When you understand that you realize
that verses 25-32 are not some sort of needless appendix but
the climax and punchline of all Jesus is saying here. For in
verses 25-32 and in His depiction of the older brother Jesus is
holding up, as in a mirror, the attitudes of the Pharisees and
scribes. They are meant to see themselves in the older brother.
And it's a sad revelation because the attitude and behavior
of the older brother is sad. There may be joy in heaven (v. 7)
over this—but not necessarily on earth. All this means that
neither the prodigal nor even the father is the primary focus
of Jesus' parable. If you stop your reading at the end of verse

---

5. John 3:13 is a bit baffling but I find B. F. Westcott's exposition clear and
satisfying (*The Gospel According to St. John* [1881; reprint ed., Grand Rapids:
Eerdmans, 1964], p. 53).

6. Don't miss the stress on the *intensity* of angelic joy. In 1858 Charles Spurgeon
preached on Luke 15:10 and underscored the joy before the angels over *one* sinner
who repents. Apparently, heaven does not celebrate globs but individuals who
repent.

24, you have messed up Jesus' parable, you have wrecked Jesus' whole intention. If Luke 15 were a joke, verses 25-32 would be the punchline, and if you dropped those verses, you would totally ruin the joke.

I do not mean by this that we should ignore verses 11-24 or even that they contain no instruction for us. Think, for example, what those verses may tell us of the 'far country' (v. 13). It is an *unstable* place: 'a severe famine came against that country' (v. 14a). Conditions can change there; it's a place where life can suddenly turn tipsy. Yet it can be a *hopeful* place, for 'he began to be in need' (v. 14b). That's not much but who knows where it will lead? It may eventually nudge him out of his love affair with the far country. And it can be a *cruel* place: 'no one gave him anything' (v. 16b). A Jewish lad working the hog farm (vv. 15-16a) is nothing but desperation, but no one seems to care. Isolation rather than community is the amenity of the far country. But of course Jesus shows us that the far country can be a *near-by* place (vv. 29-30), for, though the older son was in father's house, in disposition he was actually in the 'far country' as well. Let's go then to the climax of the parable and note how Jesus depicts him.

Jesus shows that the older brother *couldn't comprehend the Father's grace* (especially v. 30). He gets the report and explanation of the extravagant reception and it repulses him. He tells the father so: 'But when this son of yours—who has eaten up your resources with whores—has come, you butcher the fattened calf for him!' He had perhaps heard how the father had run to meet the returning son—sheer embarrassment. No Middle Eastern man with any dignity would ever dash out like that.[7] He may have been muttering about how 'dad has gone giddy over this creep.' Had his father let him take a shower, given him a change of clothes, and banished him to the county workhouse—that could be tolerated. But this! There's a certain logic in the case of furious self-righteousness. Grace—for that is what it is—just isn't

---

7. Cf., e.g., Kenneth E. Bailey, *Poet & Peasant* and *Through Peasant Eyes*, combined ed. (Grand Rapids: Eerdmans, 1983), p. 181. Bailey's insights on this parable are often illuminating, but Klyne Snodgrass thinks he sometimes assumes too much cultural carryover; see his *Stories with Intent* (Grand Rapids: Eerdmans, 2008), pp. 128-41.

'right'; it's like serving peanut butter and jelly sandwiches at a state dinner.

Others may not be so disturbed as the older brother, but the whole account has perplexed others. There's a story of a Chinese artist who wanted to paint the 'prodigal' story. His first attempt showed the father standing, waiting at the gate for the son seen in the distance. He showed the picture to a Christian friend and received some artistic criticism: 'Oh, no, you don't have it right. The father shouldn't be standing, waiting. He should be running to meet his son.' That was anathema to the artist. 'But no Chinese father could do that,' he said. Which is precisely the point, his friend replied. 'No human father would, but ....' So the next picture the artist painted showed the father running to meet his son, and, in his hurry, he had put on shoes that didn't match.[8]

In one sense the older brother is right. There is something 'wild' and outlandish about grace. It's sometimes hard to keep dignity intact when heaven throws parties and angels exchange 'high-fives' over a repentant sinner (vv. 7, 10). However, when all's said, to the older brother grace is a foreign word and has no place in his dictionary.

Jesus also suggests that the older brother *couldn't sense his own need*. He provides his father with a summary of his record: 'And I never transgressed a command of yours' (v. 29b). Now these are the words of the brother to the father in the parable, and some may object that I am reading too much 'freight' into them. We are not meant to press every detail. That's fine, but remember that Jesus is telling this to His critics (vv. 1-2), to the righteous folks who don't (think they) need to repent (v. 7). Might Jesus not intend for them to hear the older brother's protest as an expression of their own moral achievement? Are the church people and theologians not meant to hear themselves here? They've no debauchery in their record; they've played it clean; there is nothing in their lives that a tabloid could exploit. You would never catch the older brother breathing, 'I am no longer worthy' (v. 21). His mantra is, 'I have never transgressed a command of yours.'

---

8. Reuel Howe, *The Creative Years* (New York: Seabury, 1959), pp. 124-25.

The problem with such self-assessments is that they tend to be so wide of the mark, like the naïve claim we meet later in the gospel (18:21). Such self-righteousness does not know the true state of things and so lapses into false assessments. In this connection I often think of Martyn Lloyd-Jones' account of his preaching at a university mission at Oxford in 1941. Mostly students were in attendance. There was to be a meeting after the service in a separate building, a sort of 'Q & A.' The vicar and Lloyd-Jones went there, expecting to find a few students, and ran into a packed house. One well-spoken young man, after expressing some compliments, put his question: he thought the sermon could as well have been preached to a congregation of farm laborers or anyone else. What of that? This stirred up much laughter. Lloyd-Jones tells of his response:

> I said that I was most interested in the question, but really could not see the questioner's difficulty; because, I confessed freely, that though I might be a heretic, I had to admit that until that moment I had regarded undergraduates and indeed graduates of Oxford University as being just ordinary common human clay and miserable sinners like everybody else, and held the view that their needs were precisely the same as those of the agricultural laborer or anyone else.[9]

It's difficult for an older brother type to see that, though he may prefer more classy sins, he is nevertheless in the same category as the whore-hugger. And until 'he begins to be in need' (cf. v. 14), there's not much hope for him.

The older son also *couldn't enjoy the Father's intimacy* (v. 29a). His words ooze his peevish attitude. The NIV nicely captures it: 'Look! All these years I've been slaving for you.' 'Slaving' is right; the verb is *douleuō*. Very revealing, isn't it? His father was not father in his eyes but master, and he was not son but slave. To him father's house was a house of bondage, Dullsville, Nasty City. Though he was in father's house, he had no intimate relation with the father. Something

---

9. Iain H. Murray, *David Martyn Lloyd-Jones: The Fight of Faith 1939-1981* (Edinburgh: Banner of Truth, 1990), p. 77.

tragic about that. So what Jesus is showing us is that both sons were in the 'far country'; one worked the father's fields but was as far from the father as the one feeding the pigs—even though he seemed the ideal son, the moral model. The sad news is that the church pew can still be the far country. What can be more tedious, boring, dull, dead, and damning than having all the motions of religion and evidence of morality without an enjoyable relation with God?

One could also say that the older son *couldn't avoid the Father's appeal* (vv. 28b, 31-32). This older son is angry and refuses any part in the celebration, so the father goes out and 'kept pleading with him' (v. 28b).[10] And of course the father gets an earful of the son's fury (vv. 29-30) but, in spite of it, continues his plea and explanation (vv. 31-32). We might expect to see the father livid and furious at the older son's obnoxious behavior but instead he pleads with him—and after the son's tirade (vv. 29-30), he continues his plea. Verse 28b is just as astounding as verse 20b. The father doesn't just run to embrace the prodigal but goes out to plead with the Pharisee. Some sinners smell of the hog pen; but others reek of the church pew—and Jesus appeals to them as well.

Now the parable itself does not wrap things up. That is how Jesus intended it. In the story the older son couldn't avoid the father's appeal, but it *doesn't tell us his response* to the father's appeal. The whole issue is left hanging. And this is deliberate. I know I've referred to it somewhere before, but a couple of decades or more ago *Time* magazine ran a feature about the afternoon soap operas on TV. They called it 'Sex and Suffering in the Afternoon.' They discussed the problem soap opera writers faced when the week's last episode aired on Friday. There would then be two whole days in which usual viewers would be in non-soap mode, other matters claiming their attention—recreation, even church perhaps. So how can they hook viewers to be sure they will faithfully return on the ensuing Monday afternoon? They simply have a new crisis hit the fan on Friday afternoon, which is unresolved and

---

10. The imperfect verb form could also be translated ingressively, i.e., 'he began pleading with him.'

'hanging fire.' That will hook interest enough to pull their devotees back the next week.

Now Jesus is no soap opera manipulator. But He knows how to pull people into the story. If one resolves the difficulty, hearers will say, 'Oh, well, that's how it ended then!', and will disengage. But Jesus leaves the story 'unended'—we don't know how the older son reacted. That has a tendency to draw the hearer into it. He/she might then ask, 'How would *I* respond?' It's really as if Jesus said to you, 'Here, the kingdom of God has come; won't you please come in to the party?' And what would you say?

'This man welcomes sinners,' the Pharisees and scribes' complaint in verse 2, is actually a preaching of good news. But the punch-line section of Jesus' parable (vv. 25-32) preaches even better good news to me, for it says, 'This man will even welcome Pharisees!'

4

Slick, the Sly Steward

(Luke 16:1-18)

It shouldn't be that difficult. Can't we conceive that it's possible for someone to commend a specific action or particular aspect of what a person does or is, without approving all his actions or endorsing his entire character? Think of baseball. In the fifth game of the 1956 World Series Don Larsen of the New York Yankees pitched a perfect game against the Brooklyn Dodgers. No hits, no walks, no hit batters. Quite an achievement. And yet Larsen's overall record as a major league pitcher was 81 wins, 91 losses. A brilliant moment, rightly acclaimed, in that World Series victory, but, on the whole, a lackluster career. Or I think of one of my father's corny tales. Two fellows were discussing a speaker they'd just heard. The one said, 'He didn't really say anything.' The other replied, 'Yes, but he said it in an awfully nice way.' The content was vacuous but the style pleasing. Approval of part does not mean endorsement of all. So in this strange story of the devious estate-manager, his employer (and, by implication, Jesus, cf. v. 8) commends his resourcefulness, foresight, and savvy but not his morality or business ethics. Can that be so terribly difficult to sort out?

The disciples constitute the primary audience in Luke 16 (v. 1a), although there are clearly others lingering about and listening (v. 14a). Luke does not tie this material down to any specific time or place—apparently, once more, it was somewhere on that journey to Jerusalem. And the whole chapter holds together around the theme of riches or funds, whether the steward who rips off his master (vv. 1-9), the Pharisees who are money-lovers (v. 14), or the rich man who is self-absorbed in his luxury (vv. 19-31).

What is this first story? It's about a steward or estate-manager who wastes (v. 1; see same verb in 15:13; he is not viciously dishonest at this point) his master's resources, so the master requires him to turn over the books. Since he's both lazy and proud, he eliminates two future options (v. 3). Then he has his 'eureka!' moment (v. 4). He calls in each one of his master's debtors (v. 5a)—but only two examples are given. A little parabolic economy—you can divine from the two examples given (vv. 5b-7) how he operated with them all. He has them doctor their bills, so it may well be we not only have a shady steward but compliant and devious customers as well. It's because of this practice of lowering the amounts owed that the estate-manager is called 'unrighteous' (v. 8a). And we shouldn't be worried about the master's (or Jesus') commendation (v. 8), for he clearly is not praising his *integrity* but his *ingenuity*.

What I have sketched is a fairly 'traditional' approach to 16:1-9. I am aware of a barrage of assessments and articles on this passage that suggest different 'takes' on it. For example, some claim the steward actually cut out the high interest included in the bills or perhaps deleted his own commission from the charges. All of which forces me to a decision. Do I take up ten pages to explain the plethora of opinions on the parable and try to defend my own view, or do I simply refer you to those who have already done that? Since it would be difficult for me to make such a discussion interesting, I take the latter option.[1]

The concern, then, behind the parable is how Jesus' disciples (v. 1) should use 'unrighteous mammon' (v. 9), or

1. See Klyne Snodgrass, *Stories with Intent* (Grand Rapids: Eerdmans, 2008), pp. 401-19; Dave L. Mathewson, 'The Parable of the Unjust Steward (Luke 16:1-13): A Reexamination of the Traditional View in Light of Recent Challenges,' *Journal of the Evangelical Theological Society* 38 (1995): pp. 29-39 (who acknowledges the substantial contribution of my former colleague, Dennis J. Ireland, on this parable); and Robert Stein, *Luke*, NAC (Nashville: Broadman, 1992), p. 412.

what we might call secular wealth. And the main thrust of the parable is to teach that **financial resources require creative thought** (focus on vv. 8-9).

When the estate-manager made his master's debtors his own debtors, the master recognized the 'cool' move (v. 8a). Not that it was moral but it was canny, not that it was right but resourceful. The samples given show that these were big-time debtors. One indebted for 100 baths of oil (v. 6) would owe for about 875 gallons, the yield of 150 trees, thought to be equivalent to three years' wages. A hundred measures of wheat (v. 7) would come to 1,000 bushels and about eight years' wages.[2] Clearly, these debtors were not scrub-level, subsistence tenants. And they would have been delighted to have their debts substantially reduced.

I take verse 8b to be Jesus' comment. There He so much as says that those we would call unbelievers seem to be much 'sharper' than God's people in this matter of using this world's wealth. In verse 9 Jesus goes on to apply the parable: 'Make friends for yourselves with worldly wealth [lit., the mammon of unrighteousness], in order that when it gives out, they may welcome you into the eternal dwellings.' That is, use some of the slick steward's ingenuity to figure out how you can use earthly resources to benefit God's people, so that at the last they will be overjoyed and thrilled to welcome you to eternity.

It is much easier to be prosaic than creative. Imagine a college fellow asking a co-ed to go with him to a college basketball game and out for pizza afterwards. That's okay. But what if he wanted to impress her? He might say that he is going to take her 'for dinner at Dillards' (a semi-posh US department store). This will mystify her because she knows Dillards does not serve food. The evening comes, they arrive at the mall. He drives off to that part of the parking lot next to Dillards, only at the edge of the lot, quite a distance from the store. He opens the trunk (boot) and pulls out a card table and two folding chairs. He covers the table with a tablecloth, puts in place china, silver, two goblets, and cloth napkins,

---

2. Cf. Darrell L. Bock., *Luke 9:51-24:53* (BECNT (Grand Rapids: Baker, 1996), pp. 1330-31.

then reaches into a cooler for soft drinks, extracts two 'sub' sandwiches (the 'main course') and follows that later with slices of Key-lime pie. So they are 'dining at Dillards.' She may feel embarrassment—some people may be staring at this unusual spectacle at the edge of the parking lot. But you can be sure she will never forget the occasion. Not exactly the 'usual.' Whatever she thinks of this fellow, she has to admit that he put some real thought into this 'date.'

That is Jesus' initial point: put some thought, use some 'steward savvy,' to think through and come up with ways to benefit the 'sons of light' in this age, so that they'll welcome you with open arms in the 'eternal dwellings.' Jesus seems to envision folks who 'pre-arrive' you there, who are delighted when you come because of how you had helped them.

How does this work out? Obviously, some disciples can do more, some less.[3] David Gooding puts it pointedly:

> If when accounts are rendered and it becomes known in heaven that it was your sacrificial giving that provided the copies of the Gospel of John which led a whole tribe out of paganism to faith in Christ, will not that whole tribe show towards you an eternal gratitude which they will not show towards me who spent my spare cash on some luxury for my own enjoyment?[4]

Will some Ugandan believer come thanking you because you helped subsidize a biblical stewardship program that supplied micro-loans so that he and others could start self-supporting small businesses? Will a man thank you or your church for pouring funds into a Christian pregnancy counseling center? The caring advice a woman received there led her to keep her baby, a girl, who became his wife and mother of their four

---

3. G. Campbell Morgan (*The Parables and Metaphors of Our Lord* [New York: Revell, 1943], pp. 221-22) supplies an anecdote that speaks for itself: 'Many years ago I remember in the home of a very wealthy man, who was a Church member and a Christian, one morning at Family Prayers he was eloquent and tender as he prayed for the salvation of the heathen, and for the missionaries. He was startled beyond measure when the prayer was over, one of his boys, a lad of ten, said to him, "Dad, I like to hear you pray for the missionaries." He answered, "I am glad you do, my boy." And the boy replied, "But do you know what I was thinking when you were praying, if I had your bank book, I would answer half your prayers!"'

4. David Gooding, *According to Luke* (1987; reprint ed., Coleraine, N. Ireland: Myrtlefield Trust, 2013), p. 287.

children. Think it out; it's quite a project: how to make future friends by how I use 'unrighteous mammon.'[5]

In verses 10-12 Jesus makes a second application from the parable: **financial resources provide an index to character.**[6] Jesus set down the basic principle in verse 10: 'The one who is faithful in little is also faithful in much, and the one who is unrighteous [cf. v. 8a] in little is also unrighteous in much.' That is, in this context, how you handle the small stuff (money) is a clue to whether you can be trusted with greater responsibility. Verse 11 goes on, 'If therefore you do not prove faithful in worldly wealth [lit., in the unrighteous mammon], who will entrust you with the true riches?' That suggests: If you can't handle mundane finances properly, who will trust you with greater gospel responsibility or service? The Fourth Gospel provides a stark illustration. If Judas was a thief and in charge of the money box and used to pilfer what was put in it (John 12:6), should we be that surprised that a far more devastating betrayal followed (John 13:26-27)?

You will find the 'faithful in little' crops up everywhere. Some decades ago we were seeking our first pastorate and had an interview with a pulpit committee in a midwestern church. The committee had questions for us, and I had questions for them. When I began raising my questions, I noted that the committee chairman had no writing material—no folder, no notepad, no paper. In apparent desperation he opened up an empty matchbook and began scratching mini-notes on the restricted gray pasteboard interior. It struck me that a pulpit committee chairman who came so unprepared and nonchalantly to deal with a prospective pastor would do well to look for another one. It was a small matter, but it said something about *him*.

---

5. Some commentators want to make the 'friends' who welcome in verse 9 a circumlocution for God or the angels. But why re-theologize Jesus' delightful and graphic imagery?

6. A 'second' application, that is, in addition to the main one in verses 8-9. Some may argue that Luke took the material of verses 10-12/13 from some other teaching of Jesus and inserted it here because of similarity of theme. It doesn't matter much. But I vote for Jesus simply carrying on the same theme and making another application Himself. He was perfectly capable of that. Note how the beginning of verse 12 seems to hark back to the estate-manager: 'And if you do not prove faithful in what belongs to another ....'

It won't hurt to speak a little of the application of this principle. Jesus requires honesty among His servants in mundane matters, beginning with financial ones. These are easily overlooked. I recall Dr James Baird (former minister at First Presbyterian, Jackson, Mississippi) once saying that his seminary president's first word to seminary graduates was: 'Gentlemen, pay your bills!' Not 'preach the gospel' but 'pay your bills.' There were too many ghastly reports about ministers who seemed to think their position placed them above careful fulfilling of common obligations. And it was besmirching the gospel.

But 'faithful in little' pops up throughout our Christian 'culture.' What do we say of the Christian university student who gets all charged up over his 'ministry' to some high school students and yet he doesn't think keeping up on reading in his English Lit. or Medieval History courses really matters (which, one would think, were God's primary 'call' for him at such a time)? Or what of Paul's requirement in 1 Timothy 3:5? If a man's home life is in chaos and he doesn't have the guts to discipline his kids, why on earth should he have oversight as an elder in Christ's church? Or think of what Paul says in Ephesians 5:18 *and in the following context.* How do I know if I am being filled with the Spirit? Do I speak in tongues? Am I able to claim an intense, intimate experience with Jesus? From what follows Ephesians 5:18 (the flow goes through 6:9), you can tell by the tone of your marriage relationship (5:22-33), by attitudes prevalent in your home from both children and parents (6:1-4), and by the quality of your daily work (6:5-9). Marriage, home, work—doesn't sound so spiritual, mostly mundane. But it's critical to be faithful in *little*—it reveals everything.

Then Jesus makes a third application in the wake of His parable: **financial resources raise the possibility of idolatry** (vv. 13-15). Jesus raises the danger we run: 'No household servant is able to be slave to two masters …; you are not able to be slave to God and wealth [mammon]' (v. 13). Though Jesus was primarily instructing His disciples, there were Pharisees listening in on 'all these things' (v. 14), which likely includes more than verse 13—perhaps all of verses 10-13. Luke says these Pharisees were 'money-lovers' and they were, literally, 'turning up their noses' at Him, perhaps especially over the warning of verse 13. But Jesus levels them with the assertion that there is—though they may be unaware of it—an entirely different view of the matter on God's side. 'You,' he said, 'are those who justify yourselves before men, but *God* [emphatic] knows your hearts; because what is admirable among men is abominable before God' (v. 15).

We don't need to begin railing at folks about materialism. Just realize your danger whether from financial affections or something else. Don't mock Jesus. Don't think, 'Oh, that couldn't be me—I've got no hidden idolatry; why, I've not got enough money to worship it.' But idolatry is a many-headed monster. And Jesus implies it's like Velcro—it'll latch on to you quickly and hold on. Better to accept this warning (v. 13) as the grace of Jesus, to warn you. Realize there is hope in the fact that *'God* knows your hearts' (v. 15) and so can expose you and lead you to repentance. Don't 'turn up your nose' at Jesus when He says you may have an idol—He knows what it is that you tend to cuddle.

Now I have extended this treatment through verses 16-18. I know there are some catch-words links with verses 19-31 that follow, but I have a hard time cutting off verses 16-18 from the flow of Jesus' warnings to the Pharisees in verses 14-15. But any connection seems so elusive. Why does Jesus (at least in the flow of Luke's context here) suddenly go off talking 'redemptive-historical' language about John the Baptist and the kingdom of God (v. 16)? Why the stress on the permanence of the law (v. 17)? And why a few remarks on divorce that seem so tacked on (v. 18)? Connections I propose will have to be considered provisional; however, I simply can't escape the impression that verses 16-18 continue an 'answer' of sorts to the Pharisees of verses 14-15. Hence another point for our exposition: **Financial resources are not the only problem** (vv. 16-18).[7]

Jesus stresses that the Pharisees must realize 'what time they are in'—it is the time of *fulfillment*: 'The law and the

---

7. I am making short shrift of a complicated text. Bock calls verse 16 itself 'an exegetical minefield in Lucan studies.' But I can either try to put down a reasonably (?) coherent exposition or stop and discuss in exhausting detail every disputed point in these verses. Readers will find plenty of discussion in the larger commentaries.

prophets were until John; from then on the kingdom of God is being proclaimed (as good news)' (v. 16a). I think John (the Baptist) belongs to both periods; he is included in 'the law and the prophets' but also among the proclaimers of the kingdom's arrival (cf. 3:18). He has a foot in the previous age but also in the dawn of the new kingdom age. But if the kingdom has in some sense really arrived, it is also a time of *invitation*, or one might say, of opportunity. Note the last of verse 16, 'and each one must press his way into it.' I take the middle or passive verb form here (*biazetai*) to be a sort of 'softened' present tense with a hortatory or imperatival force.[8] It is then the opportune time for even Pharisees to press into the kingdom. But they must make no mistake, for this kingdom is also a regimen of *righteousness* (vv. 17-18). The kingdom does not dissolve or dispense with the commanding claims of the law (v. 17).[9] There's even more—it is under law interpreted and applied by King Jesus (v. 18). Rather than piddling around 'justifying themselves before men' (v. 15) these particular Pharisees are called to recognize what time has arrived (16a), the opportunity that is theirs (16b), and to know that entering such a kingdom means living under a regime of true righteousness (17-18). That's what I mean by the rubric, 'financial resources are not the only problem.' The Pharisees need to see that their ridicule of Jesus' stewardship teaching is simply a symptom of their far deeper problem— supremely they need to enter the kingdom of God.

Still, verse 18 is a puzzle. Granted, if as verse 17 implies, life in the kingdom is still in some sense a life under law, why should Jesus select some note on divorce seemingly out of the blue as a sample (v. 18)? Surely He didn't spy a couple of lechers in the crowd and decide to 'nail' them. Verse 18 simply seems so 'out there' and unconnected.

But we may have a hint. In verse 15 Jesus had charged these men with 'You are those who justify yourselves before men, but *God* knows your hearts; because what is admirable among men is abominable (lit., an abomination) before God.'

---

8. For discussion, see Bock, pp. 1352-53. If one takes it positively and as a flat-out statement ('everyone is forcing his way into it') it is simply not so.

9. Not, we should note, in order to use the law to establish our righteousness before God but to direct our righteous living under God.

'Abomination' is the word *bdelugma*. The same word is used by LXX to translate its Hebrew counterpart in Deuteronomy 24:4. Those who heard Jesus say verse 18 would mentally default to think of the divorce regulation in Deuteronomy 24:1-4. That text was not meant to encourage but to regulate divorce in Israel, specifically to protect the divorced wife from abuses.[10] It's a long if-if-if-then sort of text. Briefly, if a man marries a wife and is not pleased with her, he must give her written confirmation of the divorce when he sends her away; and if she then becomes the wife of another man, and if that fellow divorces her (with written confirmation) and sends her off, or if that second husband simply dies, then that first husband who originally divorced her must not take her as his wife again—it would be an 'abomination' before Yahweh. Never mind why, at this point. It just would. All I'm wondering is if the catch-word *bdelugma* in verse 15 may have brought to mind the *bdelugma* of Deuteronomy 24:4 to Jesus' mind and perhaps explain why He gave the 'divorce text' in verse 18 as a sample of law under the kingdom. Maybe. Maybe not.

At any rate, in verse 18 we must see that Jesus is not simply bringing over old covenant law; rather verse 18 goes far beyond anything in Deuteronomy 24. Jesus intensifies, interprets, and applies law in His kingdom. And He does so here in this sample. He is not regulating divorce but, one might say, accusing divorce. The thrust of Jesus' one-liner stands against the fellow who divorces as a means or license to remarry, wanting to remove his wife in order to make room for another.[11] Such a man then commits adultery against the first and proper union. Perhaps this is Jesus' version of 'abomination.' Jesus slaps a big 'A' on the chest of the man who is casual with marriage and wants to use divorce as a means of dumping a wife in order to acquire a 'new interest.' The man's 'explanation' would not matter: whether he is bored with commitment, or attracted to a new set of legs and hips, or

---

10. I am obviously over-simplifying here and omitting all sorts of questions and disputed matters.

11. See W. F. Arndt, *The Gospel According to St. Luke* (St. Louis: Concordia, 1956), p. 362. Cf. C. S. Keener, *The IVP Bible Background Commentary: New Testament* (Downers Grove, IL: InterVarsity, 1993), p. 235.

claims he's finally found 'understanding' and 'compatibility.' Instead, he crushes people, breaks promises, and commits adultery.[12] Hence Jesus sets in front of His cynical, mocking, self-justifying opponents (vv. 14-15) the new age (16a), the new opportunity (16b), and the new righteousness (17-18) they should face.

---

12. All this does not mean there are never legitimate grounds for divorce (cf. Matt. 19:9); I have deliberately limited discussion to this one-liner in Luke. For broader coverage, see D. A. Carson, 'Matthew,' EBC, rev. ed., 13 vols., 9:464-74; and J. K. Chamblin, *Matthew*, 2 vols. (Ross-shire: Christian Focus, 2010), 2:915-35.

5

Just a Little Talk with Abraham
(Luke 16:19-31)

We need to be thankful for rich people—we'd be so much poorer without them. Why, think of all the rich people Jesus (and/or Luke) introduces in this gospel: a rich farmer (12:16), a rich owner of an estate (16:1), a rich party-animal (16:19), one sometimes called a rich ruler (18:23), and a rich head tax collector (19:2). How many fewer stories we would have if it weren't for rich people!

This parable[1] about a rich man must not be severed from its preceding context. All of Luke 16 has an 'economic' bent to it, and what Jesus has already been teaching feeds into this parable. As you hear Jesus' description of this rich man, you realize he is one who doesn't give a lick about 'making friends' for eternity by means of his wealth (v. 9), that he is wholly given over to be a slave of mammon (v. 13), and that the life-style that thrills him (v. 19) and that he finds so 'admirable' is abominable before God (v. 15). In one sense, Jesus has already sketched this rich man before He introduces him. I think there are several key words that might provide the best way of working through this parable.

The first is **severity**, which focuses especially on verses 19-21, but can be extended through verse 23. Here is a

---

1. Some purist is likely to insist that the text does not explicitly call this passage a parable; but see Klyne Snodgrass, *Stories with Intent* (Grand Rapids: Eerdmans, 2008), p. 426.

sumptuous revelry and abject misery. The rich man is completely self-absorbed with his expensive 'threads,' his imported Egyptian (the usual source of 'fine linen') BVDs, and 'celebrating lavishly every day' (v. 19). It was party time all the time. But one can't help gawking at Lazarus. He has a name anyway. Apparently crippled, he had been 'thrown' down or deposited by someone at the rich man's gate; diseased and 'unclean'—'full of sores'; hungry—longing simply for scraps from the rich man's table; and helpless, likely—the mangy, half-wild dogs kept licking his sores and he could not fend them off.[2]

It seems to me that Jesus is not portraying a simple severity on the rich man's part, but a harsh, studied, deliberate, and one could even say, calculated severity. According to the story, he knew who Lazarus was (see v. 24), he could see his condition, yet there was never one move to alleviate. Lazarus was just furniture. Jesus seems to depict an intentional indifference, a heartless, cruel, and knowing neglect. Nothing unpleasant must blemish the 'good times' scenario.

Yes, as Jesus said, 'a certain man was rich' (v. 19a), but we must be clear what this does *not* mean. It was not his fault that he was rich. Jesus does not say he had no right to be rich. Jesus is not a Marxist. So far as we know he obtained his wealth honestly. Nor does Jesus imply that he should get rid of his riches; nor that he should save the world; only that he should've aided the particular man who was plainly in view in his daily life. But eating so well, it's no wonder his cholesterol got him, and he died and was buried. He finds himself in Hades and 'in torments,' whereas Lazarus has angel transport to Abraham's side (vv. 22-23). Clearly a man's earthly condition is no index to his state in the sight of God.

I don't want to unduly press the mere description of the parable but it almost appears that Jesus describes for us the

---

2. Kenneth Bailey makes a case for the canine activity being the one relief Lazarus had; see *Jesus through Middle Eastern Eyes* (Downers Grove, IL: InterVarsity, 2008), p. 385. The two particles in the Greek text (*alla kai*), however, seem to combine in a progressive sense, meaning 'and worse than all'—the pesky dogs were simply an intensifying of his misery (cf. C. L. Rogers, Jr., and C. L. Rogers III, *The New Linguistic and Exegetical Key to the Greek New Testament* [Grand Rapids: Zondervan, 1998], p. 151).

vast emptiness of mere affluence. The rich man's biography could be summed up in three statements: (1) he wore imported underwear (v. 19a); (2) he had lots of fun (v. 19b); (3) he died and was buried (v. 22b). Somehow when one reduces his whole life to a mere outline, it appears far less full and dynamic and more silly and tedious.

But we must face this 'severity.' I have argued that that of the rich man seemed harsh and intentional, but more often ours may be simply oblivious and thoughtless. But we must watch ourselves. Sometimes believers get 'application jitters' over a text like this. Someone says, 'We need to assess the needs of the homeless in our community and ....' Well, maybe. Or another suggests, 'We need to form a study committee to see whether our church can put a program in place to meet this sort of need.' No, please don't; forget the committee and program. You don't need to go looking for some outstanding sample of human wretchedness. Your 'Lazarus' might be the wife you've been neglecting, or the husband you've emotionally stiff-armed for years. Maybe your Lazarus is the child you seldom read to or pray with or play with because there are always such pressing items on your agenda; then again, 'he' may be the widow next door, whom you've never visited since the death of her husband. Who needs programs or committees for this?

Solemnity is a second word that characterizes Jesus' teaching here (vv. 23-26). We know this is a parable but when we read that the rich man is 'in Hades' and 'in torments' (v. 23a) and that he begs for the slightest relief from 'this flame' (v. 24b), we know we are dealing with the most serious matters. 'In torments' and 'at Abraham's side' seem to be the opposing alternatives. We must remember not to use a parable to draw a map of the afterlife, but at the same time we must not use 'parable' as an excuse to tone down the awful solemnity here. For example, beware of saying the rich man is only using figurative language when he speaks of 'this flame'? Well, what of it? If the language is figurative, what is it figurative of? Why do we feel the need to use figurative language? Is it not in order to express a reality that can't be grasped otherwise? You cannot dissolve realities away by blathering about figurative language.

In the confines of the parable itself, the rich man displays unrelenting chutzpah, for he seems to assume that Lazarus should be heaven's lackey for his own momentary relief (v. 24). But Abraham quickly staunches such an assumption (v. 25f.). Yet note how gracious Abraham's reply is: 'Child, remember that you received back [or, in full] your good things in your lifetime' (v. 25a). Abraham does not berate him but answers him in a very respectful way, hinting perhaps that we should deal kindly even with hell-bent people. But there can be no fingertips in water, for 'between us and you [plural] a great chasm has been put in place' (v. 26) and, because of that, there can be no 'traffic' between the two realms. That is the great solemnity because it is a great finality. There is a time and a place where nothing can be changed, nothing reversed. It is rightfully and can be helpfully sobering.

Once Robert Murray M'Cheyne stopped at a roadside quarry to get shelter from a sudden downpour of rain. These was a fire in the furnace of the engine shed where he was standing with a bunch of workmen, and 'he asked them what that fire taught them to think of.' That was all, but merely the way the words were spoken gripped the men and one was brought to faith and obedience.[3] In torments, in this flame, a great chasm—solemn indeed.

The word **sufficiency** captures the last portion of Jesus' parable (vv. 27-31). The rich man changes direction a bit. If no hope for him, he thinks of his five brothers (v. 28). But there is such a relentless arrogance about this man: he still assumes that Lazarus should be his personal errand boy (v. 27)—he should go 'testify' to his brothers so that they could avoid this 'place of torment.' But Abraham nixes the suggestion, so much as to say, 'No need of that.' He says, 'They have Moses and the prophets; let them listen to them' (v. 29). They have, Abraham says, all they need; the Old Testament is sufficient to lead them into the kingdom of God.

But, no, the rich man objects. Somehow he will not take anyone's word for an answer. He is not only lost—he is obnoxious. He will put Abraham right: 'If someone should go

---

3. Marcus L. Loane, *They Were Pilgrims* (Edinburgh: Banner of Truth, 2006), pp. 174-75.

to them from the dead, they will repent' (v. 30). They simply need a slice of drama, a sliver of the supernatural. It's as if he were saying, 'They need a visit from the "region beyond" that makes them go bug-eyed, drop their dentures, and turn to Jesus.' He is dissatisfied; his brothers need a souped-up approach. But Abraham knows better: 'If they do not listen to Moses and the prophets, neither will they be persuaded if someone should rise from the dead' (v. 31). The kingdom of God can be so insistently undramatic and low-key. Salvation is not in sensation. The brothers have the Scriptures; they have all they need; if they will receive it.

6

Millstones, Mustard, and a Cure
for Hot-stuff Syndrome
(Luke 17:1-10)

In one of our homes there was a bathroom right next to my study; it was the one I usually used. I needed new towels for that bathroom, and I wanted towels with 'strong' colors. No pastels. So I bought bright red and yellow towels. They did not fit the décor or 'ambiance' of that bathroom. But they were what I wanted—bright red and yellow. Yet anyone, not knowing my quirks yet half-conscious of décor, would look askance and be mystified over my choice of colors. It is something like that with Luke 17:1-10. We may wonder why Luke put this section here. It seems like bits and pieces (four of them), and the connections between them are not obvious, if they exist. The disciples are the audience again (v. 1), and we may assume the general setting is the journey to Jerusalem, but it looks like an odd collection of 'this and that.' Bock holds that the 'common thread' is the disciples' walk but that the sections (vv. 1-2, 3-4, 5-6, 7-10) seem to function like a collection of proverbs.[1] Other expositors see links between the sections; e.g., the duties of disciples regarding sin (vv. 1-2, 3-4), and in order to handle these the apostles ask for an increase of faith (vv. 5-6), but, even should they

---

1. Darrell L. Bock, *Luke 9:51-24:53*, BECNT (Grand Rapids, Baker, 1996), p. 1380.

carry out these duties, they must not think they should collect medals over it (vv. 7-10). Such links may be there, but they are not obvious. Even if we don't know *why* Luke selected this material or *how* it may or may not be connected, we do have *what* Jesus taught, and that must be the focus of our attention.

First, Jesus instructs us about **the peril of sin** (vv. 1-2), that is, the peril of someone causing others to sin. He says that *skandala* are inevitable. A *skandalon* seems to have a dual import; on the one hand, it is a lure, bait, enticement, and so a trap; on the other, it refers to what trips up, causes one to stumble, potentially to ruin.[2] Here the word probably refers to tripping up, so that disciples are led into sin or apostasy. Conceivably this could include persecutors who seek to make disciples renounce faith in Jesus, or it could point to deviant teaching by alleged Christian teachers, or to those luring believers into gross sin that severs their fellowship with Christ.[3]

Here we meet with Jesus' outrageous values (vv. 1-2). He combines inevitability with responsibility—occasions that lure His people to apostasy are unavoidable 'but woe to the one through whom they come.' Jesus then draws a word-picture that is almost cartoonish: 'it would be preferable for him if a millstone were hung round his neck and he had been thrown into the sea' (v. 2a). If the millstone was a donkey-driven millstone as in Matthew 18:6, it would have been terribly heavy.[4] What is Jesus saying? He is saying that it would be better for a fellow to meet a certain and cruel death before he was the means of destroying the faith of a disciple of Jesus.[5] That would be preferable to meeting the judgment

---

2. See William Barclay, *A New Testament Wordbook* (London: SCM, 1955), pp. 111-14.

3. *God's Word* (World Publishing, 1995) takes *skandalon* here as a lure to apostasy: 'Situations that cause people to lose their faith are certain to arise. But how horrible it will be for the person who causes someone to lose his faith!' (v. 1). 'Be on your guard,' in verse 3a, may look back to verses 1-2; i.e., be on the alert, on the lookout for such threats.

4. For background, see Michael J. Wilkins, 'Matthew,' ZIBBC, 1:113. One surmises this would require several executioners; just one trying to heave both victim and millstone would incur a massive hernia.

5. The 'little ones' of verse 2 are Jesus' disciples; in Matthew 18:6 Jesus calls them 'little ones who believe in me.'

of God for such wickedness. Jesus says it is better to die the most horrific and gruesome death than to bring disaster on one of His disciples. Nothing apparently so enrages Jesus as someone trying to pry one of His disciples loose from Him.

This severe warning of Jesus should prove an immense encouragement to His disciples, for it shows how Jesus regards His people. Not even 'one' (emphatic) of His 'little ones' should be lured from Him. If we switch the image to shepherd and sheep, this text underscores the intensity of Jesus' concern for the safety of His flock. Perhaps we can imagine His posting a sign in the sheepfold for all spiritual thugs to read: 'Beware of sheep.'

Second, Jesus commands us about **the practice of forgiveness** (vv. 3b-4). Verses 1-2 may deal chiefly with a threat to the disciples from outside, whereas verses 3b-4 focus on trouble among disciples—and Jesus points out how it should be handled: 'If your brother sins, rebuke him; and if he repents, forgive him; and if he should sin against you seven times in the day and seven times should turn to you, saying, "I repent," you must forgive him.'

By and large we don't believe this. What do I mean? Well, what frequently happens in such a case? What is the reaction to Jesus' direction, 'If your brother sins, rebuke him'? It is the equivalent of, 'Oh, I could never do that [never tell the truth?]; that would be too confrontational.' So the wronged one may confer with a pastor about the matter to see 'what should be done,' or one will whine to a Christian counselor about the situation, or discuss it with several friends over coffee. And in such ways the opportunity for repentance is taken from the offender. Even if, should the rebuke be given and the offender did repent, we may be loath to forgive, because that would mean giving up the 'superior' position we enjoy as 'the wronged one.'

But let's suppose we will give Jesus a hearing. What is He saying? He lays down a dual requirement: rebuke and forgive. 'Rebuke' does not mean 'telling him off' or reaming him out but simply disclosing the wrong he has done.[6] Rebuking

---

6. Cf. Lev. 19:17: 'You must not hate your brother in your heart. Rebuke your neighbor directly, and you will not incur guilt because of him' (HCSB). This text implies that expressing rebuke tends to dissipate inward resentment.

means you have the courage to confront the offender and not gossip to your neighbor about him. Jesus views 'rebuke' as a prelude to repentance and then forgiveness.[7] In verse 4 Jesus sketches an exaggerated scenario not to endorse gullibility but a readiness to forgive. Jesus is not saying something stupid in verse 4 but something pointed. For Jesus' disciples forgiveness is not to be a unique occurrence but an ongoing practice.

Our problem with Jesus' word here is that we are often too spineless to rebuke and too resentful to forgive. Jesus requires of us both courage to rebuke and compassion to forgive. The Christian life, as usual, demands both guts and goodness. In this segment Jesus is assuming that the church is a sinful people—folks who need to practice rebuking, repenting, and forgiving.

Thirdly, Jesus addresses **the question of faith** (vv. 5-6). Here the request comes from 'the apostles' and Jesus is called 'the Lord,' both by the apostles and Luke. They ask, 'Increase our faith.' There may well be a connection with what precedes. The apostles' request may have been motivated by the demands of Jesus in verses 3-4. The rebuke-and-forgive regimen may have daunted them. They might have thought, 'Who is sufficient for these things?' Hence their plea: 'Increase our faith.'

Verse 6 is the Lord's clarification. Note how Jesus redefines their need (something Jesus tends to do with His people). 'If you have faith as a grain of mustard seed ....' It is, Jesus says, not great faith but genuine faith that matters. Even 'small' faith can achieve difficult or unthinkable results: 'You could say to this mulberry tree, "Be uprooted and planted in the sea"—and it would obey you' (v. 6b).[8] Jesus is not encouraging you to upset the ecological balance or to get in trouble with the Environmental Protection Agency. But somehow we have a way of being so engrossed with Jesus'

7. Jesus does not deal with other possibilities here: What if, when rebuked, the offender does not repent? Can forgiveness be extended when there is no repentance? These matters are beyond the purview of this text.

8. The tree is usually thought to be the black mulberry, with an extensive root system and a lifespan of some hundreds of years; cf. David E. Garland, *Luke*, ZECNT (Grand Rapids: Zondervan, 2011), p. 681.

comical picture that we fail to hear what He says. It's as if we become mesmerized, wondering how that mulberry tree will do now that it's been plopped down in the Mediterranean. But Jesus is more concerned with mustard seeds than with mulberry trees. Leon Morris has summed it up well:

> Jesus' answer turns them from the thought of a less and more in faith to that of its genuineness. If there is real faith, then effects follow. It is not so much great faith in God that is required as faith in a great God.[9]

What implications might we draw from Jesus' answer in verse 6? In one sense, isn't He saying that it doesn't matter 'how much' faith you have? In fact, concern over the quantity of faith may be wrong-headed. Adolf Schlatter actually held that there was a 'false, faithless notion' combined with the apostles' request. They were seeking their support in the strength of their faith rather than looking to God as the object of faith.[10] To the same effect 'Rabbi' Duncan once passed on what Sandy Macleod said at the close of a 'question meeting.' They had been discussing the distinction between true and counterfeit faith. When they were done, Sandy Macleod said:

> All that is very well, but in analysing and scrutinizing your faith there is danger of neglecting the Object of faith. Was your faith crucified for you? Or were ye baptized in the name of your faith?[11]

Perhaps then you should pause before repeating the apostles' request. A request for increased faith could be unfaithful. What makes all the difference is the object of faith, not the quantity of faith. For faith by definition clings to God, casts itself upon God's power, rests in God's strength, relies upon God's adequacy. There may be a danger in this passion for

9. Leon Morris, *The Gospel According to St. Luke*, TNTC (Grand Rapids: Eerdmans, 1974), p. 256.

10. In *Die Evangelien nach Markus und Lukas*, Erlauterungen zum Neuen Testament (Stuttgart: Calwer, 1961), p. 339.

11. See David Brown, *The Life of Rabbi Duncan* (1872; reprint ed., Glasgow: Free Presbyterian, 1986), p. 472.

more or greater faith. We must not make an idol out of our faith. Our help is not in our faith or in the 'amount' of our faith but in the Lord to whom faith clings. Otherwise, we might say, 'Ah, I will be able to handle this, for I have great faith.' And so your great faith makes God unnecessary.

Finally, Jesus sketches a short and delightful parable that provides **the antidote for pride** (vv. 7-10). The parable reflects first-century Israelite culture. Contemporary readers should not see red or get bent out of shape because the master has a slave, or start ranting about social injustice. Because the master has a slave does not mean the master is cruel; the supper to be prepared wasn't unbearably late like eight o'clock at night but was the mid-late afternoon meal. Jesus' illustration simply reflected a common state of affairs at the time—even folks of modest means might have a slave, and He was emphasizing one matter, what the disciples' attitude should be toward their 'service.'

One can hardly miss the humor in Jesus' scenario. Indeed, some listeners may have been amused by His very first words—'Now who of you, having a slave' (v. 7). As noted, it was rather common for people of even moderate means to have a slave. But there were likely any number in Jesus' audience who did not. We can imagine one of them plunking his friend in the ribs at Jesus' opening words and exclaiming, 'Whoa, imagine that—having a slave!' But the humor especially appears in Jesus' contrary-to-life proposals. So the slave has been plowing or shepherding most of the day; and when he comes in, does the master hover all over him, telling him how exhausted he must be and that he must immediately come and sit down to a meal (v. 7b)? Not by a long shot. No, the slave is ordered to prepare the master's supper and serve him until he's finished—then, of course, the slave can eat and drink (v. 8). Or again, does the master fall over himself expressing how indebted he is to the slave for doing what he ordered (v. 9)? Of course not. Some may have a bit of difficulty with that. Maybe a ridiculous, non-human analogy can help. Which of you, having returned from a trip, would get out of your vehicle and say thank you to the battery for providing consistent starts, praise the headlights for their angelic radiance, pat the tires for rolling along diligently, laud the brake fluid for doing such a masterful job, and so on? You wouldn't do that, because folks would look at you and ask, 'What church does he attend?' But there it is. Do you do all that? No. Why not? Well, that is simply what a vehicle is supposed to do. And neither does a *doulos* (slave) get special credit for doing what was commanded.[12]

Then Jesus moves to His application in verse 10: 'Likewise, you also, when you have done all the things commanded you, say: "We are unprofitable servants [lit., slaves]; we have done what we ought to do."' The text makes us uneasy: 'You have done all the things commanded you' and 'we have done what we ought to do.' One senses that there is more than appears in those words. It reminds me of going into Sunday School when I was about ten years old and sitting beside a lad a bit older. Archie had on a green-and-white striped bow tie. Then he showed me that he could make a brown rubbery-looking worm come out the side of his bow tie! There was a tiny rubber 'hose' or line that ran down underneath his shirt and into his trouser pocket where was a small rubber 'bulb' he could squeeze. When he did, the 'worm' came out of the bow tie. It simply looked like a bow tie, but there was 'more' there than appeared. And that is the way with this text, for it pushes us to see 'more.' We can scarcely read these words without asking in the next breath, 'But who of us does "all things that have been commanded"?' Who of us can claim, 'We have done what we ought to do'? We are hardly up to that level. So the very words Jesus uses in His 'application' suck us into thinking of the *deficiencies* in our service to Him.

Andrew Bonar used to tell the story of a Grecian painter who produced a marvelous painting of a boy carrying on his head a basket of grapes. So exquisitely were the grapes painted, that when the picture was publicly displayed in the Forum, the birds pecked the grapes, thinking they were real. The painter's friends heaped congratulations on him, but he was not satisfied. When asked why, he replied, 'I should have

---

12. The thrust of this text does not overturn such assurances as Hebrews 6:10 or Matthew 10:42, which deal with God's view of believers' service; our text deals with *our* attitude about it.

done a great deal more. I should have painted the boy so true to life that the birds would not have dared to come near!'[13]

Even should we do 'all that has been commanded,' Jesus tells us our response must be, 'We are unprofitable servants.' But, like Bonar's painter, we are aware of our deficiencies and are always having to say, 'I should have done a great deal more.' Unprofitable servants indeed. This is a cure for those stupid times in your Christian life when you tend to get hot-stuff syndrome.

13. Marjory Bonar, ed., *Andrew A. Bonar: Diary and Life* (1893; reprint ed., Edinburgh: Banner of Truth, 1960), pp. 466.

7

Foreign Gratitude
(Luke 17:11-19)

Luke is both very specific and very vague as he leads into his 'leper' episode. On the one hand, he reminds us that Jesus is on His way to Jerusalem (and to all that will come upon Him there). This notice, 17:11, is the third main 'Jerusalem reminder' after 9:51 and 13:22. Jesus' Jerusalem-work has been the major concern since 9:31, and through these Jerusalem-reminders the cross casts its shadow back over Jesus' journey. Yet in locating the immediate episode Luke is not very precise. Jesus is apparently on the border between Samaria and Galilee, perhaps moving to the east, and as He enters 'a certain village' He meets up with a bunch of lepers. We don't need the name of the village; it's not necessary to be precise about that; no need to supply such particulars.

Naturally we are always wondering how a specific passage, like 17:11-19, fits into Luke's overall scheme. One can't always be sure of the connections, but since Luke 're-sets' the Jerusalem journey at 17:11, it seems one could take that point as the start of a new segment. Since 17:20-37 focuses on the coming of the kingdom, it may be reasonable to place all of 17:11–18:8 under a 'kingdom' rubric, with 17:11-19 highlighting the *scope* of the kingdom (it has room even for Samaritans), 17:20-37 its *coming*, and

18:1-8 its *justice*.[1] But for now we must deal with these ten lepers.

First off in this text we see **a distant healing for desperate men** (vv. 11-14). Ten lepers had bonded together in their common misery that overcame their (probably Jewish) scruples about Samaritans. The 'leprosy' was almost certainly not what we call leprosy (Hansen's disease) but was akin to various conditions like psoriasis, lupus, ringworm, and favus.[2] Such maladies rendered a person ritually 'unclean,' and Leviticus 13–14 take a great deal of space outlining procedures for priests (as the 'medical officers') to follow in both diagnosing and restoring lepers. Luke says, 'They stood a long way off' (v. 12b). That was a leper's tragedy. He was isolated from his community and family; he could not allow others to get near him (Lev. 13:45-46). If his loved ones provided him with food, they would likely have to leave it at a designated place, but there could be no contact or association. However, these men seem to know something about Jesus and what He can do, for they holler for Him to 'have mercy' on them (v. 13). And they seem to have confidence in His power, because when He sends them off for priests' inspection they went, 'and as they went, they were cleansed' (v. 14). So Luke depicts their isolation (v. 12), their desperation (v. 13), and their confidence (v. 14).

Imagine the scene ten days later in the home of leper number five. He's eating supper with his family. The priest's certificate declaring him 'clean' lies on the kitchen counter. He's telling his wife and children all about it. 'We hollered out to Jesus, and Jesus did it; we knew we were cleansed as we were running along to the priests! Now I have my life back.'

---

1. David Gooding (*According to Luke* [1987; reprint ed., Coleraine, N. Ireland: Myrtlefield Trust, 2013], p. 301) sums up Luke's material from 17:11–19:10 under the heads of the coming of the kingdom and entry into the kingdom. I would slightly alter his textual divisions, allotting 17:11–18:8 to the former, and 18:9–19:10 to the latter. There is also a sort of catch-word connection between 17:11-19 and the previous parable in 17:7-10. In verse 9 the master does not thank his slave and in verses 16-18 most of the lepers do not thank Jesus. The one is not obligated to give thanks, the others are, but don't. I owe this observation to my friend and pastoral colleague, Chris O'Brien.

2. See DJG, 1st ed., pp. 463-64.

Quite a number of versions render verse 12b, 'they stood at a distance.' And it was a 'distant' healing. Ronald Wallace plays on this 'distance' idea, pointing out that the distance consisted of more than literal space.[3] There was, tragically, a distance in their relationship to Jesus. They receive benefit from Jesus and yet feel no necessity to seek Jesus further. They would acknowledge the power of Jesus but, as verse 17 shows, they have no interest in the person of Jesus.[4] Likely there are any number in the visible church today who have only a 'distant' relation to Jesus.

Secondly, in verses 15-16 we see **the right response from the wrong source**. One of these lepers stopped in his tracks—when he realized he was no longer a leper (v. 15a). The priest inspection could wait; a compulsion seized him and he 'returned, with a loud voice giving glory to God' (v. 15b). Sure of his healing, he enjoyed the first act of his freedom—not standing at a distance but falling on his face right at Jesus' feet, 'giving him thanks' (v. 16a).[5] In addition to his compulsion and freedom we now hear of his identity—he was a Samaritan (v. 16b). Luke adds this as a sort of 'kerplunk' at the end of the sentence. Almost as if to say, 'Now what do you think of that?' Samaritans were generally despised by Jews, even regarded as apostates, and to have one depicted as showing a model response to Jesus' gift is more than a mild surprise. It is as shocking as Jesus' story in 10:25-37, in which a Samaritan's active compassion condemns the studied indifference of a priest and Levite.[6] So one's natural reaction on hearing Luke's final note in verse 16 is, 'No, there's something wrong with that,' or, 'That should not be!' Then we realize that such a reaction really means, 'That is not what I

---

3. Ronald S. Wallace, *Many Things in Parables/The Gospel Miracles* (Grand Rapids: Eerdmans, 1963), pp. 148-50 (2nd part).

4. Cf. Alfred Edersheim, *The Life and Times of Jesus the Messiah*, 2 vols. (reprint ed., Grand Rapids: Eerdmans, 1967), 2:330-31: 'The lesson conveyed in this case is, that we may expect, and even experience, miracles, without any real faith in the Christ; with belief, indeed, in His Power, but without surrender to His Rule.'

5. Commentators commonly point out that this is the only reference to giving thanks to Jesus in the NT (cf. Alan J. Thompson, *Luke*, EGGNT [Nashville: Broadman & Holman, 2016], p. 270). The implication of the text is clear: the way you 'give glory to God' is by 'giving thanks' to Jesus. Luke subtly edges you toward the deity of Jesus.

6. Luke by no means whitewashes Samaritans. He notes their resistance to Jesus in 9:51-53.

expect,' or, 'I would never have imagined that.' In short, 'What a surprise!' Which is precisely the point: the kingdom of God is cluttered with surprises. If we see this Samaritan's faith (see v. 19) here, should we be so astonished when Luke's second volume reports scores of Samaritans embracing the gospel (Acts 8:4-25)?

This text brings to mind some of the attitudes afoot during the 1949–52 revival on the Isle of Lewis. That revival centered in the Church of Scotland, which caused some problems among the Free Church, especially for the ministers. Well, the Church of Scotland was a 'broad' and more liberal church, at least on the mainland, and so most all of the Free Church ministers held aloof from or opposed the revival. One testimony told of a Free Church elder who was 'altogether opposed to the revival.' He had prayed for revival, but 'of course, it could not come through the Church of Scotland!'[7] The Lord had begun His work in the 'wrong' church. And here the 'wrong' leper had rightly responded to Jesus. It is the glory of God that He 'wrongly' gathers in such unexpected trophies of His grace.

Thirdly, we hear **a sad question about an aborted response** in verses 17-18. In face of the Samaritan's fervent gratitude, Jesus asks, 'Were not ten cleansed? But the nine—where are they?' (v. 17). Why only a minority report? Only a 'foreigner' (v. 18) came back 'to give glory to God.' Neither Jesus nor the text specifies that the other nine were Israelites. That's an assumption that a reader tends to make—and it may well be on the mark. But the problem is not national identity but absent gratitude. By his response the Samaritan showed that he was more taken with the Healer than with the healing. This was obviously not the case with the nine. Jesus might well say to them as He did to some of the '5,000' crowd in John 6:26, 'You seek me, not because you saw signs, but because you ate of the loaves and got your fill.' The situation is different but the trouble is the same: people can love Jesus' benefits but care little for Jesus Himself.

The heart of the matter rests in that clause, 'to give glory to God' (v. 18). Sadly, we have almost made that a ceremonial

---

7. See Colin and Mary Peckham, *Sounds from Heaven* (Ross-shire: Christian Focus, 2004), pp. 120-21, 183.

cliché, something we sprinkle about as evangelical fluff in our prayers and exhortations. Actually, it is what reveals us. I have often been struck by the stark sadness of that clause in Romans 1:21 (in the AV with which I grew up): 'neither were thankful.' The text actually records the whole response of those who could know God to some degree: 'they glorified him not as God, neither were thankful' (v. 21, AV), which was the first step on the road to their twisted thinking and darkened understanding (v. 21b). What we may consider an optional extra is rather an essential necessity. Os Guinness has written that Romans 1:21 is a sober reminder that 'rebellion against God does not begin with the clenched fist of atheism but with the self-satisfied heart of the one for whom "thank you" is redundant.'[8] That comment can summarize Luke 17 as well—and ought to both sober and scare us.

Finally, in verse 19 we hear **a deeper assurance for a grateful disciple**. Here is this Samaritan on his face at Jesus' feet. Jesus tells him to 'get up, go; your faith has saved you.' Some may dispute translating *sōzō* here as 'saved'; it can be taken as 'has made you well' or the like (as, e.g., NIV, ESV, NET). But the latter is not as fitting here as it may seem; I agree with Bock:

> The allusion must be to the full saving faith of the Samaritan, since the deliverance related to the healing had already occurred and that healing was something shared with the other nine. What the man receives here the others do not.[9]

This 'formula,' 'Your faith has saved you/made you well' occurs four times in Luke's gospel—of a sinful woman (7:50), a woman with a hemorrhage (8:48), the Samaritan here (17:19), and a blind beggar (18:42). So James Edwards observes:

> The benediction is never used of a Pharisee or Jewish leader, but only of sinners, outsiders, the unclean and needy, for 'of such is the kingdom of God.'[10]

---

8. Cited in James M. Boice, *Romans: An Expositional Commentary*, 4 vols. (Grand Rapids: Baker, 1991), 1:164.

9. In *Luke 9:51-24:53*, BECNT, 1405.

10. *The Gospel According to Luke*, PNTC (Grand Rapids: Eerdmans, 2015), p. 486.

Our Samaritan then received an assurance both deeper and higher than anything the nine others received. Which doesn't surprise us, for we have often found that those who come to Jesus always receive far more than they imagine.

8

When the Kingdom of God Comes
(Luke 17:20-37)

You have to hand it to the Pharisees—they brought up worthwhile questions.[1] When is the kingdom of God coming? (v. 20). I suppose we could summarize Jesus' answer as: the kingdom of God is both already and not yet—and you must be sure to respond rightly to what I tell you about it.

First, we have this encounter of Jesus with some Pharisees. Here Jesus speaks of **the kingdom and secrecy** (vv. 20-21), perhaps with quote marks around 'secrecy,' since the idea is that the kingdom is not an absolute secret but rather is 'not obvious.'

When the Pharisees asked their question, they 'were concerned about the mighty act of the heavenly Kingdom to crush the Roman might, punish the Gentiles, exalt Israel, and establish God's reign in all the world.'[2] They were thinking of the kingdom in its more consummated (or consummating) form. Jesus tells them the kingdom (at least the way He is speaking of it now) does not come 'with observation,' which likely means,

---

1. Verses 20-37 simply 'begin' and it's hard to know what link, if any, there is with what precedes (though note my comments at the beginning of the previous chapter). Luke indicates no change of scene, no geographical location, and, seemingly, no thematic connection. We cannot simply assume, as Bock seems to do (*Luke 9:51-24:53*, BECNT, p. 1409), that these Pharisees had witnessed the healing of the ten lepers (vv. 11-19). Nevertheless, attentive readers may remember that 7:22 indicates that the cleansing of lepers was a sign of the presence of the kingdom.

2. G. E. Ladd, *Jesus and the Kingdom* (New York: Harper & Row, 1964), p. 132. Cf. the pseudepigraphal Psalms of Solomon 17:21-46; 18:5-9 (1st century b.c.).

not with the sure-fire, tell-tale, cosmic-smoking, history-shaking signs you are thinking of. Rather, Jesus says, 'The kingdom of God is in the midst of you' (*entos humōn,* v. 21b).[3] The kingdom is already here; it's right in front of you. It has arrived in Jesus' own ministry and work (see 11:20!). Relatively speaking, the kingdom has not arrived with fireworks; it has arrived quietly, almost 'secretly,' in a somewhat subdued way. The kingdom is here because the *King* is here.

We are accustomed to this mode of thinking. For example, imagine some sort of international consortium. When the Brazilian diplomat arrives, they might quite naturally announce, 'Brazil is here.' In his capacity in that situation he represents Brazil, so that, in one sense, he 'is' Brazil. So in our text. The kingdom is here because Jesus, the king, is here. The presence of Jesus indicates the presence of the kingdom.

The Pharisees can be our teachers here. They can tell us that it's possible to be concerned with the kingdom but to ignore the king; it's possible to be fascinated with last things while neglecting the first thing. The Pharisees did not realize how close the kingdom was, 'in the midst' of them, in Jesus, in its hidden, quiet form.

At verse 22 there's a change of audience. Verses 20-21 had been directed to the Pharisees, but now verses 22-37 carry teaching for the disciples. On the Pharisees He pressed the 'already' of the kingdom, but to the disciples the 'not yet' of the kingdom; He speaks of the consummation of the kingdom or, in part, of what leads up to that. Hence in verses 22-25 He focuses on **the kingdom and suffering.**

Jesus says there will be suffering for His disciples: 'Days will come when you will long to see one of the days of the Son of Man, and you will not see (it)' (v. 22). 'The days of the Son of Man' probably refers to the time when Jesus reigns and rules in His kingdom. They will long to enjoy just one of those days. Jesus implies that the reason for such longing will be because of difficulties and sufferings they will face, the hatred and hardship that will come their way simply because they belong to Him. The pressure and the conflict will be so

---

3. Not 'within you,' as the NIV has it. Jesus could hardly say that to the Pharisees. For 'among' or 'in the midst of,' see David Garland's reference to Matill's work (*Luke,* ZECNT [Grand Rapids: Zondervan, 2011], p. 698).

severe that they will long for 'one of the days of the Son of Man'—and they 'will not see it.' Note that Jesus does not actually go this far—but He comes close to saying that His present disciples would not see His coming in their lifetime.

Jesus is not saying it is wrong to long for the days of the Son of Man, but He is warning disciples not to allow their desire to lead them into error. Some will be around who are only too glad to feed fantasy, to stir hype with their 'He's there!' or 'Look—he's here!' (v. 23a). Jesus tells us not to fall for it (v. 23b); don't let, He implies, the desire for relief lead you into all sorts of weird, wild speculations, or even to be open to them. Don't let desire father deception. Jesus provides the corrective for all this nonsense in verse 24: when the Son of Man comes you will know it. It will be like those times when lightning flashes and lights up the whole horizon from end to end. That is, His coming will be public, visible, and unmistakable. No one who sees it will have to stand there and ask, 'You know, I wonder if this could be the second coming?'

But the stress in this section is on suffering. And no sooner does Jesus speak of his no-doubts-about-it glorious coming than He inserts His customary caution: 'But first he [the Son of Man] must suffer many things and be rejected by this generation' (v. 25). This is the divine plan, it 'must' (*dei*) be this way. And this is the proper order—'first'; first suffering (25) and then glory (24). Jesus had repeatedly underscored His coming suffering (9:22-23, 31, 44-45; 12:50; 13:33). There's almost a certain pathos about verse 25. Jesus is speaking about His glorious coming but cannot help intruding a 'But first' into it all, insisting that the coming kingdom only comes at great cost. Combining verses 22 and 25, Jesus is telling us that our calling (v. 22) is to suffer many things as has our Lord (v. 25).

Our faith then is hardly 'the opiate of the people.' It's as if Jesus is saying: Do not allow a combination of wishful thinking and fervent desire and difficult circumstances to lead you to grasp at false straws (v. 23); when the Son of Man comes, you'll know it (v. 24); meanwhile, your task is to endure suffering as I have (v. 25; see Acts 14:22).[4]

---

4. Though the keynote in this section is on suffering, we should not ignore the realism and sanity Jesus commends in verses 23-24. He is clear in verse 24: what we call the second coming will be a public, universal event and you'll have no need for the

Thirdly, Jesus teaches about **the kingdom and secularism**
(vv. 26-33). The 'doctrine' Jesus highlights has to do with the
preoccupation of the world (vv. 26-30). He refers to the times
of Noah and Lot. We are accustomed, from OT testimony,
to regard such times as periods of premier wickedness (see
Gen. 6:5-8, 11-13; 13:13; 19:4-14). Jesus does not contradict that
testimony but places the emphasis elsewhere. Luke uses a series
of verbs in the imperfect tense, indicating what the people were
continually doing. In Noah's day, then, 'they were eating, they
were drinking, they were marrying, they were being given in
marriage, until the day Noah went into the ark' (v. 27). And
it was just like that in the days of Lot: 'they were eating, they
were drinking, they were buying, they were selling, they were
planting, they were building' (v. 28). Nothing wicked about
these activities in themselves. But those things were the sum
total of their lives. Jesus does not hammer on their wickedness
but their *preoccupations.* They were completely absorbed in
their own interests. Whether they are depraved is momentarily
beside the point—they are simply 'secular.' As the flood and
fire and sulfur caught them by surprise—that's how it will be
when 'the Son of Man is revealed' (v. 30).[5]

There is also a warning in this text for professing believers
in our day, at least in the west. It is easy to assume that it's

nightly news to tell you of it. This means, among other things, that Jesus did not come
back in 1923 in northwest Siberia disguised as an Orthodox priest. There have been
more than a plethora of here's-the-Messiah and kingdom-around-the-corner movements.
For historical perspective, see Norman Cohn, *The Pursuit of the Millennium* (New York:
Harper Torchbooks, 1961). Jehovah's Witnesses said that Christ returned to earth in
1914 but was invisible and not in physical form. Over the years they have had to engage
in retrenching and revising their end-time speculations (see Walter Martin, *The Kingdom
of the Cults*, rev., updated ed. [Minneapolis: Bethany House, 2003], pp. 72, 104-6). Or
there were the 'Millerites,' who claimed Christ would return sometime between March
21, 1843 and March 21, 1844, but no, that didn't happen. Some then revised the date
to October 22, 1844—but, no, that proved wrong as well—and so others claimed that
his 'coming' was a coming into the heavenly, not earthly sanctuary (see Martin, pp. 538,
540-43). It seems there is no cure for the 'There-he-is, here-he-is' disease.

5. J. C. Ryle (*Expository Thoughts on the Gospels: St. Luke*, 2 vols. [New
York: Baker & Taylor, 1858], 2:244) draws an inference (an accurate one, I think)
from this text: 'It is hard to imagine a passage of Scripture which more completely
overthrows the common notions that prevail among men about Christ's return. The
world will not be converted when Jesus comes again. The earth will not be full of
the knowledge of the Lord. The reign of peace will not have been established. The
millennium will not have begun. These glorious things will come to pass *after* the
second advent, but not before.'

non-Christians who are always preoccupied with their own 'stuff' and, as we say, are only gazing at their own navels. But there's a word here to the modern disciple. You too are liable to be so taken up with brushing your teeth, choosing your earrings, closing real estate deals, building houses, going to work, getting through school, passing your exams, taking kids to music lessons, running Junior to Little League, going to church, the beauty shop and the grocery store, text messaging, mowing the yard, finding a new hair salon, paying the orthodontist, getting allergy shots, that it's almost like you're living in Sodom. It's the frenzied pace of one thing after another that loses sight of the coming of the Son of Man.

If Jesus' doctrine deals with the preoccupation of the world (vv. 26-30), His 'application' focuses on the detachment of the disciple (vv. 31-33). Jesus gives two pictures of the urgency that should grip a disciple when 'the Son of Man is revealed.' If he should be up on the flat roof of his home and his 'stuff' is in the house, he must not 'go down to get it' (v. 31a). Same thing if he's out working in the field—he doesn't turn back to retrieve anything (v. 31b). There's a certain urgency demanded, but more than that—a detachment. If the coming of Jesus really matters, it should lead you to sit loose to all else. Jesus is pressing us here on our *affections*. Verse 31, we could say, contains positive pictures, but in verse 32 Jesus makes a 'negative' allusion: 'Remember Lot's wife' (see Gen. 19:23-26). Yahweh's agents could try to get Mrs Lot out of Sodom but couldn't get Sodom out of Mrs Lot. She 'looked back'; her eyes followed her affections.

In verses 26-33 Jesus says that is the way it will be when the Son of Man comes. It will be a re-run of Noah and Lot times. People will be absorbed in their own interests, wholly taken up with the normal stuff of life, and so they cannot be looking for a Savior—or a Judge. The kingdom meets secularism.

In the last segment (vv. 34-37) Jesus warns about **the king- dom and separation**. In spite of difficulties in interpreting this section, the main picture is clear. When Christ comes again, when the kingdom begins to fully come, it will involve separation, even at the most intimate levels (vv. 34-35). Jesus gives a night-time and a day-time scenario. In the former, two (husband and wife?) will be in one bed, one will be 'taken' and the other 'left.' In the latter case, working in the day replaces the previous picture of resting at night. Two women (the verb construction is feminine) are grinding grain together, one is 'taken,' the other 'left.'[6]

Then we face the enigma of verse 37. The disciples respond with a question: 'Where, Lord?' And we wonder just what they are asking. Then there is Jesus' strange answer: 'Where the body is, there also the vultures will be gathered together.' There are all sorts of 'takes' on this verse. It seems to me that the disciples' query picks up on the 'will be left,' in the sense of 'left to judgment.' If so, they ask where judgment will occur. Jesus' response may mean judgment will occur wherever it needs to occur, just as surely as vultures can find available prey.[7] Some may object that that is a terribly grim sort of reply. The answer to that is: Of course it is. If Jesus is speaking about judgment, how could it be other than grim? Judgment cannot be made palatable.

However, we do not need to nail down verse 37 precisely in order to 'get' Jesus' main point. We only need to pay attention to His pictures in verses 34-35. What is the upshot of those verses? Are they not telling us that association with Jesus' followers will not deliver one from judgment? Intimacy or camaraderie with Jesus' disciples does not protect from judgment. For the kingdom, when the Son of Man comes, will involve *separation*. This does not mean that your case is hopeless. You may not be a disciple of Jesus, but if you are reading this now, and if the Son of Man has not yet come, you can now bow to Him and enter His kingdom.

---

6. There is no verse 36 in modern English versions, as there was in AV/KJV. It has poor support in the Greek manuscript tradition and so is not likely a part of the original text.

7. One faces a cafeteria of proposals on verse 37. See the commentaries of Marshall and Bock for the range of interpretations on tap. Exhaustive discussion is not possible, or useful, here.

9

Prayer's Day in Court
(Luke 18:1-8)

Let's say the radiator in your car is defunct. You might
go to an auto junk yard with its acres of smashed-up
vehicles, hardly an aesthetic venue. But there you find a
model like yours with the right side totally crushed in, but
its radiator is in pristine condition. In that mass of mangled
specimens you have found something useful, just what you
needed. That's something like some of Jesus' characters in
His parables—they may be such unpromising rogues and yet
they offer something useful. Like this magistrate in our text.
He seems a low-down, self-serving political knave. In real
life someone like this might have been appointed to the local
bench by Herod, or perhaps he would be a Roman municipal
appointee. Qua the analogy, we may wonder what we could
ever salvage from this cynic, but in Jesus' story he becomes
our instructor in prayer.

We should note that Jesus is focusing on a particular kind
of prayer. Luke seems to continue on from 17:22-37 and so in
18:1 reminds us that the disciples are still the main audience
('to them' in 18:1 picks up 'to his disciples' in 17:22). And the
context of 17:22-37 seems to color 18:1-8. There (17:22) Jesus
implied that His disciples would be driven to desperation as
they endured the pressures, assaults, and opposition of the
world around them. So in the parable Jesus tells of a widow
suffering wrong and indifference, which is precisely what

God's 'elect' (18:7) as a body will also be facing. So the prayer Jesus speaks of is particularly prayer that goes on pleading with God to put things right for His people as they suffer wrong in this world. Prayer seeks its day in court. Its plea is, 'Let your kingdom come.'

On to the teaching. Jesus begins by making a general point—one that is implied rather than directly stated: **Jesus assumes that you will likely have trouble with prayer.** 'Now he spoke a parable to them, pointing out that they must always pray and not lose heart' (v. 1). As with the next parable (18:9, and that of 19:11) Luke tells us exactly why Jesus told the parable. But this statement recognizes that there are times when prayer will be hard, when we will be tempted to leave off praying and give it all up. There's a healthy realism seeping out of this text. Richard Bewes put it well:

> At certain times prayer seems arid and unproductive. I have noticed with young believers that a typical 'sticky' period occurs two years or so after the initial decision to follow Christ. But this is normal Christianity! It is easy enough to pray when life with Christ is novel, exciting and eventful. But to persist in prayer when everything is flat—that indicates *real* progress.[1]

There may be times when we have no emotional energy, no warmth of feeling, for prayer. A creeping conviction of pointlessness slithers into our mind, and we find our motivation has sprung a slow leak. But Jesus says His disciples '*must* always pray.' So this is where what I call 'Anyway Christianity' has to kick in. You don't feel like praying; you may imagine it is useless to do so, but you do it *anyway*. You do it because Jesus says so. His disciples 'must always pray.' There is often simply a certain doggedness about the Christian life. Yes, we are likely to have our troubles over prayer, but, if I may twist the children's song,

> I must go on to pray,
> this I know,
> for Jesus tells me so.

---

1. Richard Bewes, *Talking about Prayer* (Ross-shire: Christian Focus, 2000), pp. 18-19.

Jesus assumes that you will likely have trouble with prayer. And there's a kind of back-handed comfort in that.

Secondly, in this parable **Jesus depicts the situation of His people in this world** (vv. 2-5). Jesus shows the lot of His people in the circumstances of the widow. The widow He imagines would not necessarily have been old. She could even have been reasonably young, since Jewish girls might be married by their mid-teens. We hear nothing of her specific difficulty. But her plea is, 'Grant me justice [*ekdikēson*] from my opponent!' (v. 3). That term, either as a verb (vv. 3, 5) or a noun (vv. 7, 8), appears four times in the parable. She seems to be under some kind of attack, and she wants a decision from the judge that secures her right(s) and thereby provides protection from whomever was after her. Since she is a vulnerable widow and likely without resources, the opponent may have been trying by legal hanky-panky to filch her out of property. As I noted, Jesus hasn't filled in particulars. What seems clear is that she is being wronged, she is defenseless, and she wants the judge to put things right in her case.

In His 'application' of the parable, Jesus parallels the widow's circumstances with those of God's people at large. God's 'elect' also 'cry out to him day and night' for vindication (v. 7). This 'justice' or 'vindication' (*ekdikēsis*) also includes vengeance (cf. Rom. 12:19, 'Vengeance [same word: *ekdikēsis*] is mine, I will pay back, says the Lord'). The idea is that if God is to bring justice/vindication to His people, He must bring vengeance on their enemies and those who assault them.[2] God puts thing right for His people by putting down those who wrong His people. But this justice or vengeance is not something believers are to try to pull off for themselves—they are to wait for God to do so (Rom. 12:19). But this waiting is no wishy-washy, weak-knee affair, as Revelation 6:10 shows. There God's martyrs plead 'how long?' for God's avenging vindication. They are a people who suffer wrong in this world, and who get stomped on and ignored and despised, and therefore they cry out for the God of Psalm 94 to show up. This widow in the parable is a microcosm, a mini-sample, of what Christ's people face in

---

2. Vengeance is a category of justice and is not to be equated with viciousness or vindictiveness.

this world. Sometimes we can see such trouble more clearly when it's boiled down to an individual case.

For example, in Lahore, Pakistan, Amir Masih, a gardener and a Christian, went to a police station. There had been a minor theft at his employer's home and Amir went voluntarily to the police to give a statement that would clear his name. But Amir died as a result of torture inflicted by the police. They tried to force a confession from him for an offense he didn't commit. Amir's brother said that police urinated on Amir while cursing him for being a Christian. All that and torture and death. Or there's Suzan Der Kirkour, 60, a Syrian Christian and retired schoolteacher who had remained in that now largely desolated land and in her village for the sake of her pupils. But one July day Islamic militants took her, raped her repeatedly, torturing and stoning her to death. Post-mortem examination indicated her ordeal had gone on for about nine hours.[3] Such sufferings are not occasional but common for Jesus' people in this age. The intensity and severity of wrongs inflicted may vary, but legions of Christ's people face this regularly. And so they keep crying out, 'How long … until you judge and avenge our blood?' (Rev. 6:10). This widow in the parable represents the church of Jesus in this world. This church longs for one of the days of the Son of Man—and has not yet seen it (17:22).

Thirdly, **Jesus assures His people of God's intervention and relief** (vv. 6-8a). Jesus calls us to hear what the unjust judge says (v. 6). And what did he say? 'I will give her justice' (v. 5). Oh, but what a pile of persistence lurks behind that statement! Well, the widow 'kept coming to him,' without let-up. One might picture it all. She accosts him on his way to the town gate in the morning. She corners him in the market during the day ('Ah, picking up a few almonds and pomegranates, eh, your honor? Now about …'). She comes by his house 'after hours' in the late afternoon. She haunts social occasions and appears beside him as he starts out for home. If he deals for some livestock or purchases provisions, she pops up at his elbow. He begins to get jumpy, because no matter where he is, she'll appear and punch her 'replay'

---

3. Reports via Barnabas Aid.

button. So at last he confesses that though he has neither piety nor compassion (v. 4b; that is, this will go against his 'principles'), 'yet because this widow keeps pestering me, I will grant her justice, so that by her infernal coming she will not wear me out' (v. 5).[4]

Jesus points out there is both a contrast and a parallel between God and the judge. The parallel is that the judge says, 'I will grant her justice' (v. 5a), and Jesus says that is precisely what God will do for His people (v. 7a). And yet there is such a contrast in attitude and character—Jesus' words in verse 7 contain one of His how-much-more arguments (i.e., if a scumbag judge would give such a widow justice, how much more will God …). Yet Jesus may also be saying that there is a parallel in the way justice comes. But for this we will need to descend into the abyss of translation difficulties.

Much debate hovers over the last clause of verse 7 (lit., 'and he delays/waits patiently over them'), especially over how it links up with the first of the verse. Bock lists twelve views of the matter, Marshall contents himself with discussing nine! A check of English translations demonstrates this diversity. Much depends on how one takes the conjunction *kai* ('and') at the first of the clause. It takes on various nuances beyond that of a simple conjunction. Suffice to say that here I think it has the sense 'And yet,' or 'Even while,' which are very close to what is called a 'concessive' use (= 'though').[5] Hence I translate: 'And will not God surely bring about justice for his elect who cry out to him day and night, though he delays long over them?' Implied answer: Yes, He will.

The other problem has to do with the expression *en tachei* in verse 8a. It can be translated 'quickly,' but is the stress more on manner or time? If time, then it means God will bring justice soon; if manner, it means it will come abruptly,

---

4. 'Wear out' translates a Greek verb that means 'to strike in the eye,' 'to give a black eye to' someone; used figuratively, it means to batter down or to wear out. My prosaic description makes it all seem so serious—and it is; yet verses 4-5 carry their own spark of humor.

5. Cf. A. T. Robertson, *Word Pictures in the New Testament*, 6 vols. (Nashville: Broadman, 1930), 2:232; M. Zerwick, *Biblical Greek* (Rome: Pontifical Biblical Institute, 1994), p. 153 (sect. 455); C. F. D. Moule, *An Idiom Book of New Testament Greek*, 2nd ed. (Cambridge: CUP, 1971), p. 178; and David E. Garland, *Luke*, ZECNT (Grand Rapids: Zondervan, 2011), pp. 711-12.

suddenly, or swiftly when it happens. Though it may be the minority view, I think the sense is quickly in terms of manner.[6] The analogies in the preceding context seem to support this: in the Noah scenario the flood came suddenly (17:26-27), just as the destruction came on Sodom (17:28-30). Verses 7-8a, then, say that God will certainly put things right for His elect even though He seems slow to do so, and when He acts, He will do so swiftly.

There *is* then a parallel between God and this scurvy judge: justice does come though it was 'delayed.' Yet there is a huge contrast as well, a how-much-more, for God is nothing like that stone-hearted judge and His people are not regarded as irritating pests but are His 'chosen ones' (elect). The point is that the coming of the Son of Man and of God's justice is certain but not immediate. And in the meantime, 'his elect' go on living with this paradox. I think of a small-scale parallel, of a Moroccan soldier captured by separatist guerrillas in 1979 and held captive until November of 2003, when he was at last released and could get married to his fiancée. The groom said he had 'blind confidence' in his betrothed and was convinced she would wait for him. And so it was—with an engagement of twenty-four years. There was an utter certainty on his part and yet an agonizing delay.[7] That is the paradox God's people live with—and they go on crying out to Him day and night because there is no one else to whom they can go.

Finally, we note that **Jesus calls His people to perseverance in faith and prayer** (vv. 1, 8b). We must remember Jesus' whole purpose in telling this parable (v. 1). And we must remember the kind of prayer He speaks of—not prayer for a new job or for your house to sell or for your kid to get accepted into a certain university, but for God to give justice to His weary and beaten-down people. God's people live in a world in which they are assailed, assaulted, and sometimes annihilated, and so, in face of that, they must never give in, lose heart, or throw

---

6. This sense fits better with some of its uses in LXX (e.g., Deuteronomy 9:3 (make Anakim perish quickly), 28:63 (quickly removed from the land) [check crit. apparatus for the copies that include *en tachei*]; Joshua 8:18, 19 (ambush rises up quickly); Psalm 2:12 (his wrath suddenly kindled). See also Klyne Snodgrass, *Stories with Intent* (Grand Rapids: Eerdmans, 2008), pp. 459-60.

7. Noted in *World* magazine, January 17, 2004, p. 8.

in the towel; they must keep praying for God to put things right. This prayer requires unrelenting tenacity.

It's like the time when there were two elderly sisters who were huge fans of movie star Bette Davis. In 1960 Davis and her husband Gary Merrill were touring the US, doing readings of Carl Sandburg poems. Their schedule called for an appearance in the sisters' small town. The latter ladies arrived at the theatre in high excitement. As the show began and Davis came on stage, the women were mesmerized. They followed every movement, hung on every word. Suddenly one of the sisters put her hand to her chest, lost consciousness, and died of a heart attack. As medics took her out of the theatre, her sister refused to go with her. Rather, she stood up and begged the Merrills to carry on. When the show ended, there was a huge ovation and Davis invited the surviving sister up on stage. As she took her place beside Davis, she told her, 'I adored your performance, and my sister would have too if she hadn't died two hours ago!'[8] That is dogged tenacity! Not even the death of a sister will keep her from pursuing her purpose.

That is the sort of disposition Jesus wants in His disciples in their prayers for God's righteous regime. They must not give in or lose heart in this matter. Such is Jesus' concern behind His question in verse 8b: 'Only when the Son of Man comes, will he find this faith upon the earth?' Literally, the text has 'the faith,' but the faith Jesus speaks of is the faith that shows itself in persevering prayer. And so I have translated, 'this faith,' i.e., this kind of faith I've just been talking about. Jesus' question is especially urgent if, as Matthew 24:12 says, 'the love of many will grow cold.' Jesus' question doesn't exactly suggest He expects to meet a 'Jesus bandwagon' at this coming. He queries whether at that time He will find people praying in this way. Will Jesus find a people still praying, 'Thy kingdom come, thy will be done on earth as it is in heaven'? Or will our love have grown cold?

Our parable tells us that even godless, heartless politicians have their use—if they teach us to go on praying.

---

8. Paul F. Boller, Jr., and Ronald L. Davis, *Hollywood Anecdotes* (New York: William Morrow, 1987), pp. 406-07.

10

The Presbyterian and the Publican
(Luke 18:9-14)

We come now to the second of the two parables at the first of chapter 18. This second parable, however, has links with a good bit that follows. It looks like 18:9-30 hang together, for the infants and children of 18:15-16 reflect the position of the tax collector (18:13), while the commandment-keeper of 18:21 re-incarnates the Pharisee of the parable. If 17:22–18:8 focus on the coming of the kingdom at the last, 18:9-30 keys in on entering the kingdom in the present, and that 'entry' is variously described as justification (18:14), receiving and entering the kingdom (18:16-17), and inheriting eternal life (18:18—which is also parallel to entering the kingdom, 18:24-25, or being saved, 18:26).[1] Indeed, one could say that all of 18:9–19:10 hang together around a theme like 'gathering the true people of God,' who include the justified (18:9-14), the overlooked (18:15-17), then a contrast—the moral but lost (18:18-30), then, positively again, the blind who sees (18:35-43) and the son of Abraham (19:1-10).

But back to our parable. Why the title, 'The Presbyterian and the Publican'? Because 'the Pharisee' already has a bad reputation with us, equivalent to 'hypocrite,' but generally in the first century he would likely have enjoyed a certain

---

1. Alan J. Thompson, *Luke*, EGGNT (Nashville: Broadman & Holman, 2016), pp. 281.

esteem. He represents the moral churchman, and so I have dubbed him 'the Presbyterian' since that is my own 'franchise.' But he could equally be tagged, for modern equivalents, the Pentecostal, the Baptist, the Anglican, etc. So there is this story about the 'Presbyterian' and this low-life publican or tax collector. We've got a clear distinction here, we might think, between the righteous and the unrighteous; but we'd better press the 'hold' button, for *we may not be judging righteous judgment about righteousness*, we may be seeing as man sees. This is very tricky business; so let's not think Jesus' parable of the Pharisee and the tax collector, of the Presbyterian and the publican, is some simple, obvious ditty with little for us to heed. We must ask what Jesus teaches us here.

First, Jesus teaches us **how deceptive our self-righteousness is**. As noted, to us 'Pharisee' connotes hypocrite while in the first century a Pharisee would generally be regarded as the embodiment of piety and spiritual earnestness. However, the Pharisee in Jesus' story appears so crassly self-righteous that we want to place ourselves at a vast distance from him. But it's not that simple; this whole affair can be deceptive. How might you know if you are self-righteous?

Well, there can be a *symptom*. We may recognize a hidden disease by its visible symptoms. Luke reveals one in his 'purpose statement' of verse 9: He 'spoke this parable to some who trusted in themselves that they were righteous and were despising others.' Then note how this plays out in the parable, in the Pharisee's thanksgiving that he is 'not like the rest of men … even like this tax collector' (v. 11). If you have a fuel oil tank and wonder how much is in the tank, you may check a gauge that tells you. It's an indicator. And 'despising others' is a corollary of self-righteousness, a symptom of it, a companion to it. Of course, if one is 'not like the rest of men,' one's standard of comparison is other people, and if we are comparing ourselves among ourselves, we are not wise (cf. 2 Cor. 10:12).

If you are despising others, however, it is likely that you trust in your own righteousness, and when you do that, you almost *must* despise others because, if they are equal to you, you cannot regard yourself as quite so 'righteous.'

Let's go from commenting to a little meddling. You might say, 'But I simply cannot stand self-righteousness! I abhor ….'

In that very statement you may be 'despising others,' at least if it's not simply self-righteousness you abhor but self-righteous folks. Do you see it? You could be so self-righteous that you despise the self-righteous! And are, therefore, completely unaware of your own self-righteousness.

There is also a peculiar *danger* in this parable and in the way you react to it. A kind of curious double reverse takes place. For you may look at Jesus' characters and instinctively refuse to identify with the Pharisee ('That's not me!') and, for whatever reason, you identify with the publican—and despise the Pharisee! So you may fall into the pit of self-righteousness, for you may find yourself so much as saying, 'Oh God, I thank you that I am not like that arrogant Pharisee, tooting his own horn, itemizing achievements, loathing other people.' Maybe that doesn't occur in your case as you read the parable. But for many inside the household of faith, the danger and problem here is: if you identify with the publican, do you despise the Pharisee—and what does *that* say about you?

Another possible pointer to self-righteousness has to do with the *sphere* in which it appears. 'The Pharisee stood (and) was praying these things about himself' (v. 11).[2] Our self-righteousness may appear in the holiest of exercises. The Pharisee's prayer is really quite subtle. Some of us perhaps think this prayer is so much cant and 'baloney'; perhaps, but we should give him the benefit of the doubt. It's subtle, for (at least verbally) he ascribes to God the credit and praise that he is not like other men. 'God, I thank you that I am not like the rest of men' (v. 11). He seems to have some sense of the grace of God. Looking at this tax collector who, for all the Pharisee knows, may be a swindler and who knows what else, he shakes his head in gratitude and whispers, 'There, but for the grace of God, go I.' Observe the obvious: it is in *prayer* that his self-righteousness expresses itself. You see what this means? *Religion is very deceptive.* Though you may despise the slightest scent of self-righteousness, the reek of it may cling to you. How deceptive our self-righteousness is.

---

2. Does 'by/about himself' (*pros eauton*) go with 'stood' or 'was praying'? I opt for the latter; see Thompson, pp. 281-82, for discussion.

Jesus also underscores **how shallow our righteousness is** (vv. 11-12). Jesus puts a prayer in the mouth of the Pharisee. And from that we should take note of the achievement of his 'righteousness.' It consists not merely of the negatives of verse 11 but of the positives of verse 12. His was a sacrificial religion (fasting) and a generous religion (tithing). It affected his stomach and his wallet at least. And yet notice the focus of his righteousness. It has to do with tangible externals (fasting, giving) and in what he refrains from. Seems to be no searching of motives or thoughts or desires or hidden reasonings. No attention to depth matters. For example, fasting twice per week. Monday and Thursday were the usual fast days. But why would he fast then? Might it be because those days were also market days, when country folks came to town and when these Pharisees might more likely arouse attention and admiration for their piety?[3]

But perhaps the most revealing matter is what we might call the *basis* of his righteousness. Here, I think, Ronald Wallace has hit upon a telling observation. You may think he is psychologizing too much, but, if he is, it is likely accurate psychologizing. He notes that this parabolic Pharisee teaches us that we 'should not lay too much stress on our religious feeling.' He goes on:

> The Pharisee had beautiful religious feelings when he went to the temple. He felt right with God and with life. So comforting were his religious feelings that he felt sure he was in the Kingdom of God; his heart told him so. But his heart told him a lie.[4]

Wallace's comment conjures up the scene from *Pilgrim's Progress*. Christian and Hopeful wait for a young fellow to catch up with them. When he does, they converse and in the process Christian asks him why he is persuaded that he has left all for God and heaven. He answered, 'My heart tells me so.' The young man claims that his heart and life agree together, and Christian asks who told him that. He responded, 'My heart tells me so.' And his name was: Ignorance.

---

3. Alfred Edersheim, *The Life and Times of Jesus the Messiah*, 2 vols. (reprint ed., Grand Rapids: Eerdmans, 1967), 2:291.

4. R. S. Wallace, *Many Things in Parables/The Gospel Miracles* (Grand Rapids: Eerdmans, 1963), p. 104.

How shallow and flimsy our righteousness is. What then are we to do? Where can one go or what can one do to get flushed out of his/her Pharisaism? Must I then take up the words of the tax collector (v. 13)? Maybe. And maybe not. For one can do a dramatization, an imitation, of the publican; one can take his lines and not share his attitude or desperation — which would be another form of shallow righteousness. It is probably best if we simply recognize that our righteousness is shallow. What good can that do? It may be the beginning of humbling yourself, so that God can exalt you (v. 14). Maybe we need to start praying prayers like:

> No day of my life has passed that has not
>   proven me guilty in thy sight.
> Prayers have been uttered from a
>   prayerless heart;
> praise has been often praiseless sound;
> my best services are filthy rags.
>
> But in my Christian walk I am still in rags;
>   my best prayers are stained with sin;
>   my penitential tears are so much impurity;
> I need to repent of my repentance;
> I need my tears to be washed.[5]

Thirdly, Jesus shows us **how offensive our Lord is** (v. 14). Here in the wrap-up of the parable, Jesus declares: 'I tell you, this man [in v. 13] went down to his house justified rather than that other fellow.' Some in our contemporary western culture might be quite upset with Jesus and, according to the overly-used buzzword, find Him 'offensive.' If His words are offensive, they are also revealing. The sheer audacity of Jesus, for one thing. He has the gall to declare who is justified, who is 'in the right' with God, and who is not. Who gave Him that right? Who does He think He is? Telling us who is 'justified' and who is not! He seems to assume He has the right to judge.

But there's more. Jesus seems to make life an upside-down-cake by what He says. If He had said that the Pharisee

---

5. Arthur Bennett, ed., *The Valley of Vision* (Edinburgh: Banner of Truth, 2002), pp. 136, 150.

went down justified and that the publican was 'struggling' with it, folks could handle that, but Jesus flipped things on their ears. Pharisees (and remember, don't read 'hypocrite' automatically into this, for by and large their peers respected them) were devoted to the practice of godliness in the details of life. For them the Bible was not to remain some dated artifact but the repository of God's will to be squeezed into the pores of life. They were the people you wanted for next-door neighbors, for Little League coaches for your kids. They were the pro-life contingent, who attended small group Bible studies. They were ones who guarded 'conservative values.'

And you know something about tax collectors. One especially needed to be wary of those involved in taking tolls from travelers at custom check points. The Romans farmed out tax collection and these fellows made their living and profits by collecting more than was due, ripping off people, especially on *ad valorem* taxes. The rabbis denied tax collectors the right to appear as witnesses in court, hence confining them to the same class as gamblers, robbers, the violent, shepherds, and slaves. But now Jesus seems to stand this whole system of decency on its head when He says His tax collector 'went down to his house justified.' Here Jesus seems to be the One who 'justifies the ungodly' (Rom. 4:5)—that deliriously glorious phrase that ought to catch your corn flakes in your windpipe. But whether you like it or not, there it is: Jesus decides who is righteous; it doesn't depend on your feelings or achievements.

Is there any way Jesus might say this of us? 'This man, this woman, went down … justified.' It all depends if, with the publican, we believe in a miracle: 'But the tax collector stood a long ways off and refused even to lift his eyes to heaven but kept hammering his chest, saying, "God, let there be an atonement for me, the sinner"' (v. 13). We should follow his plea. Notice *the anguish he feels*: he won't lift his eyes, keeps beating his chest. This latter was usually only something women would do; only a matter of *extreme* sorrow or anguish would lead a man to act this way.[6] Notice *the*

---

6. Kenneth E. Bailey, *Poet & Peasant* and *Through Peasant Eyes*, combined ed. (Grand Rapids: Eerdmans, 1983), p. 153 (2nd part).

isolation he knows: he calls himself, literally, 'the sinner.' The Greek has the definite article and sometimes that has no special significance. But here, it may be, he is seeing himself as 'the sinner,' i.e., as if he is the only person in the universe. There is no 'or even as this Pharisee' in his words. He stands before God all by himself; he is 'the sinner.' And then note *the provision he cries for*: 'Let there be an atonement for me.' I think the usual 'Be merciful to me' is too weak. Jesus places these men at the temple, likely at the hour of prayer. There was the daily burnt-offering in the morning and late afternoon. The verb used (*hilasthēti*; cf. *hilastērion*, Rom. 3:25, and *hilasmos*, 1 John 2:2, 'propitiation') has to do with turning away wrath by means of a sacrifice. Since the setting is the temple, is it such a great reach to imagine that the tax collector thinks of the lamb offered morning and evening there? As if to say, 'Oh, that there was an atoning sacrifice for me!', one that would be a sacrifice that would take his place and absorb his judgment. Hence I hold he is asking for more than mercy and translate, 'Let there be an atonement for me.' He cries for something beyond himself and outside himself.

After my first year of college, I and several fellow students worked for a while on a summer construction job. We shared a small apartment and concocted our own meals. One of our number was the son of missionaries serving in Pakistan. Whenever he would refer to Pakistan, he would call it 'out there,' which it was, in relation to Kansas, where we were. But it got a bit aggravating. We'd be eating and he'd rail a bit about the mildness of the ketchup and then go on about how 'out there' they had ketchup with some kick to it. After a bit we got rankled. We loathed hearing about how 'out there' this was better or that was better. And that's what offends us, isn't it? That being right with God rests on something beyond us, something 'foreign,' something outside of us, something 'out there.' It rests on whether there is an atoning sacrifice that turns away wrath.

If Jesus is offensive, thank God, He becomes even more offensive: He even justifies Pharisees who have come to pray like publicans!

11

Jesus and the Little Shavers
(Luke 18:15-17)

In the ancient world childhood was not for sissies. No need to wax sentimental over children—they had a dangerous time of it. It is estimated that only fifty per cent of children lived past age ten.[1] If David Garland is right that six of every ten children died before the age of sixteen,[2] then one might surmise that a number of the parents who brought infants to Jesus might well lose them in their first year or so. Perhaps that mixed some urgency into their coming.[3] Such mortality was not simply an Israelite problem—it has been estimated that in Rome, for example, 30 per cent of all babies died within their first year, only 49 per cent of children lived to their fifth birthday, and only 40 per cent of the population lived to the age of twenty.[4] Childhood was more desperate than cute.

We'll touch later on why Luke may have placed this episode here, but there's something that stands out right at the first that we simply must notice: **the approachability of Jesus** (vv. 15a, 16a; see also our first observation in the

---

1. See C. Reeder, 'Child, Children,' DJG, 2nd ed., pp. 109.

2. In 'Mark,' in ZIBBC, 1:264.

3. I doubt we can be sure exactly what kind of benefit parents expected from Jesus' touch (the text doesn't say), but clearly they thought it was important that they ask Him to do so.

4. Edwin M. Yamauchi and Marvin R. Wilson, *Dictionary of Daily Life in Biblical and Post-Biblical Antiquity* (Peabody, MA: Hendrickson, 2017), pp. 285.

exposition of Luke 15). Jesus is clear about His attitude. 'Allow the children to come to me and don't prevent them' (v. 16a). He has time for wee ones. But verse 15a may be even more telling. 'They were bringing to him even their infants that he might touch them.' Think what those parents must've been thinking—or *assuming*—about Jesus. There had to be something about Jesus that indicated He was 'approachable.' Who in that day would necessarily assume He would care a lick about infants unless, somehow, they simply *sensed* that He would? And why would they sense that unless it was obvious in His demeanor? Otherwise, why would they venture to bring them? They assumed Jesus would welcome their little ones; they assumed He was approachable. What a grand assumption and what a superb Savior!

Not everyone values approachability. Once Abraham Lincoln's wife, Mary, was complaining to Noah Brooks, the newspaperman, about her husband. 'He's so like a child,' Mrs Lincoln began. 'I sometimes wonder if he understands even that he is the President. I cannot teach him—he will see them all, mere servants, washerwomen—anyone. He talks with anyone who will come, the wounded, office-hunters, women with dead or wounded boys; and the more ragged they are, the longer he will sit and hear them.'[5] Mrs Lincoln's frustrated complaint is, ironically, a fine commendation. And it's not only children's parents who find Jesus like this, but any of His disciples who know Him well know that as they come to Jesus, they never meet a cold shoulder but always a beckoning hand.

We also meet here **the congregation of Jesus**—infants and children and 'such ones as these' (v. 16b). Here we need to look at verses 15-17 in light of their context. For now, we'll confine ourselves to 18:1-17. To be sure, the infants/children here in verses 15-17 are 'real' characters, whereas those characters in verses 1-8 and 9-14 are 'parabolic' characters. But surely the collection is significant. Here is a congregation of no-counts: a widow, a tax collector, and infants. Luke seems to be telling us something by his placement of these segments in series, as if it's sort of vintage Jesus to pull such types together.

---

5. Burke Davis, *They Called Him Stonewall* (New York: Fairfax, 1988), p. 375.

But this is the sort of thing Christ does repeatedly (so we won't forget). Who would have given a second—or even a third—thought to those eighteenth-century Bristol coal miners? They were known for their brutality, were 'a pitiable and neglected people' with the piles of coal around them and the squalid huts they lived in. But George Whitefield went and preached to them in the open air, to some thousands of them, the unwashed faces surrounding him. Whitefield reported that one could tell when they came under conviction: one could 'see the white gutters made by their tears which plentifully fell down their black cheeks.' Hundreds of these convictions issued in sound conversions.[6] Who would have thought? But Jesus gathers His people even from the coal mines. So Luke 18 simply underscores what Paul told the Corinthians. 'Well, just look at yourselves,' he so much as said, 'you are hardly the cream of civilization.' And then the explanation:

> But God chose the things the world calls foolish that he might put the wise folks to shame; and God chose what the world regards as weak that he might put the strong to shame; and the insignificant things and the despised things God chose—the 'nothings,' that he might set aside the 'somethings,' so that no flesh could boast in the presence of God (1 Cor. 1:27-29).

Jesus seems to be doing the same. He seems to delight in desperate widows, anguished tax collectors, and insignificant children.

Next, we get a glimpse of **the servants of Jesus** in verse 15b: 'And when the disciples saw it, they began to rebuke them.' This doesn't mean the disciples were crabby ogres or innate child-haters. It may well be that their intrusion was meant to protect Jesus. Perhaps they wanted to save Him from excessive 'people-fatigue.' Or maybe they were a bit irritated at the way people kept imposing themselves on Jesus, giving Him no relief. Think of well-known figures in sports or politics or entertainment in our own day. How difficult it must be for them to go out for a meal or attend a public event

---

6. Arnold A. Dallimore, *George Whitefield*, 2 vols. (Westchester, IL: Cornerstone, 1979), 1:263.

as a spectator without being recognized, talked to, asked for an autograph and so on. It brings on a certain tiredness—and here the disciples apparently want to spare Jesus that.

However, Jesus' response (v. 16) shows that though the disciples thought their action was clearly right, in this case it was wrong-headed. Here is a pattern that should put Jesus' disciples in any age on alert. We may be sure about how our service to Christ should play out—and then find our whole assessment has been wrong. Here the disciples were so definite in their response but utterly indifferent to the needs of children. David Gooding helps us to see at least one way in which this text should come home to us:

> [I]t is when, like the apostles, we start engaging in 'Christian work' that we are liable to fall into the temptation of thinking that it is more important to attract 'leaders' and 'magnates' to Christ rather than the Mrs Mopps of this world.[7]

All our 'service' then always needs to be placed before Jesus, so that He can correct our calculations and purge our perceptions.

Lastly, we hear **the application of Jesus** in verses 16b-17, as He instructs from this episode. Once more it is helpful to pull in the larger context. I agree with Earle Ellis' observation that Luke likely and deliberately contrasts the children with the Pharisee in the preceding episode (18:11-12) and with the religious ruler in the following episode (18:18, 21). These men want to merit the kingdom.[8] So Luke has the children here in a structural 'sandwich.' Part of what Jesus means then in verse 17 by 'receiving the kingdom of God as a child' is that a child doesn't go around crowing about fasting twice a week and tithing everything he gets, nor does he make impossible claims like 'All these I have kept from youth.' A child doesn't mess with merit.

We should not miss the implication of verse 16: 'Allow the children to come to me … for the kingdom of God belongs to

---

7. In *According to Luke* (1987; reprint ed., Coleraine, N. Ireland: Myrtlefield Trust, 2013), p. 310.

8. E. Earle Ellis, *The Gospel of Luke*, NCB, rev. ed. (London: Oliphants, 1974), p. 216.

such as these.' Jesus implies that those to whom the kingdom belongs are those who have 'come to (Jesus).'[9] They come to Him with the dependence of a child.

In verse 17 Jesus drives home His statement in verse 16b. Here He speaks both of 'receiving' the kingdom and 'entering' it. To 'enter' it one must receive it 'as a child.' This phrase could mean 'as a little child receives it' or 'as though one were a little child.' It's important that we not become schmaltzy about little children and conjure up their commendable traits that we may imagine they show. David Garland put it well when he says that Jesus

> does not refer to some inherent quality in children, such as their imagined receptivity, humility, trustfulness, lack of self-consciousness, transparency, hopefulness, openness to the future, simplicity, freshness, excitement, or any other idealized quality that commentators often attribute to children. None of these virtues were associated with children in first-century culture, and they reflect a contemporary, sentimental view of children.[10]

He goes on to say, 'In light of the preceding parable of the tax collector who pled for mercy from God out of his helplessness, Luke must have had in mind the child's total helplessness and dependence on others, which explains the mention of "infants" [*brephē*, v. 15].'[11] In Augustus Toplady's words: 'helpless, look to thee for grace.'[12] That is the position of a 'child,' of one who will both 'receive' and 'enter' the kingdom of God.

---

9. Alan J. Thompson, *Luke*, EGGNT (Nashville: Broadman & Holman, 2016), pp. 284-85.

10. David E. Garland, *Luke*, ZECNT (Grand Rapids: Zondervan, 2011), p. 729.

11. Garland, p. 729.

12. From his hymn, 'Rock of Ages.'

12

The Lethal Commandment
(Luke 18:18-30)

Airports are fascinating—that is, if one is not rushed, harried, or panicked about making a connecting flight. But if one has plenty of leisure between flights, 'people-watching' can be both fun and educational. And Luke allows us to do some people-watching before we arrive in Jerusalem. He shows us a 'good' man who is sad (18:18-30), a blind man who can see (18:35-43), and a lost man who is found (19:1-10). Right now we focus on the first of these. This 'good man who is sad' (18:18-30) stands in his moral achievement in contrast to the helpless infants of 18:15-17; and in his blind naivete (18:21) he is the polar opposite of the blind man who could 'see' (18:38-39) even before he could see (18:43)! The major concern in this section remains the same: whether one is 'justified' (18:14) or 'receives' the kingdom (18:17) or has eternal life (18:18).

First off, verses 18-19 force us to deal with **words and meaning**. A ruler, perhaps from the Sanhedrin, asks Jesus, 'Good teacher, what can I do to inherit eternal life?' (v. 18). Then Jesus replies, 'Why do you call me "good"? No one is good, except one—God' (v. 19). You could almost drown in the ink spilled over Jesus' reply.[1] Many scholars hold that

---

1. Before you do, make sure you work through the rigorous study by B. B. Warfield, 'Jesus' Alleged Confession of Sin' in his *Christology and Criticism* (1932; reprint ed., Grand Rapids: Baker, 2003), pp. 97-139.

Jesus is putting distance between Himself and God, but I think that misreads Jesus; rather He is finagling to get this ruler to think through what it may mean to call Him '*Good teacher.*' Leon Morris has put it well:

> *No one is good but God alone* is not to be understood as a repudiation of the epithet *good* as applied to Himself. If that was His meaning, Jesus would surely have said plainly that He was a sinner. Rather He was inviting the ruler to reflect on the meaning of his own words. What he had just said had implications for the Person of Jesus. If He was good and if only God was good, as all rabbinic teaching agreed …, then the ruler was saying something important about Him. So far from repudiating the deity of Jesus, as some hold, the question seems to invite the young man to reflect on it.[2]

Jesus is not making an overt statement but tempting the man to think more deeply and carefully about what he said. It was probably obvious that he was using 'good' too casually, perhaps as a mere piece of flattery.

However, there is something more in Jesus' words than what reflects on Jesus. I don't think you will usually find it discussed in commentaries. But Jesus told him, 'No one is good.' Was not this word directed to the ruler? Was he not meant to ponder that? Did not those two Greek words (*oudeis agathos*) include and describe the ruler? Shouldn't he have questioned his own flawless morality (v. 21) and taken to heart Jesus' description of his condition? He has cause for double deliberation: What does it mean if Jesus is really 'good'? Where am I left if I am one of those who are not good?

Next, we find **knowledge and ignorance** in verses 20-21. Jesus tells the ruler: 'You know the commandments' (v. 20a) and proceeds to itemize five of them from the love-your-neighbor section of the Decalogue (v. 20b). The man is clearly disappointed, apparently impatient, perhaps even exasperated with Jesus' answer.[3] 'All these' [emphatic], he

---

2. *The Gospel According to St. Luke*, TNTC (Grand Rapids: Eerdmans, 1974), 267. See also Knox Chamblin, *Matthew*, 2 vols. (Ross-shire: Christian Focus, 2010), 2:945 (including fn 6).

3. And perhaps some Christian readers are disappointed with Jesus here. Their

replies, 'I have kept from (my) youth' (v. 21). To exaggerate somewhat ... this was like attending a writers' conference and being told to begin by printing one's name as legibly as possible ten times. His 'What can I do' (v. 18) had in view something far beyond this elementary level. 'Been there, done that,' was his assessment.

But some readers will be appalled at his attitude. How, they will think, can he say he has kept all these commandments from his youth? How can he *know* the commandments and yet really be so *ignorant* of them? Has he no sense that the sixth commandment condemns attitudes that lay behind murder (Matt. 5:21-22)? Doesn't he understand that the seventh commandment can be violated simply in one's imagination (Matt. 5:27-28)? Does he not grasp that the eighth commandment requires not merely honesty but industry and generosity (Eph. 4:28)? Has he never fought with the tenth commandment? Has he never experienced how this law that forbids sin actually stimulates it (Rom. 7:7-8)? He has never felt the razor edge of the law slicing deep into the abyss of his conscience. 'All these I have kept.' How tragic to see a man who knows the commandments but not himself.[4]

We can now move on to a third segment, **demand and exposure** (vv. 22-23). Jesus doesn't pick at this man. He doesn't complain about his superficial view of the law. He moves on. 'You still lack one thing,' He tells him (v. 22a). The ruler's hopes rise. Here, then, is the 'thing I can do' that I was asking about (v. 18), he thinks. Actually, Jesus was going for the jugular: 'Sell all that you have and give it round to the poor, and you will have treasure in heaven, and come, follow me' (v. 22b). The 'one thing' was too much. He became 'very sad, for he was terribly rich' (v. 23). Jesus' demand was a test case, a litmus test, that exposed his *first commandment* problem. As someone has said, his problem was not that he had great possessions but that they had him. Here was a

---

reaction may be—pardon the anachronism—'Why doesn't he just quote Acts 16:31 to him?' Why, some may wonder, does Jesus mess with the law? Answer: Because Jesus doesn't shoot Bible bullets at people but wants to get them to see and feel their need. Remember 10:25-28.

4. Some may think the Westminster Larger Catechism too thorough, but questions/answers 101-149 might have helped this ruler.

commandment he had not kept. He was an idolater; he had another God; he was exposed.

Dr Alexander Whyte was minister of Free St. George's in Edinburgh in the later nineteenth century and following. He was known for his sometimes vivid and even terrifying imagination. Once he was preaching on this ruler and followed him, as his biographer says, 'right out of the Gospel story.' Whyte depicted him plunging down the inferno and just as he was about to disappear in its bottomless abyss, Whyte, who had been leaning over the pulpit as though 'watching him with blazing eye,' shouted: 'I hear it! It's the mocking laughter of the universe, and it's shouting at him over the edge, "Ha ha! Kept the commandments!"'[5] A graphic way of exposing the emptiness of any such claim.[6]

While we are dealing with this 'demand and exposure,' we should probably deal with the 'insensitivity' of Jesus. That is the unpardonable sin of our age. Let someone be wicked or virtuous or mad—it doesn't much matter. But being 'insensitive' raises critics almost from the dead. And Jesus is insensitive here. He exposes the man's idolatry and gives no palliative care. He makes him very sad and leaves him that way. And yet there were certain gifts Jesus was offering him if he could only see. Making him sad was a gift—if for once he could see himself as he was, there might be hope. So truth was Jesus' gift. And there is also a gift in Jesus' call, 'And come, follow me' (v. 22c). Those words are actually a promise. Oh, the idolatry has to be dealt with, but if he sells all, he'll still have Jesus! It's as if Jesus says, 'I will be enough for you.' In any case, Jesus didn't pamper the man's self-image. Jesus doesn't necessarily care about your 'feelings.' Jesus disappointed this man, made him sad. How will you respond if you meet the insensitivity of Jesus?

In the aftermath of this interview, verses 24-27 focus on **impossibility and hope**. Jesus begins with a difficulty before He gets to the impossibility. As He sees the ruler's sadness, He

---

5. G. F. Barbour, *The Life of Alexander Whyte* (London: Hodder and Stoughton, 1923), pp. 300-01.

6. This whole encounter makes two matters clear: (1) one can be very religious and/or moral and not have eternal life; and (2) one can be a person of solid outward morality *and* also of deep, hidden idolatry.

exclaims, 'How difficult it is for those having wealth to enter into the kingdom of God!' (v. 24). He follows this up with a (in one sense) comical picture meant to suggest impossibility: it's easier for a camel to go through a needle's eye than for a rich man to enter the kingdom of God (v. 25). Audience reaction sets in: 'Who then can be saved?' (v. 26). The thinking likely is that the rich are rich by the blessing of God and if those so blessed cannot make it, what hope is there for Joe the plumber, Mac the carpenter, or Sophie the washer-woman? Part of Jesus' answer is, 'None.' Whether a rich ruler can be saved or Joe or Mac or Sophie—well, Jesus seems to put all that in the category of what is 'impossible with men' (v. 27a). But omnipotence overwhelms impossibility: the matters that are impossibilities for men 'are possible with God' (v. 27b), so possible that God can bring even a rich person into His kingdom. Stein has put it well:

> For Luke salvation came from God, and God can break the hold that riches have on a person. By God's grace it is possible to give up all and follow Jesus as Luke 18:28-30 reveals, and it is even possible for a rich man to enter God's kingdom as 19:1-10 reveals.[7]

We need to hear this. We are so prone to think salvation is a man-thing, primarily a matter of human response, that we've forgotten that 'salvation is the Lord's affair' (Jonah 2:9). We sometimes need shaken to remember that the gospel is not merely facts about God (though it is that) or the truth about God (though it is that), but 'the-power-of-God-unto-salvation' (Rom. 1:16). The gospel is power, such power that it can wrench bluebloods and no-counts out of darkness and plant them in the kingdom of light.

Now Peter has a comment apparently on this ruler-situation, and that leads us into the last segment which I call **naivete and assurance**. Now nearly everyone, it seems, feels a right to psychologize Peter, so why shouldn't I have that privilege as well? Some may think Peter is speaking with a bit of pride in verse 28 ('Look, we [emphatic] have left our

---

7. Robert H. Stein, *Luke*, NAC (Nashville: Broadman, 1992), p. 459.

own stuff and followed you') as if in contrast to the ruler (cf.
v. 22). But I rather think Peter is simply being reflective and
matter-of-fact—making what one could almost call a naïve
observation.[8] And probably seeking re-assurance. This Jesus
gives in verses 29-30: 'In truth I tell you, there is no one who
has left house or wife or brothers or parents or children for
the sake of the kingdom of God, who will not get back many
times over in this age—and in the age to come, eternal life.'[9]
I won't go into the details but please catch the punch of the
answer: commitment to Jesus will never impoverish His
disciples. They will receive back 'many times over' even in
this age.[10] This text is actually very close to what Paul calls
'the surpassing worth of knowing Christ Jesus my Lord'
(Phil. 3:8). Why would anyone dream of leaving such prized
possessions (v. 29) unless convinced that Jesus gives 'many
times over'?

8. Other expositors (e.g., Arndt, Bock, and Plummer) take a similar view.

9. Remember Jesus' words here were spoken first of all to the Twelve. They
had literally left such things/people in order to be with Jesus. To be with Him involved
extended time(s) away from all that mattered most to them. Note that 'house' is
the only non-personal entry Jesus mentions here among the 'sacrifices.' But don't
imagine that leaving 'wife,' for example, meant severing a marriage relationship (Mrs
Peter, after all, later traveled with her husband, 1 Cor. 9:5). Yet Jesus' statement
takes in more than the Twelve, as His 'There is no one' implies.

10. How this may be is not spelled out in Luke's account, but there is a hint of
it in Mark's (cf. Mark 10:30 with Mark 3:31-35).

13

Clarity and Density
(Luke 18:31-34)

These verses beg for separate treatment. But they are not separate: in light of verses 28-30, these verses show that 'Jesus also has forsaken all for the sake of the kingdom.'[1] Quite a contrast as well, between the benefits disciples get (vv. 29-30) and the sufferings Messiah endures (vv. 32-33). And this is actually the seventh prediction of Jesus' sufferings in Luke (see 5:35; 9:22; 9:43-45; 12:50; 13:32-33; 17:25).[2] Here we stand on holy—and instructive—ground.

Note, first of all, that Jesus speaks of **the certain fulfillment of His destiny** (v. 31). 'We are going up to Jerusalem,' He tells the Twelve. This journey to Jerusalem has been in view since chapter 9, in fact since the Moses-and-Elijah discussion about Jesus' 'exodus' that He was to fulfill in Jerusalem (9:31). So the journey is about to reach its end, in the place where Jesus must perish (13:33). It is in connection with Jerusalem that Jesus mentions the predictions of Scripture. There 'all the things written by the prophets about the Son of Man will be accomplished.' The 'all things' includes both His distress and His deliverance, both His sufferings and the ensuing glory (vv. 32-33) that the prophets speak of. Jesus

---

1. E. Earle Ellis, *The Gospel of Luke,* NCB, rev. ed. (London: Oliphants, 1974), p. 217.

2. Leon Morris, *The Gospel According to St. Luke,* TNTC (Grand Rapids: Eerdmans, 1974), p. 269; so too Ellis, p. 218.

is not embarrassed by what we call the Old Testament. (It was, after all, His Bible). He simply assumes the truthfulness and accuracy of its messianic predictions. The fact that they dated from some or several hundreds of years before simply indicates that His mission was not some ad hoc affair cobbled together in desperation but a divine *plan* determined and predicted long before.

We are usually impressed by those who can conceive a plan and actually execute it. Robert Dick Wilson was for some years a highly-respected Old Testament and Semitics professor at Princeton Seminary. In his student days, while doing advanced study in Berlin in the early 1880s, he designed a plan for his life: he would divide his subsequent life into three blocks of fifteen years each. The first fifteen years would be taken up studying the original languages of Scripture and certain cognate languages. The second fifteen would zero in on biblical textual matters in light of his studies, and in the last fifteen years he hoped to write up what he had learned. For someone who knew twenty-six languages that might be quite a lot. When Wilson died at seventy-five, most all his 'forty-five-year plan' had been achieved.[3] We are impressed by something like that, for there are so many non-humanly-controlled variables that wreak havoc on such schemes. But the pieces of God's redemptive plan involving the Son of Man are not recent formulations. They were announced through the prophets hundreds of years previously and written down (hence they can be checked)—and all these things 'will be accomplished.' At Jerusalem. There is no doubt about it. Jesus does not blush to presume upon the truthfulness of God's 'Old Testament' word.

Secondly, Jesus discloses **the terrible intensity of His sufferings**: 'For he will be handed over to the gentiles and he will be ridiculed and abused and spit upon and, when they've flogged him, they will kill him—and on the third day he will rise again' (vv. 32-33). These verses parallel Matthew 20:17-19 and Mark 10:32-34, but in the seven references to Jesus' sufferings in Luke, this is the climactic one and most

3. W. C. Kaiser, Jr., 'Robert Dick Wilson,' in *Bible Interpreters of the Twentieth Century*, ed. W. A. Elwell and J. D. Weaver (Grand Rapids: Baker, 1998), pp. 74-75.

detailed. The verbs (hand over, ridicule, abuse, spit on, flog, kill) both itemize and so intensify what Jesus will face in Jerusalem.

We must not divorce these verses from verse 31. Such sufferings had been 'written by the prophets' as well. One thinks, for example, of Isaiah 50:6. One must see it in an over-all context. Isaiah 50:4-9 is one of the 'Servant songs.' The first of these passages about 'the Servant of Yahweh' is in 42:1-4, where it is clear, among other things, that this Servant is a royal figure, a king, because He will bring forth justice to the nations. The second song in chapter 49 identifies the Servant as 'Israel' (49:3) and yet not Israel: He is Israel-in-concentrate, but is not the nation Israel since His mission is to restore Israel to Yahweh (49:5-6). In the third song (50:4-9) the Servant speaks in the first person and has a prophetic ministry ('how to sustain the weary with a word,' v. 4), but then He goes on to describe His suffering:

> The Lord Yahweh has opened my ear,
> and I, I did not rebel;
>> I did not turn away.
>> I gave my back to smiters,
>>> and my cheeks to ones plucking out my beard;
>> I did not hide my face from scorn and spit.
> But the Lord Yahweh helps me;
>> therefore I am not disgraced … (vv. 5-7a).

There's a certain abruptness that catches us by surprise. The suffering was Yahweh's will for the Servant (v. 5a); the Servant was submissive to that suffering willed for him (v. 5b); and the suffering is shameful and intense (my back, my cheeks, my face, plus scorn and spit, v. 6) yet mysterious (the rationale for the suffering is not spelled out here). One can be forgiven for thinking Isaiah 50:6 lies behind Jesus' words here in Luke.

We might also note Isaiah 52:14. It is a difficult text. It is part of the fourth Servant song in Isaiah; in fact, it's part of 52:13-15 which is a preview-summary for the whole song as it depicts both the suffering and success of the Servant. Verse 14 describes reactions to his suffering:

> As many were appalled at you
> —so disfigured,
>> his appearance did not seem that of a man
>> nor his form that of the sons of man.

The idea is that his sufferings had so ravaged him that he didn't even seem to be a specimen of humanity. This too may have played into Jesus' description here in Luke.

Jesus' design was to awaken the Twelve to what would take place in Jerusalem. Hence the climactic and detailed description of the sufferings that awaited Him. But shouldn't these verses 'awaken' us as well? Do we ponder as we should the mockery, torments, and cruelty Jesus endured for us? To be sure, Christian history contains examples of those who 'over-indulged' in morbid fixation on Jesus' sufferings. But can't some of us run into another danger? Can we almost de-crucify Jesus, thinking of His sufferings almost as a doctrinal concept and not the inhuman blow-upon-blow He endured for us? Why would Luke include 'the terrible intensity of his sufferings' unless to move us to a response like:

> Lest I forget Thy thorn-crowned brow,
>> lead me to Calvary.
> Lest I forget Gethsemane;
> lest I forget Thine agony;
> lest I forget Thy love for me,
>> lead me to Calvary.[4]

Finally, in verse 34 Luke reports the non-reception of Jesus' words when he relates **the amazing density of His disciples**. The NIV captures the text well: 'The disciples did not understand any of this. Its meaning was hidden from them, and they did not know what he was talking about.' Commentators frequently point out that there are three statements of the disciples' non-comprehension in this verse. As if Luke is wanting to hammer the point home. Here's a fascinating mix of divine mystery and human frailty. Part of the reason they didn't 'get it' is because it 'was hidden' from them. The verb form here is sometimes called a 'divine

---

4. From 'Lead Me to Calvary,' by Jennie Evelyn Hussey.

passive,' an indirect way of speaking of God's activity. They wouldn't see it until God made it plain to them. And yet there seems to be the sense that they *ought* to have comprehended. It's not that the Twelve did not understand the nouns and verbs of Jesus' words but that they could not grasp how that could fit with Jesus' mission or their conception of Jesus' mission. We may wonder how such clarity (vv. 31-33) could meet with such density. How could it 'go right by' them?

But in a way it's not so hard to understand. One of my friends was once on a presbytery committee charged with dealing with some problems in a local church within the presbytery. This local church was distinctive in that, though it was a part of our denomination in the United States, this church itself was made up of ethnic non-westerners. My friend told me that the committee ran into a strange trend, apparently a cultural difference. He said that they would discuss matters with the church leadership, reach conclusions and assume that all would proceed on those lines. But, when they conferred again, my friend said it was as if everything was back at point zero and the local leaders assumed all issues could be negotiated all over again. For my western friend, it was as if everything that had been said and decided simply 'went by' the local leadership.

That seems to be the case with the disciples here. Jesus' plain words just got no traction with them. We can understand the disciples since we're wrapped up in our own weakness (cf. Heb. 5:2). Some of us can think of 'blind spots' we've had about the Lord's truth or about the Christian life, and had them perhaps for years before the Lord showed us our error. And then we look back and ask ourselves, 'Why didn't I see that? Why did that go right by me? Why was I so dense?' Always plenty of material for repentance.

14

Jericho Grace
(Luke 18:35–19:10)

Jericho—seventeen or so miles northeast of Jerusalem, six miles north of the Dead Sea and to the west of the Jordan River. Jericho is both old and low. Settlements date back to 8,000 b.c., and it sits in that colossal geological ditch, the Rift Valley, at about eight hundred feet below sea level. It was, in former days, a city that carried a curse (Josh. 6:26) but later enjoyed a surprise of Yahweh's grace (2 Kings 2:19-22). And, now as Jesus comes, it is the place of grace again. Two episodes show how grace has come to Jericho.

The first tells of **a blind man who can see** (18:35-43). The setting is simple: Jesus is 'in the vicinity of Jericho.'[1] And 'a certain blind man was sitting by the road begging' (v. 35). This man is very definite about what he wants—to see, or perhaps, 'to see again' (v. 41). And what Jesus did in restoring his sight (v. 42) showed what 'time' it was, for this was what was to

---

1. There's always been a bit of a brouhaha over Luke's account (v. 35) and those of Matthew (20:29) and Mark (10:46). The latter place this encounter when Jesus is leaving the town, while Luke has it when Jesus enters Jericho. However, Stanley Porter ('"In the Vicinity of Jericho": Luke 18:35 in Light of its Synoptic Parallels,' *Bulletin for Biblical Research* 2 [1992]: pp. 91-104) argues cogently that Luke's verb and preposition (*eggizō + eis*) do not indicate movement (entering) but location ('in the vicinity of'). Hence no conflict with Matthew/Mark on that score. The blind man episode occurred as He was leaving Jericho (as Matthew and Mark have it) but Luke has chosen to relate it *before* the Zacchaeus encounter, perhaps because he wanted Zacchaeus to form a kind of climax, especially with its huge punch-line in 19:10.

occur in Yahweh's final day of deliverance (see Isa. 35:5-6).[2] The point is the same as in Jesus' response to John the Baptist in 7:22. These miracles are signs that the final age has already broken into the present time. They are a clear preview of what is to come. But the really significant matter here is that this blind man could see (vv. 38-39) *before* Jesus restored his sight! He stands in contrast to a preceding cast of characters, all of whom were 'blind': the Pharisee in Jesus' parable who touted an impeccable resumé (vv. 11-12), the ruler who imagined he had kept the commandments (v. 21), and the disciples who simply couldn't see what Jesus plainly told them (v. 34).

He could see who Jesus was. Twice as he cries out, he calls Him 'Son of David' (vv. 38, 39). He assumes Jesus is the messianic king of David's line. How did he hear that, how did he know that, how did he come to that conviction? I don't know. He could see his own need. 'Have mercy on me' is his plea. The LXX uses the very same verb form (*eleēson*) some eighteen times in the Psalms in pleas to Yahweh, where it usually translates the Hebrew *ḥānan* ('to show grace').[3] He is certainly not demanding something that is his right but pleading for what he needs in his helplessness. And he could see that one must defy social pressure to lay hold of Jesus. Those in the fore part of the crowd tried to 'shush' him up, 'but he [emphatic] kept crying out[4] all the more' (v. 39). He made a regular ruckus. Opportunity ('Jesus of Nazareth is passing by,' v. 37) and desperation (v. 41b) meet in that moment, and there's no way he's going to calm down. 'The crowd's attempt to silence his cries says to him, "You do not matter to anyone, and least of all to someone important like Jesus".'[5] But he turns a deaf ear to the crowd's social analysis.

Let's pause a moment here. If you are already a Christian, you may think this pericope has little to do with you. But people who can 'see' are repeatedly raising this cry. It brings together the identity of Jesus (Son of David) and the

---

2. Cf. Ps. 146:8—although there is no instance of recovery of sight in the OT revelation.

3. Hatch and Redpath, *A Concordance to the Septuagint*, 1:450.

4. I take the imperfect tense here as indicating continuous or repeated action.

5. David E. Garland, *Luke*, ZECNT (Grand Rapids: Zondervan, 2011), p. 741.

emergency of my need ('show grace'), even if perhaps I can't specify what precise form of grace I need. Don't you find you have to raise this cry again and again—because of doubts and fears in your own soul or because of matters in your family or marriage or because of the press and load in your work or calling or because of reverses in your or a loved one's health or because of the sudden murkiness that's occurred about your future plans? Do you ever get beyond this? 'Jesus, son of David, have mercy on me.' We never get beyond the need for Jericho grace.

Now there's another citizen in Jericho—**a lost man who is found** (19:1-10). Jesus made waves when He told Zacchaeus that He 'must' lodge with him (v. 5). The spectators started griping about that (v. 7). Folks in the crowd were apparently pro-Jesus, but it seemed Jesus could 'mess up' so easily. One can rather understand people's repugnance. Zacchaeus was a 'head tax collector and rich' (v. 2). He was a sort of internal revenue agent with other agents under him. The tax collecting involved was in the form of tolls and custom charges for transport of goods. A port of entry like Jericho would have any number of caravans and/or transported goods coming through. These would be assessed according to value and, of course, valuation was in the eyes of the tax collector. As my father used to say, 'Figures don't lie, but liars do figure.' That was the trouble with most tax collectors—and so people regarded them as low-lifes and scuzz-balls.[6] Profits beyond what was actually required in their quota went into their pockets. So they were despised, and here is Jesus deliberately hobnobbing with one of them.

Jesus made an amazing assessment of His visit. 'Today,' He said, 'salvation has come to this house' (v. 9). Salvation came not because of what Zacchaeus promised to do (v. 8)— what he would do was rather the *evidence* of salvation.[7] Rich Zacchaeus then stands in contrast to the rich ruler in 18:18-23, for the 'salvation' shows that here a rich man has slithered

---

6. For a good overview, see T. E. Schmidt, 'Taxes,' DJG, 1st ed., pp. 804-07.

7. Zacchaeus vowed both generosity (v. 8b) and restitution (v. 8c). The fourfold restitution goes beyond the requirement of the law (full restitution plus a fifth); cf. Leviticus 6:1-5; Numbers 5:6-7.

through the eye of the needle into the kingdom (18:24-25)![8]
Nor is Zacchaeus being a 'son of Abraham' (v. 9b) a matter
of merit. It is a matter of propriety—even he is one of the
covenant people, one of the lost sheep of the house of Israel.
And Jesus is fulfilling Yahweh's word in Ezekiel 34:16 in
bringing the lost among the covenant people back to the Lord.

But none of this might have happened. So far as we
can tell, Zacchaeus' purpose was to see Jesus (vv. 3-4), to
get above the crowd, which is what trees are for. Can you
imagine Zacchaeus talking with Mrs Zacchaeus over supper
that night? 'So I got up in that tree,' he says, 'and Jesus went
by on the road, not twenty feet from me, and went on his way
to Jerusalem; but I got a good look at Him.' Such an imagined
scenario allows us to see what makes all the difference—the
initiative of Jesus. 'And when he came to the place, Jesus
looked up and said to him, "Zacchaeus, hurry on down, for
today I must stay at your house"' (v. 5). Jesus knows his name,
takes the initiative, and speaks of a divine 'must.' Everything
turns on this. What if Jesus simply went on? The lost didn't
find his way—Jesus found him. The words of an anonymous
hymn say it well:

> I sought the Lord, and afterward I knew
> he moved my soul to seek him, seeking me;
> it was not I that found, O Savior true;
> no, I was found of thee.[9]

This account reminds us of how important incidental details
can be—'Jesus looked up.' I think of that story of William
Thomas in the community in South Wales where Martyn
Lloyd-Jones had his first pastorate. William Thomas was
perhaps close to seventy years of age, and basically a filthy-
talking, nasty, old drunk. But he overheard some men in the
pub talking about the preaching at the chapel, something
about there being 'hope for everybody,' and Thomas was
curious to check it out. The first Sunday he lingered outside
the church fence and lost his nerve. The next Sunday night
he found they were already singing and he was too late.

---

8. Tiede, cited in Bock, *Luke 9:51-24:53*, BECNT, p. 1514.
9. *Trinity Hymnal* (1990), No. 466.

The third Sunday evening he was nervously loitering round the gate when one of the men welcomed him and said, 'Are you coming in, Bill? Come and sit with me.' He did, and he understood the message, and came to faith that very night.[10] It all seemed so incidental and yet, in one way, everything hung on those words, 'Come and sit with me.' Seems like they were part of a Savior's seeking and saving the lost.

We'll soon be dealing with Jesus' triumphal entry into Jerusalem (19:28-44), but if we really see 'Jericho grace,' we might say the triumphal entry had already happened at Jericho.

---

10. Iain H. Murray, *David Martyn Lloyd-Jones: The First Forty Years 1899-1939* (Edinburgh: Banner of Truth, 1982), pp. 222-23.

15

Putting the Brakes on
(Luke 19:11-27)

It was the first week of August 1914. The German Kaiser told departing troops, 'You will be home before the leaves have fallen from the trees.' On the other hand, Russian officers expected to be in Berlin in six weeks. One of them asked the Czar's physician whether he should pack his full-dress uniform for the entry into Berlin—or should he simply allow it to be brought by the first courier?[1] Such were some of the attitudes on the eve of what would become World War I. That's what we usually prefer—the quick fix, the immediate solution. That's the way folks in Jesus' entourage felt as He neared Jerusalem: 'they were thinking the kingdom of God was going to appear immediately' (v. 11b). And Jesus had to teach them otherwise. We long for instant relief, but in His kingdom Jesus invites us to—and insists on—the long haul.

Let's turn aside for a moment to say that we are entering, or are about to enter, the last section of Luke's gospel. Everything from 9:51 to at least 19:10 has been correlated around the 'journey' to Jerusalem. Scholars differ about precisely where in the text that journey terminates, but it's apparently at some point in the latter two-thirds of chapter 19. Jerusalem is quite prominent in Luke; he mentions it thirty-

---

1. Barbara W. Tuchman, *The Guns of August* (New York: Bonanza Books, 1982), pp. 119-20.

two times in his gospel over against thirteen for Matthew
and eleven for Mark. And of course what happens now in
Jerusalem is supremely crucial—in the original root-meaning
of that word. So, to recover our perspective, note our overall
outline for the gospel:

Back now to 19:11-27. I think this segment might be captured
by means of several key words and the teaching emerging
from them.

The first key word is **correction**, which indicates **how much
of Jesus' work consists of correcting our wrong perceptions**
(vv. 11-12). Verse 11 is the third time Luke tells us specifically
why Jesus told a parable (see 18:1, 9). 'He spoke a parable
because he was near Jerusalem and they were thinking the
kingdom of God was going to appear immediately' (v. 11b).
Hence the parable begins, 'A certain man, a nobleman, went into
a far country to obtain a kingdom for himself and to return' (v.
12). Odd to us perhaps, but familiar to Jesus' hearers. 'To obtain
a kingdom' here means to be granted the right to reign. Herod
the Great had traveled to Rome to be confirmed in his reign,
as did his son Archelaus.[2] The analogy in the parable indicates
there will be an interim between the nobleman's journey to
the far country and his return. There will be a time when he
is not 'on site.' There will be a time when Jesus is away before
He returns as king and the kingdom comes in its fullness. It
will not 'appear' now in its consummated form in Jerusalem.

However, there is a paradoxical truth about the kingdom
in the larger context, and we must take account of it. Verses
28-48 immediately follow our present segment; those verses
report the triumphal entry of Jesus into Jerusalem and
His royal-like jurisdiction over the temple. So our chapter

---

2. A delegation of Jews protested Archelaus' appointment, but Augustus made
him ethnarch anyway with the 'carrot' of kingship if he proved worthy. He ruled
with such harshness and brutality that later a group of both Jews and Samaritans
(imagine that) pleaded for his removal (cf. v. 14). Rome banished him to southern
Gaul in A.D. 6 and appointed a procurator in his place. Cf. DJG, 1st ed., p. 322.

proclaims a dual truth about Jesus and the kingdom: Verses 28-48 suggest the king *has* come, while verses 11-27 tell us that it is not yet time for the kingdom to come in its *final* form.

There were, then, some folks who were 'trigger happy' over the kingdom and suffered from a sort of kingdom mania. And, in one sense, Jesus is saying: Relax, there will be *time* for you to serve in the kingdom. The thrilling climax of the kingdom's arrival is not now; now is the time for plodding along as you wait for the king's return. This context reminds me of a stint of study in Jerusalem some years back. One of the fellows in our group was from Northern Ireland, and this was during 'the troubles' there. We were therefore eager to quiz Rob about it all. He told us much about conditions there, but then, as if making a summary statement, he said, 'But you've got to get on with the 9-to-5, you know.' He was saying that in all the turmoil and unrest, one still had a routine one had to maintain; there still had to be a certain ordinariness about life. It seems to me that that is Jesus' emphasis here: you must yet wade through ordinary days as you serve the king and wait for Him.

Hence Jesus goes about His correcting work here. Have you noticed that that is what the whole New Testament tends to do? It is largely a 'correcting' book. It naturally starts with Jesus. Didn't Jesus have to correct Peter's distorted view of what the Messiah was to be (Matt. 16:21-23)? Do 'grace' and 'freedom' mean that we can simply go on sinning? Romans 6 and 2 Peter and Jude knock that down. What is Paul doing in 1 Corinthians 15? Isn't he essentially saying, 'What do you mean there's no resurrection?' Or there's the Jesus-plus heresy; what Jesus has done is not enough; I must add my religious or moral pittance to it; and Galatians puts that down. Or there's the Christ-is-deficient heresy and so we have Colossians. There are errors and confusions about hope and the second coming and so 1–2 Thessalonians sets us straight. Is a mere profession of faith a genuine faith? So we have James. Is suffering really a normal component in the Christian life? Among many others, 1 Peter sets us right.

Beyond even the particular problem here in our parable, haven't you found that Jesus has spent a good deal of time *correcting* you over the years? Maybe it's been on the nature of the Christian life. Maybe He's had to show you that Christian living does not consist in the amount of Christian busyness or the number of Christian activities you participate in (and which can simply exhaust you). Has He ever brought you to see that maybe what's more important is that you focus on the 'church that is in your house,' that you spend your time there being prophet, priest, and king in your own home? Or perhaps He has had to change your impressions or misconceptions about prayer, and perhaps break up some of your rigid thinking about it. Jesus exercises a ministry of correction toward us, and thankfully it goes beyond the precise concern of this parable.

Secondly, this parable focuses on **calling**, or **how important faithfulness is, in the interim, as we wait for the kingdom** (vv. 13-19). Before departing, the nobleman in the parable summons ten slaves,[3] gives them ten minas, apparently one per slave (v. 13a), and tells them to 'do business' with the funds while he is gone (v. 13b).[4] A mina constitutes about three-four months' pay for a worker, hence not a humongous amount, significant but not massive.[5] The slave is simply to do what the master has told him to do while he is 'away.'

Jesus shifts to the king's return and the slaves' reports (vv. 15ff.).[6] There are two highlights we should note here. One is to see how a disciple's faithfulness stirs the pleasure of Jesus (vv. 17, 19). Note especially verse 17. The first slave has reported his success and the king exclaims, 'Superb! Good slave! Because you have proven faithful in a smallest matter, have authority over ten cities.' Aren't we to see that fidelity thrills Jesus? The Lord really does take delight in His people (cf. Ps. 149:4). Some of us as parents know something of this. I recall one of our sons, who teaches high school history and

---

3. Once again, don't let the mention of 'slaves' (*douloi*) send you off on a 'social justice' tirade. They are part of the cultural setting of the time, and, in any case, such 'slavery' is not to be equated with the harshness or brutality of some of the nineteenth-century American variety nor of Nazi forced-labor camps.

4. Lit., 'while I am coming' is a part-for-the-whole expression, covering the time of his departure and return (see W. F. Arndt, *the Gospel According to St. Luke* [St. Louis: Concordia, 1956], p. 392).

5. There is a good bit of overlap between this parable in Luke and that in Matthew 25:14-30. For all their similarities, I think they are distinct and so focus only on Luke's here. For those wanting to pursue the issue, see Klyne Snodgrass, *Stories with Intent* (Grand Rapids: Eerdmans, 2008), pp. 523-24, 529-31.

6. Though there were ten slaves (v. 13), Jesus only needs three to make His points.

coaches the tennis team, telling us that one of the players asked if they could have a Bible study. So our son met with one or two of his tennis players early in the morning one day a week to study 1 Peter. That's not an earth-shattering affair in one sense, but can you imagine the joy it brings to a father's heart to hear his son is doing that? So why wouldn't Jesus be delighted over the faithfulness of His disciples?

There is a second highlight here: our faithfulness faces the hostility of the world (v. 14). Not everybody loves this king. This is a part of the context in the parable that is easily ignored. There seems to be no reason for the citizens to hate this nobleman (v. 14)—they just did. But this means that the king's servants must openly and publicly declare their loyalty in a hostile environment of those who hate their master and don't want him to reign.[7] The king's servants must carry on in a king-hating world. So as the king's servants, we serve between the smile of Jesus and the frown of the world, and we must decide which we value most.

The third segment deals with **consequences** and teaches **what a sobering destiny awaits those who reject Jesus' kingship** (vv. 20-27). The latter part of the parable deals with this 'other' slave (vv. 20ff.) and ends with the king pronouncing doom on his enemies (v. 27). The latter seems particularly harsh and brutal: 'Only these enemies of mine who did not want me to reign over them—bring (them) here and slaughter them before me.'

What are we to make of that grizzly sentence? We must remember the 'coloring' of the parable. Here is a Near Eastern king who has a significant rebel presence in his realm. It is no surprise then to find out he eliminates them. How does this carry over to Jesus and His kingdom? We don't necessarily transfer all the pictorial elements of a parable into our doctrinal formulation. What is the doctrine involved here? Is it not essentially that of 2 Thessalonians 1:8-10a? Which says:

> He will punish those who do not know God and do not obey the
> gospel of our Lord Jesus. They will be punished with everlasting

---

7. James Edwards (*The Gospel According to Luke*, PNTC [Grand Rapids: Eerdmans, 2015], p. 538) and Kenneth Bailey (*Jesus Through Middle Eastern Eyes* [Downers Grove, IL: InterVarsity, 2008], pp. 401-2) stress this note in the parable.

destruction and shut out from the presence of the Lord and from the majesty of his power on the day he comes to be glorified in his holy people (NIV).

In the parable Jesus seems to *depict* how eternal ruin awaits you if you reject Him as king over you (vv. 14, 27); in the epistle the apostle *declares* much the same. And we may say that not all the pictorial elements of a parable are to be carried over into a doctrinal formulation, but the fact is that many folks will gag at Paul's doctrine as much as at Jesus' picture. And there's a reason for that: it is simply impossible to describe final judgment pleasantly and attractively. It is intended to be awful, to scare you, even offend you, if in that way it can get your attention.

Yet this part of the parable also shows that not all who oppose the king are *blatant enemies*; some are *false servants* (vv. 20-26). Some expositors hold that in spite of the third servant's words (vv. 20-21), nothing happened to him. That is hard to believe on two counts. Strictly speaking, of course, within the confines of the parable that may be so. But there's no doubt where this servant 'belongs' given (1) his hostile view of the king (v. 21), and (2) the king's own words, 'You wicked slave!' (v. 22). He lost more than a mina, for he despised the king as much as those in verse 14. Not all Christ's enemies are outside—any number of them are within the ranks of his servants. Somewhat like the situation in 1777 when the American colonies were carrying on their revolution against Britain. Benjamin Franklin and John Adams were in Paris, where, as members of the 'American Commission,' they were lobbying for French support. The third 'American' on the commission was Dr Edward Bancroft, New England physician, warm friend of Franklin's, secretary to the commission, hard-working, fluent in French—an amazingly capable man. But what neither Franklin nor Adams ever knew was that Bancroft was a British spy, raking in 500 pounds a year from the Crown for his services. Anything of importance connected to or decided by the American Commission was known in London within days.[8] Apparently a patriot, actually a spy. It's similar in Jesus' ranks.

---

8. David McCullough, *John Adams* (New York: Simon and Schuster, 2001), p. 201.

Jesus then is teaching us what a sobering destiny awaits those who reject His kingship, and, whether we make allowances or not, verse 27 is a hard note on which to end. There are ways of dealing with such unwelcome words. The prophecy of Isaiah ends with such a severe word:

> As they leave, they will see the dead bodies of the men who have rebelled against Me; for their maggots will never die, their fire will never go out, and they will be a horror to all mankind (Isa. 66:24, HCSB).

But when the passage is read in the Jewish synagogue, verse 23 is repeated after verse 24 in order to end on a more tolerable note:

> All mankind will come to worship Me, from one New Moon to another, and from one Sabbath to another, says the LORD (Isa. 66:23, HCSB).

I have even heard preaching instructors advise along such lines, saying that we should not leave folks in despair or with bad news but should give them some word of grace or hope to hold on to. But why? Why not leave them in despair if that is what they need? Final judgment is never pleasant and cannot be described pleasantly. Nor should we have our minds turned away from it. It *is* the note on which Jesus ends.

16

Jerusalem: Triumph and Tragedy
(Luke 19:28-48)

Luke seems in no hurry for Jesus to get to Jerusalem. In verse 28 He is 'going up' to Jerusalem, in verse 41 He 'drew near' the city. Of course, He does 'enter,' but even then it is specifically the temple that He enters (v. 45). Jerusalem in this passage is a mixed 'read': it is the scene of triumph (in the Lord's arrival, vv. 35-38) and of tragedies (in the Lord's opponents, v. 39, the Lord's lament, vv. 41-44, and the Lord's temple, vv. 45-46). We can consider the passage under three heads.

First, notice **the acclaim of Jesus** (vv. 28-40). He is close to Bethphage and Bethany (v. 29). Bethany is 1.7 miles east of Jerusalem on the east slope of the Mount of Olives, while Bethphage is likely to be located near-by, a little to the north of Bethany.[1] Jesus sent two disciples to (apparently) one of these villages to procure a colt. Luke does not explicitly link this colt to the prophecy of Zechariah 9:9-10 as do Matthew (21:4-5) and John (12:14-15), though the following scenario (vv. 35-38) hints he might have had that in mind.[2]

---

1. A. D. Riddle, 'The Passover Pilgrimage from Jericho to Jerusalem,' in *Lexham Geographic Commentary on the Gospels*, ed. Barry J. Beitzel (Bellingham, WA: Lexham, 2017), pp. 402-5.

2. We should note that Zechariah 9:9 shades the joy it speaks of with realism. The frequent rendering 'victorious' or 'having salvation' may be meant in a passive sense, 'having been saved.' The adjective rendered 'humble' often describes

Now Jesus knows everything about this colt (v. 30) — and those who may be watching it (v. 31). If anyone asks the two why they are untying the animal (and they do, v. 33), the duo are to play their trump card: 'The Lord has need of it' (vv. 31b, 34). The reader faces a conundrum here. Is this an instance of Jesus' supernatural knowledge or was this only a matter of some previous arrangement Jesus had made with the colt-owners? Considerations can be marshalled for both options. However, it seems to me that when Luke says in verse 32 that they 'went off and found it just as he had said to them,' he himself favors the first option. He wants to stress the uncanny accuracy of Jesus' word. I tend to think Luke would want his readers to ask the question, 'Did Jesus just know that or did He set that up beforehand?' I think maybe he would want readers to ponder the mystery, to begin to ask, 'Who then is this?' The gospel doesn't always approach us by direct assertion but by subtle suggestion; sometimes it wants to lure us to ponder Jesus by facing us with a mystery.

What is not mysterious, however, is that Jesus is making a calculated move. He carefully plans what is to take place. By His colt-requisition He is deliberately setting the stage for the 'triumphal entry.' It was not merely the spontaneous eruption of His disciples' enthusiasm; He Himself had 'set it up.'[3]

The 'whole multitude of the disciples' (v. 37) join in the pageant of Jesus' arrival. It is a public disclosure (vv. 35-38) of Jesus' kingship, as the crowd hails Him in the shout of Psalm 118:26a, 'How blessed the one who comes — the king — in the name of the Lord!' (v. 38a).

Psalm 118 is the thanksgiving of a victorious Davidic king with a bit of dash and drama (cf. my previous discussion at 13:35). The psalm seems divided into 'parts,' sometimes the king speaks as 'I,' sometimes the congregation (or others at the temple) speak as 'we,' 'our,' or provide more general responses. One might map out the bulk of the psalm like this:

'afflicted' people. Zechariah may be sketching a strange sort of king—one who is afflicted and had to be saved or rescued. If so, then the shadows of the cross fall on this joyful announcement. See Joyce Baldwin, *Haggai, Zechariah, Malachi*, TOTC (Downers Grove, IL: Inter-Varsity, 1972), p. 165.

3. Cf. Arthur A. Just, Jr., *Luke 9:51-24:53*, Concordia Commentary (St. Louis: Concordia, 1997), p. 744, fn 3, citing Nolland.

King's testimony, vv. 5-7
  Congregational response, vv. 8-9
King's testimony, vv. 10-14
  Congregational response, vv. 15-16
King's testimony—and request, vv. 17-19
  Congregational (or official's) response, v. 20
King's testimony, v. 21
  Congregational response, vv. 22-27
King's testimony, v. 28

In the second 'I' section, the speaker tells how 'all nations surrounded me' (v. 10) and three times he exclaims, 'In the name of Yahweh I cut them off' (vv. 10, 11, 12)—not because he was so slick or powerful but because 'Yahweh [emphatic] helped me' (v. 13b). It makes most sense to take this 'I,' then, as a king, under assault from surrounding nations and yet, by Yahweh's help, victorious over them.[4] That king then asks for access to Yahweh's house in order to give thanks for his victories (v. 19), and there the congregation welcomes him with—among other words—'Blessed is he who comes in the name of Yahweh' (v. 26a). And that is the cry of the crowd of disciples as Jesus rides down the Mount of Olives. They had seen His mighty works (v. 37b) and now they take up the cry of the Psalm, welcoming the victorious Davidic (messianic) king (v. 38).

At this point a bit of irony appears in Luke's story. Some of the Pharisees vent their displeasure at this enthusiastic demonstration. 'Teacher,' they demand, 'rebuke your disciples' (v. 39b). That is: Don't let them carry on like this, making such audacious, inflammatory claims. 'The rebuke of the Pharisees represents the real attitude of Jerusalem toward Jesus. He is not now Messiah triumphant but Messiah

---

4. I do not know why some Psalms commentators (J. A. Alexander, Leupold, Allen Ross) are so insistent that the 'I' = the people of Israel in post-exilic times, when the 'I-we' segments so naturally fit a king-people pattern in a pre-exilic setting. Incidentally, the 'hymn' (Matt. 26:30; Mark 14:26) Jesus and His disciples sang after the Passover meal may have been Psalms 115–118 (if the practice was that early). If so, think how bracing and moving verses 17-18 must have been for Jesus ('I will not die, but I will live, and tell the deeds of Yah; Yah has disciplined me severely, but he has not given me up to death'). For a fresh and nourishing exposition of Psalm 118, see Philip S. Ross, *Anthems for a Dying Lamb* (Ross-shire: Christian Focus, 2017), pp. 125-46.

rejected.'[5] The irony arises if we remember Psalm 118. For there the people revel in the astonishing turn-around in the king's victory: 'The stone the builders rejected has become the cornerstone!' (v. 22).[6] In Psalm 118, the 'builders' are those nations who tried to decimate and destroy the king and his people (Ps. 118:10-13). But here in Luke's gospel, the 'builders' who oppose the King are not pagan nations but the spiritual leadership within Israel (v. 39)!

But Jesus is not about to 'shush up' the acclaim of this throng of disciples. He tells these Pharisees, 'If they keep silence, the stones will cry out' (v. 40). It's as if Jesus says: This is a 'have-to' situation; it simply has to come out. If you stifle their praise, it will break out elsewhere—you can't stop it; you suppress their acclaim, and the stones will let loose with it. Is that what you want—rocks screaming at you? That may seem a bit over the top, but you must catch this note of 'unstoppability' in Jesus' answer.

It's like the 1954 Cotton Bowl football game between Alabama and Rice. Rice was backed up near the end zone, but one of their backs ran around end down the right side of the field eluding and outdistancing defenders—he was going to go all the way for a touchdown. But suddenly, as he ran past the Alabama bench, a figure darted out and tackled the runner. It was Tommy Lewis, an Alabama player who was not currently in the game. It was illegal, of course, and they awarded Rice the touchdown. But look at it from Tommy Lewis' perspective: here's an opponent, racing in the clear for a score, going right by the Alabama bench; Tommy Lewis simply can't stand it; to think this fellow will score; a compulsion seizes him; he must stop him! It *had* to be done. Illegality aside, the principle stands. Jesus was saying there was plainly this necessity, this inevitability, about the acclaim He was receiving.

---

5. E. Earle Ellis, *The Gospel of Luke*, NCB, rev. ed. (London: Oliphants, 1974), p. 224. Ellis also adds: 'The central division of Luke opened with Jesus' rejection in Samaria (9:53). It closes with his rejection at Jerusalem' (p. 225).

6. This verse is simply a pictorial or proverbial expression. There is no reason to imagine any suggestion about the re-building of the temple in connection with it. If I were to say to several companions, 'Let's get the ball rolling,' a hearer would not assume we were in an athletic contest; it is merely an expression urging on whatever activity needs doing.

Now these people have a lot more to learn about the kind of king Jesus is to be. There is still much ignorance mixed in with their praise. But at least they are glad to say Jesus is the king who comes in the name of the Lord—and that's far better than being one of the 'builders' (v. 39).

Secondly, note **the anguish of Jesus** in verses 41-44. Luke has a different sequence here than all the other gospels (e.g., Matt. 21, Mark 11, John 12). Luke jars us by placing the lament of Jesus immediately after the praise of His disciples. This is hardly the climax we are expecting:

> (41) And when he drew near and saw the city, he lamented[7] over it, (42) saying, 'If you had known on this day, even you, the things that make for peace! But now it has been hidden from your eyes. (43) For the days will come upon you when your enemies will throw up earthworks against you and will circle round you and will hem you in on all sides, (44) and they will dash you and your children in you to the ground, and will not leave one stone on another in you, because you did not know the opportunity of (God's) visiting you.'

Jesus grieves over the blamable ignorance and consequent blindness of Jerusalem (vv. 41-42) and then over the ruin and judgment she will experience because of it (vv. 43-44). Time was when King David went up the Mount of Olives weeping, when he was forced to escape the city (2 Sam. 15:30), but Jesus weeps as He comes in apparent triumph into the city. Naturally, 13:34-35 might suggest we should have been prepared. But still it discombobulates a reader to take in verses 38-39 and then to get hit with verses 41-44. It does not seem like a proper climax at all, there's something 'wrong' about it.

When I was about fourteen, we were going to move. My father was leaving one pastorate and taking up another. He had served the one he was leaving for eleven years, and, as is sometimes the custom, the church held a 'farewell dinner' for our family. It's an occasion when, besides the food, people

---

7. The verb *klaiō* means to lament with sobs, whereas *dakruō* (as in John 11:35) means to shed tears (Arndt).

can express their appreciation and gratitude for, in this case, my father's ministry. Though there may have been some sadness over his leaving, still, on the whole, it's a positive and 'feel good' occasion. And before the evening draws to a close, my father is to make a few remarks. I don't remember all he said; hopefully he expressed some thanks. But I do recall one comment. He told them, 'If I had known some time ago what I know now, I would not be leaving.' What was that? What did that mean? Were there some church politics or something that had gone on? Don't know. But think of the effect of that. Here's an occasion that's supposed to be mostly sweetness and light, and my father drops that 'bomb' in the middle of it. Folks probably asked themselves, 'What didn't he know?' 'What did he find out?' 'What was going on?' 'What did he mean by that?' As I recall, my father didn't explain. He just allowed it to hang there. But one isn't supposed to do that; it's not appropriate. But it didn't seem to bother my dad.

That is a bit like Luke's placing Jesus' anguish right after the 'triumphal entry' section. It doesn't seem fitting. So why would He do it? Perhaps to shock us into seeing how horrid and ruinous it is to reject and repudiate the Son of Man who came to seek and to save the lost. Maybe the only way Luke can get you to see this is by 'wrecking' his narrative, by forcing you to hear the agonizing anguish of Jesus.

Then in verses 45-48 we meet with **the authority of Jesus**. Unlike Mark who has the temple clearing on the next day after a night spent in Bethany (see Mark 11:11-17), Luke 'moves it up' and reports it right after the 'triumphal entry.'[8] There is nothing devious or wrong about Luke's report. He chooses to omit the night in Bethany in order to place the temple episode right next to the 'entry' episode, and does so to show Jesus coming as king on His way into the city and then *acting as king* when He enters the temple. The king does not merely come but comes to His temple. What He does there shows that He assumes the temple is *His place*. We are watching the authority of Jesus in living color.

Too much 'color' for some. There are four key words we can use to summarize this section and, clearly, the first is

---

8. Matthew's sequence (21:12-17) is like Luke's.

violence. 'And when he entered the temple, he began to throw out those selling' (v. 45). No 'Beg your pardon' or any of that. Jesus was not nice. He threw them out. There will probably always be a hand-cream contingent that feigns horror at Jesus' act. We cannot help them much. It was violent.

The second word for this episode is *restoration.* Verse 46a implies this idea, but we need to back up a moment and fill in some background. For a major festival like Passover (in this case), worshipers came both from Israel itself but also included Jewish pilgrims from all over the Roman world. Jerusalem may have had a population at the time of 80,000, but the influx of Passover pilgrims might push the total to 200,000.[9] Most worshipers could not bring sacrificial animals with them, so there was a 'market' for purchasing locally provided and approved sacrificial animals. In our text this was taking place in the temple complex in the 'court of the Gentiles,' a huge 35-acre area in which non-Jews could come.[10] There's some evidence that this bazaar in the Court of the Gentiles was a relatively recent innovation. Apparently there were four markets on the Mount of Olives where worshipers could obtain sacrificial victims, but Caiaphas & Co. set up a market in the temple as competition with these traditional markets.[11] If so, all the more reason for Jesus to vent His wrath on such wheeling and dealing.

It is in this situation that Jesus quotes Isaiah 56:7. In Isaiah 56 Yahweh promises that a day will come when 'foreigners' and other rejects ('eunuchs') who become Yahweh's servants will be made 'joyful in my house of prayer' and then explains: 'for my house shall be called a house of prayer for all peoples' (v. 7). But how could it be a house of prayer amid all the clutter and clamor, all the bargaining and bickering, of an oriental market? Hence Jesus' action was a restoring work, reclaiming

---

9. See Eckhard J. Schnabel, *Jesus in Jerusalem: The Last Days* (Grand Rapids: Eerdmans, 2018), pp. 107, 458 n 21; ABD, 3:753; ISBE, 3:677. Josephus' figures in his *Jewish War* (2.14.3) are likely exaggerated.

10. For the ground plan of 'Herod's temple,' see NIDB, 5:506; for a graphic showing the relative size of the Court of the Gentiles, see *Archaeology Study Bible* (Crossway, 2017), pp. 1544-45.

11. See W. L. Lane, *The Gospel According to Mark*, NICNT (Grand Rapids: Eerdmans, 1974), pp. 403-4, 406.

His Father's house for its intended purpose. Or was it strictly His Father's house? For when Jesus quotes 'My house shall be called a house of prayer' one senses that Jesus' 'my' is a reference to Himself. Is He making a claim? Is He saying that the temple is *His* house? And therefore He purges it of perversions?

Condemnation also describes Jesus' action. This seems implied in verse 46b when He alludes to Jeremiah 7:11 — 'you [emphatic] have made it [= 'my house'] a cave of thugs.' In Jeremiah 7 the prophet was railing against the men of Judah who would practice idolatry and break Yahweh's commandments then come to worship in the temple. As if they were a bunch of rogues running wild and then coming back to the safety of their 'hideout,' the temple. So they made the temple 'a cave of thugs.' Here Jesus tells these temple marketeers that they are turning the temple into a cave of thugs or 'a den of robbers.' I think He means they are not making it a refuge for robbers, as in Jeremiah 7, but 'the actual place in which they can commit their greed-driven acts.'[12] Some scholars downplay this shystering and profiteering but there seems to be sufficient evidence for it.[13] So, for Jesus, their clamor defeats the purpose of the temple and their profiteering defiles the holiness of the temple.

The fourth word is *threat*. There may not be a direct threat on Jesus' part here, but His allusion to Jeremiah 7 suggests one. After Yahweh had reamed out Jeremiah's contemporaries for their superstitious, rabbit-foot attitude toward the temple (Jer. 7:4), He then told them to take a trip to Shiloh where the tabernacle had been in previous years and which He had allowed the Philistines to devastate (cf. 1 Sam. 4). And Jesus' action here seems to portend that a greater 'cleansing' is coming, another Shiloh-reenactment.

Such is the authority of Jesus — authority He has over the worship of His people. We ought not to think that Jesus'

---

12. Michael L. Brown, 'Jeremiah', EBC, rev. ed., 13 vols, 7:161.

13. See J. Jeremias, *Jerusalem in the Time of Jesus* (1969; reprint ed., Peabody, MA: Hendrickson, 2016), 49; also Alfred Edersheim, *The Life and Times of Jesus the Messiah*, 2 vols. (reprint ed., Grand Rapids: Ferdmans, 1967), 1:368-70; and Knox Chamblin, *Matthew*, 2 vols. (Ross-shire: Christian Focus, 2010), 2:1013-14. I have found Chamblin's whole exposition of the temple cleansing to be the most satisfying of any (2:1007-16).

scrutiny is limited to a first-century temple but realize it extends to our worship assemblies today. And one of the sad affairs is that there is many a church that is no longer 'a house of prayer.' One can enter churches that may have a brief prayer at the beginning and a 'wrap-up' one at the end, but for the most part there is no prayer in the worship. You will starve before you will find a prayer of confession or a time allotted for intercessions. We may be happy to crank up the amplifiers and go on singing 'praise songs,' but let us not give time for the arduous and careful work of prayer. Jesus likely has much cleansing work yet to do in our gentile churches.

17

Facing the anti-Jesus Coalition
(Luke 20:1–21:4)

Two Yugoslav representatives are meeting Hitler and Ribbentrop in Vienna in late March 1941. There they sign an agreement submitting their nation to the Third Reich. However, almost as soon as they return to Belgrade, their government is overthrown in a coup. The new regime offers to sign a non-aggression pact with Hitler, but, clearly, it did not plan to play puppet to the Nazis. This threw a monkey wrench into Hitler's plans and threw Hitler into one of the wildest rages of his life. He would even postpone his planned assault on Soviet Russia for four weeks in order to crush Yugoslavia with 'unmerciful harshness.' And so it was. On April 6 the attack began. For three days and nights Luftwaffe bombers ranged over Belgrade at roof-top level. The city had no anti-aircraft guns. The German attack killed 17,000 civilians, wounded many more, and left the city smoking rubble. They had 'offended' Hitler, he was 'ticked off,' and they reaped the whirlwind.[1]

That is the kind of pattern we meet in Luke 20. Jesus' entry as king but especially His ruckus in, and purging of, the temple court had so riled and infuriated the Jewish leadership that they came after Him, in this chapter, wave upon wave

---

1. William L. Shirer, *The Rise and Fall of the Third Reich* (Greenwich, CT: Fawcett, 1960), pp. 1078-83.

and from every sort of angle. Jesus has aggravated them to the hilt and they are ready to be rid of Him (19:47). Until that time, they come at Him in every way, seeking to discredit and trap Him. He is facing the anti-Jesus coalition. Because the whole chapter (plus 21:1-4) centers on these conflicts, I think it better to treat the text as a whole instead of breaking it up into smaller sections. We'll sacrifice some detail but hopefully see the larger picture.

First of all, in verses 1-19 Luke highlights **the enmity Jesus exposes**. The interruption came while Jesus was teaching and preaching in the temple complex (v. 1; cf. 19:47a). Since His purge of the marketeering there (19:45-46), Jesus has now 'reclaimed the temple for its legitimate use as a center of revelatory instruction.'[2] But this does not inhibit this seething Sanhedrin committee. They demand to know the sort or source of the authority Jesus has assumed. Why such a demand unless they hope to goad Him into making a claim that they might label 'blasphemy'? Jesus plays the game by counter-questioning them: the baptism of John— from heaven or from men? (v. 4).[3] This sends them into an unholy huddle. Should they give the 'safe' answer (v. 5), which they didn't believe (cf. 7:29-30), Jesus would nail them for their unbelief. Yet if they said what they actually thought, the consequences would be both unpopular and likely lethal (v. 6). So they are both faith-less and gutless. Here was a moment of opportunity if they could but see it, a moment to question their unbelief and to disdain their fear of man. How Jesus had revealed them to themselves if they but had eyes to see it. If nothing more they should have despised themselves for their wimpy unbelief that couldn't even face the fear of man. So they did the unthinkable—they lost face (v. 7) and confessed agnosticism.

Jesus, however, has not finished with them. He tells the people a parable (v. 9), a parable this theological task force knows is meant to depict them (and their kind; v. 19). 'The

---

2. Joel B. Green, *The Gospel of Luke*, NICNT (Grand Rapids: Eerdmans, 1997), p. 699.

3. The 'baptism of John' is a 'cipher for the whole of John's message' (Green, 701). To say 'From heaven' would implicitly mean accepting John's testimony to Jesus (3:16-17; cf. 7:18-23).

lord of the vineyard' in Jesus' story entrusts its care to 'tenant farmers' and goes away.[4] At intervals he sends a slave to collect some of his proceeds or profits, but these slaves are all treated with an increasing degree of contempt and harm (vv. 10-12). At last he decides to send 'my son, the one I love' (v. 13) with the hope they will respect him. But this only stirs their greed: he is the heir; if they kill him, they will have 'the inheritance' (vv. 14-15a). His hostile hearers (v. 19) don't need a volume on the interpretation of parables to catch Jesus' point. There is such a thin veil over the parable that it is transparent. It's like Joseph's dreams in Genesis 37. Joseph for some reason couldn't keep from spilling his dreams to his brothers: we were binding sheaves in the field and your sheaves gathered round and bowed down to my sheaf (Gen. 37:7); or, the sun, moon, and eleven stars were bowing down to Joseph (v. 9). None of his brothers had to ask him, 'What on earth could that mean, Joseph?' It was all clear—some things don't need any interpretation. Jesus' opponents were the climactic batch in a long history of Israelite leadership rejecting Yahweh's servants. Only now they are going to kill the Son the 'owner' loves (v. 13). Jesus exposes their enmity. He says to them, 'I know what you are going to do.'

But we must allow Jesus to finish the parable. He does that with a question: 'What then will the lord of the vineyard do to them?' (v. 15b). He immediately answers, 'He will come and destroy those tenants and will give the vineyard to others' (v. 16a). Jesus' audience can't help themselves and blurt out, 'Oh no! Not that!' (v. 16b). But, Luke says, Jesus 'looked straight at them' and so much as asked them what Psalm 118:22 meant. He quotes it: 'The stone the builders rejected—it has become the cornerstone.'[5] We've already alluded to this Psalm and even this text in the previous chapter. The statement in this verse may be a kind of gnomic or proverbial statement expressing radical reversal. We've already argued that in the context of the psalm the 'builders' likely refers to the hostile

---

4. For the vine or vineyard as an emblem of Israel, see, e.g., Isaiah 5:1-7; Psalm 80:8-18.

5. I take the reference as a cornerstone rather than a capstone. A cornerstone was a huge stone used at the base of two walls which gave stability and anchorage to the structure.

nations that attacked the Davidic king of Israel. However, he 'cut them off' and won the victory over them. The one they despised became the 'cornerstone.' But in this context, in view of Jesus' parable, we meet a shocking irony: the 'builders' who reject God's chosen One are not hostile pagan nations but Israel's religious leadership! And Jesus goes on to point out what will be in store for them (v. 18). We might say Jesus plays on this 'stone' idea: He has noted the *rejected* stone ('the stone the builders rejected,' v. 17b) that is also the *triumphant* stone ('it has become the cornerstone,' v. 17c) and so becomes the *perilous* stone ('Everyone who falls on that stone will be smashed to pieces, and on whomever it falls, it will grind him to powder,' v. 18).[6] Jesus *threatens* these leaders with nothing less than final ruin, and yet in that same threat He *appeals* to them. With His parable it's as if He says, 'We all know, don't we, what's going on here and what you are planning?' Then with His 'stone' text (vv. 17-18) He says, 'But do you realize what it will *cost* you?' Is that not also an appeal to these enemies He exposes? Mercy is hidden in that severity.[7]

Next, Luke tells us of **the answers Jesus gives** (vv. 20-40). Now devious agents and theological skeptics accost Jesus to trap Him or hold Him up to ridicule. The first encounter centers on a *political* question (vv. 20-26), the latter on a *theological* one (or, if we want to be snooty, an 'eschatological' one; vv. 27-40).

With sincere looks, furrowed brows, and smelly flattery (vv. 20-21) the lackeys pose their loaded question: Is it lawful for us to pay taxes to Caesar or not? (v. 22). Bock paraphrases their intent: 'Are God's people exempt from paying such a tax to a foreign power? Jesus, are you loyal to Israel, looking for its independence, or should we knuckle under to Rome?'[8] They are trying to gore Jesus on the horns of a dilemma: answer

---

6. Cf. David Gooding (*According to Luke* [1987; reprint ed., Coleraine, N. Ireland: Myrtlefield Trust, 2013], pp. 336): 'There is no vineyard anywhere in the universe where creatures may usurp the authority of the owner and of his son and then continue forever to enjoy the grapes.'

7. We must also remember that Jesus' parable here (vv. 9-16) is not merely a parable with a bite (v. 19) but is also a Christological claim. When the vineyard owner speaks of 'my son, the one I love' (v. 13), Jesus is asserting who He is.

8. D. L. Bock, *Luke 9:51-24:53*, BECNT (Grand Rapids: Baker, 1996), p. 1611.

pro-Roman and Jewish folks will be disenchanted with Him; answer anti-Rome and Roman authority will be quick to condemn Him (if they expose him). But if they are crafty (cf. v. 23), Jesus is craftier: 'Show me a denarius,' He asked (v. 24). As soon as they did, He had won the game of 'Gotchya!'

We're getting ahead of ourselves, however. We should talk about that denarius. It was the usual daily wage for a laboring man. But the emperor's denarii were special. They were likely produced at the imperial mint in Lyons, were officially the emperor's property, and Jews, for example, *had* to use this coin; it was the one *required* for paying the poll tax in all provinces. The poll tax was likely a denarius per year per person.[9] The front of the coin depicted a bust of Tiberius decked with the laurel wreath, 'the sign of his divinity,'[10] with the inscription, 'Tiberius Caesar, Augustus, son of divine Augustus.'

Back to the scene. Jesus is the one laying the trap. If they were to avoid stepping into it they should have answered His request for a denarius with a firm 'We don't carry them.'[11] But they don't. They have one with the likeness and legend of Caesar on it. If they were so all-fired disturbed over subservience as God's people to a foreign power and to a self-deifying ruler, what on earth were they doing with his currency in their pockets, currency by which they would pay the tax and also are buying and trading from day to day? 'By accepting imperial money they have profited by the financial, economic and legal order of the empire.'[12] Hence they 'owe' Caesar for this. 'So then pay back to Caesar the things that are Caesar's' (v. 25). End of debate.

Well, not quite. We must take in the rest of Jesus' punchline: 'and (give back) to God the things that are God's.' Here Jesus 'nails' us. But often we don't see it, and we don't hear Him. We read verse 25 and think what a slick answer it was; and we talk about responsibility to the state, or we throw around talk about

---

9. C. S. Keener, *A Commentary on the Gospel of Matthew* (Grand Rapids: Eerdmans, 1999), p. 525 (drawing in part on Lane).

10. Ethelbert Stauffer, *Christ and the Caesars* (London: SCM, 1955), p. 124.

11. F. W. Danker, *Jesus and the New Age*, rev. and expanded (Philadelphia: Fortress, 1988), p. 320.

12. Stauffer, p. 130.

two kingdoms, or ramble on about the secular and the sacred, or even raise the difficulties that we may face when these two realms conflict. And we don't hear Jesus. 'Pay back to God the things that are God's.' When He said that He minimized Caesar, He trivialized Caesar, He set him in the shade. I don't know if I can do what Jesus requires. What does it mean to pay back to God the things that are God's except to offer to Him all that I am and have? Jesus' demand here costs far more than we typically imagine as we sit in front of this text.[13]

Don McClure spent some time after graduating from college getting some first-hand 'missions' experience in the Sudan. He was teaching some Sudanese boys. He wrote home, telling how some of his students had 'begun to comb their hair on the same side as I do and, as much as they are able, to dress like me.' One of them, he said, asked him if it cost a lot to dye his hair red (McClure was red-headed). McClure said it was very costly and then, rolling up his trousers, he told him it was even more expensive to make the hair on his legs the right color![14] That's the way this text is. It is far more demanding and 'expensive' than we commonly think. So easy to take verse 25 as sort of a principial solution for our church and state dilemmas and be deaf to Jesus' demand.

In this matter—surrendering all we are and have to God—I tend to think of Deuteronomy 10:12-13. Was Moses perhaps speaking a bit tongue-in-cheek? He begins with, 'And now, Israel, what is Yahweh your God asking of you except,' and then he continues, [except] 'to fear Yahweh your God, to walk in all his ways, and to love him, and to serve Yahweh your God with all your heart and with all your being, to keep the commandments of Yahweh and his statutes ....' It's as if Moses says, 'Now this is all very simple and elementary, nothing complicated about this at all—this is really all that Yahweh asks of you.' And then you read verses 12-13 and you see how basic and simple it is! What does Yahweh ask of you? Well, just everything. That's all. 'Give back to God the things that are God's.' And who can ever do that?

---

13. David Garland (*Luke*, ZECNT [Grand Rapids: Zondervan, 2011], p. 802) has rightly picked up Jesus' emphasis here.

14. Charles Partee, *Adventure in Africa* (Grand Rapids: Zondervan, 1990), p. 27.

Next, Jesus answers the theological question posed by the Sadducees (vv. 27-40).[15] Luke tells us all we need to know about them at the moment: they deny the resurrection (v. 27). And they come to Jesus with what J. C. Ryle called a favorite technique of skeptics, a supposed case. They allude to Moses' provision in Deuteronomy 25:5 for a man to marry the childless widow of his deceased brother and so to provide at least a son that can be counted as the deceased brother's. These Sadducees try to make 'hay' out of this. They say there were seven brothers (v. 29). Who knows if there were? At any rate, they say that the first brother died, his wife was childless, so the second brother married her but had the same fate. In fact, all seven had married her and died in the process. Then comes the real 'kicker': 'At last the woman also died' (v. 32). Really? No kidding? This is actually what makes their case so phony—no woman could have survived seven husbands! She would have given up the ghost long before. Maybe she could have survived three or 'by reason of strength' four. But seven? No—she'd have perished before that. But we must let the Sadducees present their puzzle. Hence, come the resurrection, whose wife will this lady be? (v. 33). Do you flip a coin or pull a number out of a hat? What? They mean to hold up the very idea of resurrection life to ridicule.

Jesus tells them they are operating on false assumptions.[16] They are assuming that conditions in the age to come will be precisely like those in this age. Tuesdays there will be like Tuesdays here. Not so, Jesus says. In this age people marry and are given in marriage, but those 'who are counted worthy to attain to that age and of the resurrection out of the dead' will not do so.[17] The reason for that is that in one respect they will be like angels—they will not die, and so no necessity for marriage as a means of preserving the race as was the case in a formerly mortal world.[18]

---

15. On the Sadducees, see NBD, 3rd ed. (1996), pp. 1044-45.

16. David Gooding nicely highlights the Sadducees' false presuppositions (p. 340).

17. In verse 35 Jesus distinguishes; not everyone will share in that age.

18. Some believers who are happily married in this age may feel disappointment if marriage is not an item in the age to come. We *really like* our spouses and can hardly conceive life without them. But we ourselves also need to beware of making

But all this is merely preliminary. Jesus moves on to the Sadducees' real issue, the resurrection of the dead, in verses 37-38. He takes them to what Moses said in the 'bush' passage (Exod. 3:6) when he called the Lord 'the God of Abraham and the God of Isaac and the God of Jacob.' In fact, Yahweh had identified Himself that way in that text. Jesus obviously does not mean 'the God of' construction to mean 'I am the God that Abraham, Isaac, and Jacob once worshiped,' though that would have been true. But Jesus and Moses, indeed Yahweh Himself, use 'the God of' in the sense 'I am the God who stands in relation to Abraham,' etc. So, in Moses' time, some hundreds of years after the deaths of these three patriarchs, Yahweh is saying He is the God who stands in relationship with each of them. They died long ago. But Yahweh is yet in relation to each of them, which means in some way they still exist. They are not non-entities, for God cannot be 'God' of non-entities (cf. v. 38). If they still exist in relation to God, then they will be fodder for the resurrection. What's behind this? I think it goes back to Yahweh's covenant promise to Abraham, when He assured him He would 'be God to you — and to your seed after you' (Gen. 17:7). Now if the eternal God pledges Himself 'to be God to you,' that establishes a relation that is as eternal as the God who promised it. Once Yahweh binds Himself to you to be your God, there is no circumstance, no opponent, that can sever that relation. Even in death He is still the God who holds you and at the right time will raise you to life.

It seems to me that the basic idea is similar to what we find in Paul's paradoxical reference to the 'dead in Christ' who will rise first at Jesus' second coming (1 Thess. 4:16). These believers are dead. But they are dead 'in Christ.' Which puts a bit of a spin on 'dead.' They are dead but dead in union with a living and resurrected Savior. If they are dead in union with Him, then there's a sense in which they are not absolutely, irrevocably dead — they cannot be when even in death they are joined to and exist in relation to a living Lord.

---

false assumptions. We should assume that the age to come will be more not less. Hence close relations in this age will surely in some way enjoy an even deeper intimacy and a far higher joy then than in the currently given mode of this age. We can be sure that the Lord will not use the age to come to *deprive* us.

David Gooding has summed this incident up well. He says the Sadducees assumed that 'the relationship formed between God and men in this life was only temporary.'

> But that is not so. God being eternal, the relationships he forms are eternal. Centuries after Abraham, Isaac and Jacob lived, God was announcing himself to Moses, so Christ pointed out, as the God of Abraham and the God of Isaac and the God of Jacob …. The eternal cannot be characterized by something that no longer exists. Resurrection then is not a fantasy dreamed up by the wishful thinking of less than rigorous theologians; resurrection is a necessary outcome of the character and nature of God.[19]

Thirdly, in verses 41-44 we hear **the conundrum Jesus poses**. After Jesus has fielded the barrage of questions aimed at Him (vv. 2, 22, 27-32), He goes on offense and presses His own question on them (in Matthew 22:41, 'them' = the Pharisees). Jesus' *question* is, 'How is it they say the Messiah is the son of David?' (v. 41). That would be a common opinion among His hearers. And well supported. Plenty of biblical passages could be cited for it (e.g., among others, Isaiah 9:7; 11:1; Jeremiah 23:5-6; Ezekiel 34:23-24; and Hosea 3:5). Jesus' question does not deny the assertion but sort of suspends it, as if to say, 'Perhaps we need to look at that a bit more.' The reason for that begins in the *assumption* (or simply, assertion) Jesus makes: 'For David himself says in the book of Psalms' (v. 42a) as He goes on to quote Psalm 110:1. Jesus clearly assumes that the psalm speaks of the Messiah and that David is the speaker and/or author of the psalm. He bases this latter contention on the 'heading' of the psalm, which, though printed by itself in our English texts, is actually a part of verse 1 of the canonical Hebrew text. This is crucial to Jesus' argument.[20]

---

19. Gooding, p. 340.

20. That ascription in Psalm 110 reads, 'Of David, a psalm.' Many OT scholars reject David's authorship. One common ploy is to say a court prophet is speaking and that the 'my lord' in verse 1 is this prophet referring to David or another Davidic king. This is sheer scholarly guesswork. Sometimes such scholars 'excuse' Jesus for holding David's authorship of the psalm by alleging that Jesus simply shared the opinions current among His first-century Jewish contemporaries. But that does not wash well. Any reader of the gospels knows there were plenty of matters on which Jesus did *not* share the view of His contemporaries. But there are some who seem

All this leads up to Jesus' *quotation* of Psalm 110:1:

> The Lord said to my Lord,
> 'Sit at my right hand
> until I make your enemies
>   the footstool for your feet' (vv. 42b-43).

The Hebrew text reads, 'Yahweh says to my *'adōn* (lord),' but if this were read in the synagogue they would read *'adōnai* when they saw 'Yahweh,' which would be equivalent to LXX (and the NT's) 'The Lord said to my Lord.' This one called 'my Lord' then is in some way distinct from Yahweh yet superior to David, the speaker. And so Jesus raises His *enigma* that He wants to leave with His opponents: 'David then calls him "Lord"—how then is he his son?' (v. 44). As if to say, Have you thought about that? Has that ever grabbed your attention as you read Psalm 110:1? How do you put all that together?

Isn't it the case that we can easily miss something that's right there in the text, or fail to think through the clear import of a text? When Bishop Butler (d. 1752) lay dying he asked for his chaplain and said (in a somewhat works-loaded manner), 'Though I have endeavored to avoid sin, and to please God to the utmost of my power, yet, from the consciousness of perpetual infirmities, I am still afraid to die.' His chaplain told him that he had forgotten that 'Jesus Christ is a Savior.' 'True,' the bishop admitted, 'but how shall I know that He is a Savior for *me*?' His chaplain came back with, 'My lord, it is written, "Him that cometh unto Me, I will in no wise cast out."' 'True,' Butler confessed, 'and I am surprised that, though I have read that Scripture a thousand times over, I have never felt its virtue till this moment; and now I die happy.'[21] Sometimes a text is like that. We don't always grasp it as we should.

And Jesus seems to be raising that point with His audience. Have you really thought through what 'to my Lord' in the first of Psalm 110 implies? And this shows us Jesus' *technique*

---

to think Jesus a naïve simpleton in such matters. See further, R. T. France, *Jesus and the Old Testament* (London: Tyndale, 1971), pp. 100-2, 163-69.

21. John Whitecross, ed., *The Shorter Catechism Illustrated* (1828; reprint ed., London: Banner of Truth, 1968), pp. 49.

here. He doesn't pound the text into them. He just leaves it hanging in the air. As if to say, What do you think of that? How do you suppose you can solve this conundrum? Where do you think you are to 'go' with this? Can you think outside the usual box? In an indirect, almost teasing way, He wants to enlarge their view of the Messiah, that He is not only David's seed but David's sovereign, that He has both human descent *and* divine status.

Our account ends on a huge contrast. Luke places Jesus' depiction of the narcissism of the scribes (20:45-47) beside the sacrifice of a widow (21:1-4) and so shows us **the piety Jesus commends**.[22]

Jesus speaks to His disciples though in the hearing of the crowd (v. 45) and warns them about the scribes,[23] the interpreters and teachers of the Torah. The scribes are wrapped up in appearance (robes), in recognition (fawning greetings in markets, status seats in synagogues and suppers), and in domination (v. 47). The last, 'devouring widow's houses,' may refer to their sponging on widows' hospitality[24]—and then mollifying the imposition with a little devotional mishmash. 'Religious leader' and 'ego-driven' can be synonymous expressions. They have immense privilege and so face all the more severe judgment (v. 47c).

The other scenario occurs near the women's court where the receptacles for gifts were located. A number of rich folks are throwing in their gifts—then Jesus saw a poor widow throw in two lepta (21:2). A *lepton* was the smallest coin in circulation in Israel. It was worth 1/128 of a denarius (a worker's normal daily wage). So 'a common laborer would earn one *lepton* in about four minutes of a ten-hour work day.'[25] So those two *lepta* she gave were nothing. And yet,

---

22. I am aware that some see the widow's offering (21:1-4) not as an evidence of her sacrificial giving but as a sample of the oppressive system pushed by the scribes (20:47). The scribes instruct and urge poor widows to give like this and so to utterly impoverish themselves (see the commentaries of Fitzmyer and Green). There's a certain cogency to this view, but I am unable to get around the fact that Jesus *does* seem to *commend* this widow for her giving (21:3-4).

23. See C. L. Feinberg, 'Scribes,' NBD, 3rd ed. (1996), pp. 1068-69.

24. Cf. J. Jeremias, *Jerusalem in the Time of Jesus* (1969; reprint ed., Peabody, MA: Hendrickson, 2016), p. 114.

25. Mark Strauss, 'Luke,' ZIBBC, 1:477.

as Jesus said, they were everything: 'For all these threw in among the (other) gifts out of their abundance, but she [emphatic] out of her deficiency threw in all she had to live on' (21:4). She has done more than give; she has cast herself upon God to sustain her.

This last segment reveals something about our Lord more than it reveals about the widow. It shows, as J. C. Ryle says, that it is not beneath Jesus to observe the conduct of 'a certain poor widow'; it shows that 'actions and deeds in the weekly history of a poor man, which the great of this world would think trivial and contemptible, are often registered as weighty and important in Christ's books'; it shows that 'the lives of cottagers are noticed by Him as much as the lives of kings.'[26]

Looking back over this whole section from 20:1–21:4, we could say that it presents to us Christ as 'the wisdom of God,' as He foils and answers and refutes and exposes the schemes and thinking and follies of men. Where does He get this wisdom? Who then is He? Why do you still hold back from laying hold of Him?

---

26. J. C. Ryle, *Expository Thoughts on the Gospels: St. Luke*, 2 vols. (New York: Baker & Taylor, 1858), 2:350-51.

18

Judgment on Jerusalem, etc.
(Luke 21:5-38)

Luke has already reported two of Jesus' laments over Jerusalem (13:33-35; 19:41-44), both of which indicate the dire destiny awaiting her. Now in our passage he has Jesus providing even more detail. However, Jesus speaks of far more than the coming judgment on Jerusalem—hence the 'et cetera' in our chapter heading. Jesus covers more than Jerusalem's demise. He touches on various aspects of coming things and especially of 'last things.' Since Luke has already posted some of Jesus' 'last things' instruction (see 12:35-48; 17:20-37), we should not expect him merely to punch a 'repeat' button here. Clearly, some of Luke's material here parallels the 'Olivet Discourse' in Matthew 24 and Mark 13—yet Luke casts his material in his own mold. I will not be microscopically comparing Luke with Matthew and Mark, since I think that would tend to destroy our focus on hearing Luke.

The immediate stimulus for this segment of Jesus' teaching came from the remarks by some in the crowd about how the temple was 'decked out' with such 'fine stones and offerings' (v. 5). They were speaking of 'Herod's' temple. Herod the Great, who reigned from 37–4 b.c., had instigated a massive temple rebuilding and refurbishing project. According to a later proverb, 'He who has not seen the temple of Herod has never seen a beautiful building in his life.' It *was* impressive. The temple site was some 172,000 square yards, and so the largest site of its kind in the ancient world. The retaining walls 'towered more than 80 feet above the roadways going around its perimeter and reached over 50 feet below street level in their foundation courses.'[1] Herod assembled 10,000 workers and had 1,000 priests in masonry and carpentry and used 1,000 oxen to transport stones from the quarry the two miles to the construction site. Some of the 'smaller' Herodian stones have been discovered lying in the street—the Roman soldiers had shoved these down from the western side of the temple complex in the A.D. 70 destruction. Most of them weighed two to four tons but some were over fifteen tons. The impact caved in the flagstones in the street.[2] But these are the 'puny' ones. On the western wall, for instance, below the present surface level, one can see huge foundation blocks. One of them weighs an estimated 415 tons and measures 46 x 10 x 10 feet.[3] And all this doesn't touch the splendor of the temple proper. But perhaps it's clear why folks were so enamored with such massive and opulent display (v. 5). What a shock then when Jesus tells them of coming days when there will not be one stone on top of another that will not be pulled down (v. 6)! So on to the teaching.

First, Jesus presses on His hearers **the matter of deception and the need for discernment** (vv. 7-11). Verse 7 is likely a bit breathless. Jesus' hearers react to His 'shocker' in verse 6, and ask, 'Teacher, when then will these things be and what is the sign when these things are about to take place?' (v. 7). Their 'these things' seem to refer to the temple destruction (v. 6). But Jesus' answer does not answer their question. He takes off with, 'Watch out, don't be led astray, for many will come in my name …' (v. 8a). He seems to be thinking of the matter of His coming and of the charlatans who come before Him. Hence it seems to me that Jesus wants first of all to speak *generally* of coming matters in verses 8-11. He *will* answer the query of verse 7 come verses 20-24, but the potential of deception is such an urgent matter that it must hold first place in His reply.

---

1. ABD, 6:365.

2. Randall Price and H. Wayne House, *Zondervan Handbook of Biblical Archaeology* (Grand Rapids: Zondervan, 2017), pp. 209-12.

3. James K. Hoffmeier, *The Archaeology of the Bible* (Oxford: Lion Hudson, 2008), p. 133.

It ought to strike us that the first word Jesus utters about future things is a warning not to be duped. 'Many will come in my name, saying, "I am he," and, "The time has arrived"' (v. 8). Apparently, there were plenty of such frauds in the first century itself.[4] The warning is still in effect. I recall in the late 1980s and early 1990s that a reasonably respected expositor in the Baltimore area began putting forth dates for the Lord's return. He was not claiming messiahship but thought he could say 'the time has arrived.' One would think there would be more godly cynicism about such characters, but, no, they seem to stir up their followers—until the predicted time goes by and one can only sweep up the ashes of disappointment and stupidity.

That is Jesus' first word. Then He goes on to itemize what are *non-signs* of the end. Here He also intends to put a brake on sensationalism. 'But when you hear of wars and upheavals, don't get in a panic; for these things must take place first, but the end is not immediate' (v. 9). In verses 10-11 Jesus simply expands on verse 9: 'Nation will rise up against nation and kingdom against kingdom; there will be great earthquakes, and famines and plagues in various places, and there will be terrifying things and great signs from heaven.' These are likely samples of the 'wars and upheavals.' National and international conflicts, what we call natural disasters, indeed, all sorts of terrifying occurrences. But these are *not* signs of the end (v. 9b). How often Jesus' word is not heeded. It's not all that rare to run on to some preacher who cites the increasing prevalence of wars in this century, the recurring natural disasters, and the insidious plagues throughout the world as pointers to the imminent end. Such claims fly in the face of Jesus' clear teaching. Rather such matters are the 'stuff' we can expect in the present age and, although we don't relish them, we should not get our bowels in an uproar over them. Instead we should heed Jesus' word: 'For these things *must* take place first' (v. 9b). That is a divine 'must'; it refers to what God has sovereignly ordained. Which tells us that however chaotic our times are, however crazy nations and politicians seem, however topsy-turvy our world appears, it's

---

4. See R. Meyer, TDNT, 6:826-27.

not as if everything is simply running amok. That 'must' tells us that what may look like cosmic pandemonium is yet in the grip of an ordering will. Here then is Jesus' first concern: don't be hoodwinked by sensationalists and don't go into hyper-mode over what seems an unglued world.

Secondly, Jesus speaks of **the matter of persecution and the need for endurance** (vv. 12-19). We must pay particular attention to the chronological note in verse 12a: 'But before all these things.' 'All these things' refers to the matters outlined in verses 7-11. Jesus implies that the occurrences of verses 7-11 are a bit 'down the road,' whereas *before* those things, in the very immediate future, His disciples will face conflict and persecution (= vv. 12-19). He outlines where they will be (opponents will be 'handing you over to synagogues and prisons; you will be led off to kings and governors on account of my name,' v. 12b) and who will hate them (even their closest relations and friends, v. 16, and, in fact, pretty much everyone, v. 17). Though the world may occasionally smile on disciples, on the whole they will be the objects of a sheer inborn, often raging, antipathy and derision (cf. Genesis 3:15; should we be surprised?). One thinks of Celsus' (ca. A.D. 180) rant:

> Far from us, say the Christians, be any man possessed of any culture or wisdom or judgment; their aim is to convince only worthless and contemptible people, idiots, slaves, poor women, and children .... These are the only ones whom they manage to turn into believers.[5]

So persecution (v. 12) and execution (v. 16b) will be their fare.

However, even in the middle of this suffering Jesus allots gifts to His people. The first is *opportunity*. They may be hounded and hammered and put on trial before kings and magistrates, but 'it will turn out for you to bear testimony' (v. 13). It will be better than church! In court they will have a captive audience and, when grilled, can speak freely of a crucified and risen Lord (cf. the instances in Acts 4:1-22; 5:27-42; 6:8–7:60; 16:25-40; 22:1-21; 22:30–23:11; 24:1-21;

---

5. Bruce L. Shelley, *Church History in Plain Language*, 4th ed. (Nashville: Thomas Nelson, 2013), pp. 35.

26:1-23). Their enemies, in their efforts to stifle them, will actually provide them a platform for declaring their faith.

The second gift is the *provision* Jesus makes. When they are hauled into court situations, they are not to stew and worry over how they will defend themselves (v. 14)—don't try to rehearse what you should say, 'for I [emphatic] will give you a mouth and wisdom which all those opposing you will not be able to resist or contradict' (v. 15). Jesus relieves their anxiety—He has an emergency ration for His people in the dock. In this crunch and under this pressure, they won't need to fret or agonize over how to answer. Jesus will 'give' it to them.

How many times the Lord's servants have stood before the rulers of this age and have found this 'mouth and wisdom.' One thinks of Samuel Rutherford, about 1660 and not long for this world. But the authorities wanted their pound of flesh and ordered him to appear in Edinburgh to face a charge of high treason. Rutherford's answer was: 'Tell them I have got a summons already before a superior judge and judicatory, and I behove to answer my first summons; and ere your day arrive, I will be where few kings and great folks come.' Or years earlier, in 1596, when James VI was strutting his overbearing ways and venting his complaining accusations against the Presbyterians, Andrew Melville respectfully but bluntly told him, 'You are not the head of the Church; you cannot give us that eternal life which we seek for even in this world, and you cannot deprive us of it.'[6] A mouth and wisdom.

Jesus' third gift is *preservation*. He states this in, probably, a deliberately paradoxical way. On the one hand, Jesus says 'you will be handed over' even by those closest to you and 'they will put some of you to death' (v. 16b). Then in verse 18 He says, 'Yet not a hair of your head will ever perish.' One assumes that some of those hairs belong to those put to death. But Jesus is not talking nonsense. Remember 12:4. Don't fear those, Jesus said, who kill the body and after that have nothing more they can do. That's it. How frustrating for

---

6. See Thomas McCrie, *The Story of the Scottish Church* (Glasgow: Free Presbyterian, n.d.), pp. 84-85, 250.

them. They can kill you but they can't make you extinct. So here, they may put some of you to death and yet not a hair of your head will perish.

Paradoxes like that can seem perplexing and yet be true. Consider a statement like: North is southeast of Due West. As a bare statement that may sound baffling, but not if you live in South Carolina. For then you know that Due West is the name of a small town in the western part of the state and that North is the name of a town that is actually south of Columbia in the middle of the state, but, looking at a state map, it is clear that North is southeast of Due West. Geographically the conundrum is perfectly true. I think Jesus sometimes uses paradox because He wants us to think. And what a tremendous assurance this is. You may be put to death but not a hair of your head will ever perish. Putting verse 16b and verse 18 together seems to be a promise of complete redemption in resurrection. There is just a certain indestructibility Jesus gives His people. In face of whatever they encounter, they will be preserved.

Jesus' disciples, then, in view of their conflicts (vv. 12-18), have need of endurance. 'In your endurance you must possess your souls' (v. 19). And the gifts Jesus gives in this conflict are intended to sustain that endurance.

At this point Jesus responds to the question asked in verse 7, as He speaks to **the matter of judgment and the need for escape** (vv. 20-24). The sign that Jerusalem's (and the temple's) destruction is near is when they 'see Jerusalem being surrounded by armies' (v. 20). The present participle ('being surrounded') is important and suggests an ongoing process rather than an isolated event. This in turn explains Jesus' warning in verse 21: 'Then let those in Judea flee to the mountains, and let those in the midst of her get out, and let those in the countryside not enter it.' And Jesus tells why: because these are *'days of vengeance,'* that is, days of God's vengeance on the city;[7] they are *days of distress* (v. 23), when the last thing you want is the extra burden of enduring a pregnancy or nursing an infant; they are *days of death and*

---

7. 'To fulfill all that is written' (v. 22b) may refer to OT curses for covenant-breaking (e.g., Leviticus 26:31-33; Deuteronomy 28:49-57; cf. 1 Kings 9:6-9).

dispersal (v. 24a), and *days of humiliation* (v. 24b), as Gentiles trample Jerusalem at their will.[8]

This will be a time of 'wrath against this people' (v. 23b). Come A.D. 70 Titus and the Romans would arrive and decimate Jerusalem. And yet it was all rather gradual. The Jewish revolt occurred in A.D. 66 and Vespasian (Titus' father) came in Spring of 67 and by the end of 67 had reduced all of northern Palestine to Roman control. By the first half of 68 Vespasian had established a ring of military outposts around Jerusalem. He then received news of Nero's death and a whole year transpired (June 68-into 69) when little Roman activity occurred. However, by June of 69 Vespasian had reasserted Roman dominance in southern Palestine and now all the land except three fortresses and Jerusalem itself was under the Roman thumb. Vespasian was declared emperor in July of 69, so he bequeathed the demise of Jerusalem into the hands of his son Titus. Titus & Co. arrived a few days before Passover in 70. Besieging and assaulting Jerusalem was a five-month ordeal. Stragglers from the city would be seized and crucified in full view of the city—or they would be driven back into the city with mutilated limbs, with hopes that such would demoralize the defenders. During this time the Romans ringed in the whole city with a continuous stone wall, a feat they managed in three days, posting numerous guards along it to ensure that no one escaped. So the city starved until the Romans finally broke through in August, burned the temple, butchered here-to-fore survivors, and occupied the last hold-out, the upper city.[9]

Jesus' warning (v. 21) may well have been taken to heart. Eusebius of Caesarea (ca. A.D. 260–340) asserts that the church at Jerusalem, in response to a divine revelation given before the war, got out of the city and went to live in Pella, a town

---

8. There may be a glimmer of hope in 'until the times of the Gentiles are fulfilled.'

9. I have only provided a summary of this tragic time. For further detail, see, of course, Josephus, *The Jewish War*; for a splendid digest of Josephus' account, see Cleon L. Rogers, Jr., *The Topical Josephus* (Grand Rapids: Zondervan, 1992), pp. 156-204; see also Emil Schürer, *The History of the Jewish People in the Age of Jesus Christ* (175 B.C.–A.D. 135), 3 vols., rev./ed. G. Vermes and F. Millar (Edinburgh: T. and T. Clark, 1973), 1:485-513.

east of the Jordan and some seventeen miles south of the Sea of Galilee.[10] And Josephus notes that as early as A.D. 66—even after the Jews had enjoyed a surprise victory over the Roman twelfth legion, many Jews began exiting Jerusalem in droves. In spite of that initial victory, they could see the Roman handwriting on the wall and were sure Roman might would crush the city. Until sometime in A.D. 68 folks could depart the city with relative freedom.[11]

Jesus' warning here (vv. 20-24) is similar to those in OT texts (e.g., Jeremiah 50:8-10; 51:6, 45; Zechariah 2:6-7; cf. Jeremiah 38:1-3) which call Israel/Zion to escape from Babylon and the judgment coming on her. But here the judgment will fall on Jerusalem, the 'city of God.'[12] Yet one can't help noticing how Jesus' warning is riddled with compassion. One can't help but think, who but Jesus would care about the hapless plight of pregnant women and nursing mothers in such circumstances (v. 23)? Don't we have to say that what we have here is vintage Jesus, a Savior whose compassion overflows and who longs to spare His people from needless trouble and heartache?

---

10. *Ecclesiastical History*, 3.5.3. Some may point out that Jesus tells those in Judea to flee to the mountains/hills, whereas Pella was not in the mountains but in low-lying foothills east of the Jordan. But that is mostly a quibble, if one considers the mountains a temporary refuge and Pella as a longer-term residence. Moreover, Jesus told those 'in the midst of her' simply to get out without any reference to their immediate or extended destination.

11. See Josephus, *Jewish War*, 2.20.1; W. L. Lane, *The Gospel According to Mark*, NICNT (Grand Rapids: Eerdmans, 1974), p. 468. For good measure, note that Luke 21:21 is *not* the equivalent of Matthew 24:15-16 and Mark 13:14, in spite of some similar phraseology. Jesus' words in Matthew and Mark speak of 'when you see the abomination of desolation,' then those in Judea are to flee. Some expositors hold that this refers to A.D. 70 when the Romans planted their standards with the image of the emperor on them on the temple site (e.g., Alan Cole, 'Mark,' in *New Bible Commentary*, 3rd ed., p. 970; and, at least partly, William Hendriksen, *New Testament Commentary: Exposition of the Gospel According to Matthew* [Grand Rapids: Baker, 1973], pp. 857-58). But Mark 13 and Matthew 24 do not fit the Roman conquest. By the time the Romans planted their standards in the temple, the temple was burning and only the upper city was not yet reduced. At that point it was far, far too late for anyone to flee. The whole province (cf. 'those in Judea') as well as the city had already been sealed off before that moment and flight made an impossible dream. In Luke's account Jesus speaks of what will be the Roman assault on Jerusalem; in Matthew and Mark 'the abomination of desolation' is likely a 'last-thing thing' shortly before the return of the Son of Man.

12. Incidentally, *epi tēs gēs* in verse 23 should probably be taken as 'upon the land' (i.e., Israel or Judea) rather than as 'upon the earth' (as ESV).

Fourthly, Jesus teaches about **the matter of panic and the arrival of deliverance** (vv. 25-28). The scene shifts here from the particular, Jerusalem in verses 20-24, to the cosmic and universal. Jesus speaks of 'signs' that will precede the coming of the Son of Man (v. 27), signs that are utterly unnerving—they consist of what we might call natural disturbances (signs in sun, moon, and stars, v. 25a; cf. Isaiah 13:10; Ezekiel 32:7; Joel 2:10, 31; 3:15), which along with maritime upheaval, will bring on international dismay ('dismay of nations in perplexity at the roaring of sea and waves,' v. 25b) and psychological dread, as people tremble over what may be coming next in a world seemingly unglued (v. 26). What's next is … 'And then they will see the Son of Man coming in a cloud with power and great glory' (v. 27). The 'they' refers to the perplexed and panicked people of verses 25-26. Such signs (vv. 25-26) and sight (v. 27) mean no one will yawn when the Son of Man returns. This occurs, apparently, after 'the times of the Gentiles' (v. 24b).

Just what are we to understand by this 'Son of Man'? Jesus is obviously referring to Himself, but He picks up this reference from Daniel 7:13-14. Note how Daniel describes the one 'like a Son of Man' in that vision. He clearly seems to be a *human* figure, for he stands in contrast to the vicious beasts (lion, bear, leopard) previously touted in Daniel's vision. But he is also a *divine* figure, for Daniel says that all peoples, nations, and languages are to 'serve' him. The Aramaic verb for 'serve' in verse 14 means paying reverence to deity or to a purported deity. Hence the NIV is right to translate it as 'worship.' This, of course, means he is an *individual* figure and that 'Son of Man' does not merely denote the corporate people of God. And he is a *royal* figure—he is given and has a kingdom and so will rule.[13] He is the One a distraught and terrified world will see coming.

But Jesus' disciples (i.e., those who are alive on earth at this time) are not to be petrified with fear. Rather, 'when these things begin to take place' (i.e., the 'things' noted in verses 25-26), He says, 'Straighten up and lift up your heads, because

---

13. For more detail, see my *The Message of Daniel*, BST (Nottingham: Inter-Varsity, 2013), pp. 99-101.

your redemption is coming near' (v. 28). This 'redemption' is their full and final salvation and place in His kingdom. So redemption arrives in frightful trappings (vv. 25-26), but if you know that—because Jesus tells you—it gives a certain settledness and even expectancy.

In the earlier stages of the 'Market Garden' offensive in World War II, British troops had dropped on Dutch soil and had created quite a stir among Hollanders. Young Anje van Maanen, whose father was a medical doctor in Oosterbeek, recalls receiving a phone call from some friends telling her that 'the Tommies dropped behind our house and they are on their way to Oosterbeek!' Anje put the phone down in a house that became crazy with joy. Her response? 'An invasion! Lovely!'[14] We don't usually think of invasions as 'lovely.' But if your land and people had been under the thumbs of Hitler's lackeys and legions for four years, such an invasion would mean liberation, quite 'lovely.' So too the coming of the Son of Man may bring consternation to an unbelieving world but will mean 'lovely' redemption for the flock of Jesus.[15]

Finally, Jesus raises **the matter of certainty and the need for preparedness** (vv. 29-36). Jesus will underscore the matter of certainty in verses 32-33, but first He speaks of 'signs' that indicate the certainty of these last things. He uses a mini-parable. As soon as one sees the fig tree and other trees putting out leaves, one knows summer is near; so too, 'you, when you see these things taking place, you know that the kingdom of God is near' (v. 31). By 'these things' Jesus means the occurrences of verses 25-26 (contextually, this makes the most sense). These things mean the kingdom of God is near in its full and final form. This does not mean anyone at that time can predict the day or the hour of it—they will only be general indicators that the kingdom is close at hand.

Those are the signs. Now in verses 32-33 Jesus is giving assurance of the reliability of His word. This 'assurance' note

---

14. Cornelius Ryan, *A Bridge Too Far* (New York: Simon and Schuster, 1974), pp. 260-61.

15. Luke 21 seems to suggest a general order of events: (1) A time of persecution and testimony (vv. 12-19); (2) the destruction of Jerusalem (vv. 20-24); (3) the times of the gentiles (v. 24b); (4) the coming of the Son of Man (vv. 25-28). The first likely overlaps with the second and third.

is more dominant in verse 33, but we need to spend some time with verse 32 first. What does Jesus mean when He says, 'Truly I say to you that this generation will by no means pass away until all things take place.' What does He mean by 'this generation'? Is He, as we often do when referring to our generation, speaking of His contemporaries? If so, is there something in the timing of things we have missed? I am convinced that 'this generation' does not refer primarily to Jesus' contemporaries. Prior to verse 32 here, 'this generation' occurs eight times in Luke (plus 9:41, which speaks of 'a faithless and perverse generation'), and always carries a negative tinge.[16] I am not going to take several more pages to discuss the half-dozen views scholars have proposed for 'this generation' in verse 32. I ask you to go back to the exposition of Luke 11 and re-read the 'Additional Note on 11:49-51' and note the references there. Briefly, 'this generation' carries a pejorative twist and refers not simply to people within a 30-40 year time block but to those who have been, are, and will be light-rejecting, kingdom-opposing, Messiah-spurning people. The phrase refers to a *type* of people, not primarily to their *time.* So Jesus in verse 32 seems to assure us that, at the end, unbelieving, Christ-rejecting people will still remain and will by no means escape facing the judgment of the Son of Man. Then comes the further assurance of verse 33: the created order may go 'kaput,' but Jesus' words will 'in no way pass away.' They will 'stand forever' (cf. Isa. 40:8). You can absolutely rely on what Jesus teaches about the future.

If, then, there is such certainty about these matters, Jesus' disciples must be prepared for them—they must exercise a certain vigilance (vv. 34-36). Jesus' primary demand occurs in verse 34; however, He also speaks of the *wide scope* of these final events ('for it will come upon all who dwell upon the face of all the earth,' v. 35)—it will not be some regional middle-eastern disturbance; and then He presses us with the *essential matter* ('But stay awake at every point, praying that you may be strong enough to escape all these things about to

---

16. Much like in OT texts when Yahweh refers to 'this people,' often a dis-paraging way of referring to Israel, as if placing them at a distance from Him (cf., e.g., Exodus 32:9; Deuteronomy 9:13; Isaiah 6:10; 8:6; Jeremiah 7:16; 11:14; 13:10; 14:11; 16:5; 19:11).

take place and to stand before the Son of Man,' v. 36)—which is the 'one thing needful,' to stand before the Son of Man.

But back to Jesus' demand in verse 34. He commands us to 'pay attention to yourselves' and then He raises a *double difficulty*. On the one hand, we can destroy vigilance by 'debauchery and drunkenness,' anesthetizing ourselves to truth and discipline by slobbering along in an alcoholic fog. Yet there is something else just as destructive of vigilance: 'life-related anxieties'—these too can cause that day to come on one 'suddenly' and prove a snare rather than a delight. We can be very sober folks and yet suffer from this trouble. These are by no means attitudes or activities laced with lurid wickedness. They are simply life's preoccupations with lesser matters that consume us and so we don't 'turn our eyes upon Jesus.'

Recently, I was re-reading Hampton Sides' *Ghost Soldiers*. It's an account of how in early 1945 some 120 US Army Rangers slipped behind enemy lines in the Philippines. Their mission was to rescue over 500 American and British POWs who had spent three years in an abominable Japanese prison camp near the city of Cabanatuan. Some of these were the last survivors of the Bataan Death March. There was peculiar urgency— the Japanese army was on its last legs and sometimes when forced to retreat would simply execute the POWs under their 'care.' The Rangers' assault on the camp was a success, but they had a problem with some of the prisoners. The Rangers were herding or carrying POWs to the front gate of the camp to escape; but some of the prisoners had stashed away mementos or valuables or items they wanted to retrieve from their barracks. There was no time for that. The Rangers had to refuse such attempts and force such fellows to the front gate. One of the Rangers, Marvin Kinder, was leading a prisoner by the arm toward the gate. Suddenly, the man resisted. 'I have to go back in and get some documents I hid.' Kinder denied him—they had to keep moving. 'But I need my documents,' the prisoner insisted. 'When I get back to the States, I'm going to court-martial a man who ate my cat. A beautiful cat it was! The man ate my cat, I'm telling you!' Kinder lifted the pitiful soldier up and carried him to liberty. Freedom had arrived but all he could think of was a skinny cat that some other skinny POW had consumed. Of course, given the conditions, the man was probably near to coming unhinged. But isn't it a picture of the actual trivia that so preoccupy us and close our eyes to the coming Son of Man?

Luke closes off this super-charged chapter with a routine note about Jesus' teaching in the temple during the day, going out to the Mount of Olives at night, and people flocking early to the temple to hear Him next day (vv. 37-38). These words may seem like a mere logistical notation, but, really, they are quite remarkable. For Jesus knows what is brewing in Jerusalem, as chapters 22 and following make clear. And yet here He is, simply going about His Father's business in the temple. 'I must go on my way today and tomorrow and the day following' (13:33). Days are about to come when that will be impossible, but today He can teach the people, today He can do what He has been called to do.

19

The Lord's Supper and Teaching
(Luke 22:1-38)

One can almost sense it. Perhaps it's like walking along on a municipal asphalted walking trail and, after a mile, you are suddenly aware that the asphalt has ceased and has become crushed gravel. You don't even have to look—you can 'feel' the difference immediately. That's something like entering the 'Passion narrative' in Luke's gospel (chs. 22–23). His gospel is all the story of Jesus, but when the reader nears the cross, there's a different 'feel.' There's a certain solemnity that comes over one; one almost senses he is intruding on holy ground.

Luke's report partially parallels the accounts in Matthew 26 and Mark 14, but Luke has also chosen to go his own way. 'Unlike Mark and Matthew, where the scene switches immediately to the Mount of Olives, in Luke after the Lord's Supper Jesus gives a "farewell discourse" to his disciples.'[1] In Luke's account there is a good bit of teaching, 'table talk,' at the Last Supper. I prefer to concentrate on Luke's account without constantly cross-referencing it with Matthew and Mark. Not that the latter is not a proper study, but it can become tedious and tends to destroy interest in what Luke himself wants us to see.[2]

---

1. Robert H. Stein, *Luke*, NAC (Nashville: Broadman, 1992), pp. 545.

2. There is no need to doubt the historicity of Luke's record here. It's common for some scholars to allege that the early church invented or concocted various gospel accounts. But that won't wash here. Why would the early church want to invent the

I propose to treat our passage by 'seeing double.' That is, one can look at Luke's account via sets of two. There are two kinds of preparation for Passover at the beginning (vv. 1-6, 7-13), two sets of statements by Jesus at the supper (vv. 14-18, 19-20), two problems He deals with (vv. 21-23, 24-30), and so on. I am not claiming that Luke has a 'double' scheme in mind, but as I studied the passage this pattern—like Aaron's calf (Exod. 32:24)—just came out this way.

First, we meet with **double 'preparations'** (vv. 1-6, 7-13), two preludes to the Last Supper, that center on two disciples. The first has to do with a disciple who solves a dilemma (vv. 1-6).

It was near Passover time, and the chief priests and scribes had a methodological problem: 'how they could take him out' (v. 2). They couldn't simply seize Jesus, because they were 'afraid of the people' (v. 2b). The people at large—perhaps a good number were Galilean pilgrims?—held Jesus in high esteem (19:47-48; 21:38), and the Jewish leaders were skittish of flying in the face of that popularity (see also 20:6, 19). They knew it only took a spark to start a riot. There was a reason for those extra Roman troops at Passover time. Then Luke writes a scary sentence: 'Now Satan entered into Judas called Iscariot' (v. 3). The prince of darkness found a place in the heart of one who had preached Jesus and cast out demons in His name (9:1-2). But this 'solved' the leaders' problem. Judas would know 'the how'—how he could hand Jesus over to them when no crowd was around to interfere or intimidate (vv. 4, 6). They were overjoyed (v. 5) and the deal was struck.

Look at this with priestly and scribal eyes. What a break this was! Who could've imagined a perfect solution seemingly out of nowhere. They must have thought heaven's providence had come at just the right time. Actually, it was all very grim: they were men with no hair on their chests (they are slaves to

story of Judas' betrayal or report the prediction of Peter's denial? If the early church wanted to win people to Jesus, they wouldn't do that by telling about the damnable perfidy of one apostle and the abysmal failure of another. That's not the way to impress people and win converts. But, of course, if it's true and you have nothing to hide, you simply tell it all—like Luke did. Cf. Norval Geldenhuys, *Commentary on the Gospel of Luke*, NICNT (Grand Rapids: Eerdmans, 1951), p. 569; D. L. Bock, *Luke 9:51-24:53*, BECNT (Grand Rapids: Baker, 1996), p. 1731.

fear of the people), but a satanic 'providence' seems to smile on them. Let's push the 'hold' button on this picture and look at the second 'preparation' section.

In verses 7-13 we meet with a disciple who opens his home. The day arrived—the Passover lambs were to be slaughtered.[3] Jesus directs Peter and John to go into the city and prepare for the Passover. If the big question with the priests and scribes was 'How?' (vv. 2, 4), Peter and John's is 'Where?' (vv. 9, 11). It may well be that Jesus sent Peter and John off by themselves on this matter in order to keep Judas in the dark about the location. Being in the city at night without the 'protection' of the people around Him would make Jesus easy prey for Judas' schemes (cf. John 11:57). But if Judas does not know location or street address (nor do Peter and John at the first), then Jesus' time with His men will not be interrupted. This, of course, is surmise, but a likely one.[4]

Verses 10-12 present us with another mystery similar to 19:29-34 (obtaining the colt). Is this water-lugging fellow a sample of Jesus' supernatural foresight or is he a part of a pre-arrangement Jesus made with the fellow's master?[5] Hard to be sure. I would tip toward a pre-arranged plan of Jesus, for when He says 'a man carrying a jar of water will meet you' (v. 10), it sounds as though he is on the look-out for two men and knows they will be coming around this time. He leads them to a house and to the master of the house, who has a large upper room ready. And Jesus' word is always reliable: 'they found (it) just as he had said to them' (v. 13).

---

3. Peter and John (v. 8) may have taken a lamb to the temple on the afternoon of 14 Nisan. 'Preparing for the meal would involve taking their lamb in the afternoon to the temple and joining one of three lines to have the animal slaughtered. Priests would catch the blood in gold and silver vessels, pass the carcass along the line until it reached the priest next to the altar, where it was offered as a sacrifice. When the entrails were removed, the animal was returned to the owners for roasting' (David E. Garland, *Luke*, ZECNT [Grand Rapids: Zondervan, 2011], p. 852).

4. See David Gooding, *According to Luke* (1987; reprint ed., Coleraine, N. Ireland: Myrtlefield Trust, 2013), p. 349.

5. It's almost always alleged in commentaries that a man carrying such a water jar would be unusual because women usually did that. E. Schnabel says this is not the case; he says that someone traced the origin of this erroneous suggestion to Lagrange's commentary on Mark published in 1920 (*Jesus in Jerusalem: The Last Days* [Grand Rapids: Eerdmans, 2018], pp. 203, 503); but it was partially suggested in Alfred Plummer's 1902 commentary.

Is it too wild to suggest that these two 'preparation' units may be meant to contrast two disciples? Here in verses 1-6 is one of Jesus' premier disciples who so much as says, 'I want a price for Him.' In verses 7-13 we find, in his house, one of Jesus' obscure disciples who says, 'I have a place for Him.' Isn't this latter something glorious? That Jesus has such an array of 'unknown' disciples who are willing to give Him what they have?

Secondly, we encounter **double pronouncements** in verses 14-18 and 19-20. The first has to do with Jesus' *abstinence*.

The time arrives and Jesus and the apostles (as Luke calls them here) are reclining around the table. Jesus makes a remarkable statement: 'I have earnestly desired to eat this Passover with you before I suffer' (v. 15). We will allude to the reason behind this statement in a moment, but I think we ought to let verse 15 sink in first. Jesus is speaking out of the depth of intense longings—'earnestly desired' reflects an emphatic Hebrew-like idiom. And we should not miss the 'with you.' Doesn't this verse indicate how Jesus *really liked* His disciples and cherished His companionship with them? True, none can deny they were frequently dense, muddle-headed, naïve, and foolish, but Jesus didn't merely put up with them, He genuinely prized them. We should not forget this—there may be an 'overspill' from this text about how Jesus may regard His current-day disciples, bungling as we may be.

In verse 16 Jesus explains the rationale behind His desire: 'For I tell you that I will in no way eat of it until such time as it is fulfilled in the kingdom of God.' He specially wants to eat this Passover with them because He will not be celebrating any more of them until that climactic celebration in the final kingdom. There is a similar logic between verses 17 and 18. In verse 17 Jesus takes a cup, gives thanks, and tells the disciples to share it among themselves. There were four cups of wine in the Passover tradition and this was likely the first cup that evening. Then Jesus adds, 'For I tell you, I will in no way drink from now on of the fruit of the vine until the kingdom of God comes' (v. 18).

It is easy to skate by this 'abstinence' of Jesus. Joachim Jeremias has given special attention to it. He holds that Jesus' desire in verse 15 was an unfulfilled desire, that Jesus abstained from the meal on that night in the upper room, and that His ongoing abstinence was especially a time of fasting, mourning, and intercession for Israel in her unbelief.[6] However, I think Jesus' 'reasons' in verses 16 and 18 imply that He *did* eat the Passover of verse 15 and that verse 15 then does *not* indicate an unfulfilled desire. But Jeremias' question 'Why the abstinence?' even from this Passover on still remains. I think the answer may be simpler than the one Jeremias provided, though one has to admit to some speculation when the text itself does not explicitly answer the question. Maybe there is more weight to the words 'with you' in verse 15 than we imagine? Is Jesus abstaining from this point on because He knows He will be separated from His disciples, that ere long He Himself will be 'home' (so to speak), but they will not—and so He refuses to celebrate until He can do it *with them* (again) in the fulfilled kingdom of God? That is, Jesus abstains until He can have His people all with Him at table in the kingdom.

We may have family coming in from a distance, and they have told us they will arrive at supper-time. The meal is ready, but they may have been delayed by heavy traffic or unexpected road construction. Do we go ahead and eat anyway? No, we keep the meal warm and wait; we just refuse to go ahead until our loved ones are with us. I wonder if that is not what drives Jesus. He refuses to eat and drink in the absence of His people. He so esteems His people that He will not celebrate until they have finished their course and can be with Him in that repast (note the 'with you' in Matthew 26:29). Jesus' 'abstinence' is another way in which He shows how much His people matter to Him.

The second set of pronouncements focuses on Jesus' *gifts* (vv. 19-20).[7] These verses are Luke's record of 'the Lord's supper.' The setting was a Passover meal.[8] However, at

---

6. J. Jeremias, *The Eucharistic Words of Jesus* (Philadelphia: Fortress, 1966), pp. 207-18.

7. There is a textual problem in the Greek text here. Verses 19b-20 are missing in some textual witnesses, but the evidence for accepting them as part of the original text is very impressive. For a lucid discussion, see W. F. Arndt, *The Gospel According to St. Luke* (St. Louis: Concordia, 1956), pp. 439-40.

8. For an overall sketch of the traditional Passover meal, see Danby's *Mishnah*, 'Pesahim,' 10.1-9.

this Passover meal Jesus breaks out of and goes beyond the Passover as He represents His coming death to His disciples.

We must first plow through some of the details of Jesus' words over the bread and the cup. Note the verb 'broke' in verse 19a, 'And when he took bread, having given thanks, he broke and gave to them.' That is very literal, but note that the object of 'broke' is the unleavened bread not His 'body.' Jesus breaks the bread in order to *distribute* ('and gave') it to the disciples. 'Broke'/'broken' does *not* describe Jesus' body.[9] John's gospel is quite adamant that Jesus' bones, like the Passover lamb's, were not broken (John 19:31-37; cf. Exod. 12:46; Ps. 34:20). Perhaps a good chunk of Christian hymnody needs to be revised.[10]

Of this bread Jesus said, 'This is my body, which is being given for you' (v. 19b). If one presses the first 'is,' I think it is clear that it means 'represents' or 'signifies.' Jesus in His body is right there in front of the disciples, so it is unlikely they thought the bread actually was His body.[11] The disciples were no doubt familiar with the words of the Passover liturgy, 'This is the bread of affliction which our ancestors ate when they came from the land of Egypt' (cf. Deut. 16:3). 'By no stretch of the imagination did anyone suppose that they were re-eating the very bread the Israelites had eaten in the wilderness.'[12] So wherever we 'go,' so to speak, with Jesus' words, we must conclude He was speaking metaphorically.

---

9. The idea of Jesus' 'broken body' probably arises from an inferior reading in Paul's account in 1 Corinthians 11:24, 'my body which is broken for you' (see KJV and NKJV). But the genuine reading of the earlier and better manuscripts is simply, 'my body which is for you.' Cf. Knox Chamblin, *Matthew*, 2 vols. (Ross-shire: Christian Focus, 2010), 2:1293-94.

10. I am not disputing the mangling Jesus received in the flogging and the brutality He endured (cf. Isa. 52:14), only holding that we should not load up a term for bread distribution with freight for Jesus' suffering.

11. Luther thought otherwise. At the Marburg Colloquy (1529) he took chalk and wrote on the table *hoc est corpus meum*, apparently with stress on the 'est.' The Protestants there could not come to an agreement; for details, see N. R. Needham, *2,000 Years of Christ's Power*, 4 vols. (Fearn, Ross-shire: Christian Focus Publications, 2016), 3:155-61. A full treatment of the Lord's Supper is beyond the scope of this commentary; for a very sane and (in my view) superb treatment, see Donald Macleod, *A Faith to Live By*, enlarged ed. (Ross-shire: Christian Focus, 2002), pp. 271-85.

12. Craig S. Keener, *A Commentary on the Gospel of Matthew* (Grand Rapids: Eerdmans, 1999), p. 631.

Jesus goes on to say, 'Keep on doing this in remembrance of me' (v. 19c). The verb in the present tense implies an ongoing practice, something they are to continue to do. But what does 'in remembrance of me' involve? There may be overlap here with the Passover itself, for it was to be a 'memorial' (Exod. 12:14), a 'remembrance occasion.' Surely this meant Israel was to call to mind its *costliness* (for a lamb was slain and its blood smeared on the doorposts and lintel, Exod. 12:3-7), its *protection* (for when Yahweh saw the smeared blood, He would not strike the Israelite household in judgment and death, Exod. 12:12-13), and its *liberation* (for they were set free from bondage, cf. Exod. 12:33-37; 13:17ff.; ch. 14). Does not the Christian essentially remember the same as he or she ponders the death of Jesus?[13]

Now Jesus takes the cup and says, 'This cup (is) the new covenant in my blood, which is being poured out for you' (v. 20). This cup is probably the third cup of the Passover, sometimes called 'the cup of blessing.' Jesus specifies that the cup is the 'new covenant.' Here He surely has the Jeremiah 31 prophecy in mind. I think it wise to pause and remind ourselves of what Jeremiah says about that covenant.

Excursus on 'new covenant' in Jeremiah 31:31-34

Jeremiah's new covenant prophecy is a part of 'the Gospel according to Jeremiah' in Jeremiah 30–33, where he proclaims a future and a hope for Israel and Judah. Much of the shape of that hope is condensed in this new covenant passage, where he (or rather, Yahweh) speaks first of **the failure the covenant addresses** (vv. 31-32). Watch out, for dentures may hit the floor when reading verse 31: 'I shall cut a new covenant with the house of Israel and with the house of Judah.' 'Incredible'

---

13. Some expositors hold that the 'remembrance' in the Lord's Supper was done by 'proclaiming the Lord's death' (1 Cor. 11:26). That is, using Paul's account of the supper, they see the 'remembrance' Jesus mentioned (1 Cor. 11:24, 25) as being carried out in a rehearsing or proclaiming of the story of Jesus' suffering and death when the supper was celebrated (cf. v. 26). Hence, the 'remembering' was primarily in such 'proclaiming.' The 'proclaiming' then is not in believers' action of partaking of the supper but in the normal practice of giving a verbal account of Jesus' suffering and death on such an occasion. This could be; the Passover 'remembrance' seemed to have a verbal testimony linked with it (see Exodus 12:26-27; 13:8-9, 14-16). However, I am not convinced of that 'take' on 1 Corinthians 11:26; for discussion, see David E. Garland, *1 Corinthians*, BECNT (Grand Rapids: Baker, 2003), pp. 548-49.

is an over-used word in my country. If the interior of your auto is reasonably clean, a passenger may say it is 'incredible.' It's not. But this is. Have you read Jeremiah's prophecy? The 'covenant people' are in rebellion big-time and so far gone that Yahweh forbids Jeremiah to pray for them. Yet here He's going to cut a new covenant with them. Why, why is He doing this? Why does Yahweh still insist on messing with Israel? Hasn't He yet learned how perverse they are? Can you catch the shock in this text? Can you see that, by rights, there ought to be no new covenant?

Yahweh is not in the least naïve about His people. This new covenant will 'not be like the covenant I cut with their fathers'—He refers to the covenant at Sinai (Exod. 19-24). There will be something distinctive about this covenant. In the Sinai covenant there was no lack of intimacy on God's part ('on the day when I took hold of their hand ...,' v. 32b) and there was no lack of grace ('But I had married them,' v. 32d),[14] but a lack of fidelity on Israel's part. It was the covenant 'they [emphatic] broke' (v. 32c). The fault was not with the covenant but with the people (Heb. 8:8-9). Here were people who failed. Israel was a major covenantal train wreck. The new component in the new covenant is not that it has grace while the former one did not, for the fact is clear that the former covenant was suffused with grace; what is distinct is that the new covenant *will not be sabotaged by human sin*. Part of the newness of the new covenant consists in the fact that it will overcome and defeat the failure and fickleness of God's people. This is the covenant that wins the victory over sinful human inability.

Then in verse 33 Yahweh speaks of **the law the covenant embraces**: 'For this is the covenant which I will cut with the house of Israel after those days, says Yahweh: I shall place my torah [law, instruction] within them and I will write it upon their hearts, and I shall be God to them and *they* [emphatic] will prove to be my people.'[15] The new covenant then is not without law

---

14. B. K. Waltke, TWOT, 1:119.

15. Note the covenant is 'with the house of Israel,' which summarizes the formula in verse 31 that the covenant is 'with the house of Israel and with the house of Judah.' Contemporary Gentile believers must not assume that the covenant is all ours and that Israel has no more place in it. It is, strictly speaking, *their* covenant. We must not think we can high-jack this covenant as our own—rather we piggyback on

but includes law; it does not dismiss law but ingrains law. And yet putting torah 'within them' and writing it 'upon their hearts' is not actually what is new about the new covenant, for this was already an OT ideal and, apparently, a matter of OT believing experience. Skeptics can check Deuteronomy 6:6; 11:18; 30:14; Isaiah 51:7; Psalms 1:2; 37:31; 40:8; 119:11, 24, 34-36, 77, 92, 143, 174. What is new here, in verse 33, about the new covenant is not the elimination of law, for the law is at the heart of the new covenant; it is not the internalization of the law, for that was both a conceptual and an experiential reality for Yahweh's true people under the Sinai covenant; what is new is the *scope* and *success* of the law-keeping under the new covenant, so that the covenant marriage-relation is *not* broken but holds faithfully by *mutual* fidelity (as the text indicates—'I shall be God to them and *they* [emphatic] will prove to be my people'). This will be true not merely of a few but of 'the house of Israel.'

Verse 34 expands on verse 33 (Note the initial 'And ...,' which NIV, NASB, CSB omit); here is the result of Yahweh's writing His law on Israelite hearts, here is what it leads to, here is what it will be like—hence Yahweh speaks of **the future the covenant promises** (v. 34a). No more exhortation to obedience will be needed. Note the individual cases ('each his companion, each his brother') which explode into the emphatic *'all of them* will know me,' and all of them exhaustively, 'from the least of them to the greatest.' Note that 'know Yahweh' and 'will know me' involve/s not merely intimate personal communion but living in right, just, compassionate conduct, as Jeremiah 9:23-24 and 22:15-16 show. This will be true of all of them, the whole house of Israel. This will go a good way toward fulfilling Isaiah 11:9 and Habakkuk 2:14.

I'm not sure we're always aware of the scope of verse 34a; we have a tendency almost to equate the new covenant to the NT age. Here I think William Dumbrell provides a helpful corrective and is worthy of extended quotation:

> Yet the immediacy of the new situation to which v. 34 refers us seem[s] to take us beyond all biblical personal experience; the limitations of the purely human situation have been transcended.

Israel's privileges in that covenant. We must never forget that we are gentile add-ins to the Israelite olive tree (Rom. 11).

The era to which Jeremiah points here and its characterization by the absence of need of any human instruction, brings with it the concept of changed natures, indeed perfected human natures ....

It is not a Christological point of view that is being offered here, as though we are being specifically presented with the series of covenant contrasts which the death of Jesus, as ushering in the New Covenant, will resolve. In Jeremiah, we are looking beyond the New Testament age to the community of the end-time, to a situation when the kingdom of God has finally come and God is all in all ....

The New Covenant age is something which lay not merely beyond the circumstances of the return from exile to which Jeremiah immediately spoke, but, we suggest, beyond the New Testament age as well.[16]

All of this leads to the climactic clause of the prophecy in verse 34b: 'for I will forgive their iniquity and their sins I will remember no more.' Here is **the forgiveness the covenant needs**. The whole new covenant rests on 34b. If this is not so, none of the covenant provisions can come about. Now let us return to the upper room and Luke 22.

* * * * *

Jesus called the cup 'the new covenant in my blood' (v. 20b). Note those last three words. Did you notice what was 'missing' in Jeremiah 31? Oh, it was hinted at—three times Yahweh said that he would (literally) 'cut' the covenant. That expression probably arose from the practice of killing an animal as a part of confirming a covenant. Clearly, 'the blood of the covenant' was a major item in the Sinai covenant in Exodus 24. Half of it Moses threw against the altar (propitiating God?) and half he threw over Israel (claiming the people?). But there is no death, no sacrifice, explicitly connected with the new covenant in Jeremiah 31. So Jesus will provide **the sacrifice the covenant awaits**—the cup represents the Jeremiah 31 covenant '*in my blood.*' Hence Jesus indicates that the new covenant is *inaugurated* with His

---

16. W. J. Dumbrell, *Covenant and Creation* (Nashville: Thomas Nelson, 1984), pp. 181-83.

death, even though it has not yet been consummated (see the quote from Dumbrell above).

Observe also that Jesus speaks of His blood as 'being poured out for you' (v. 20c). That preposition 'for' has generated some debate. It is the Greek *hyper*, which often means 'in behalf of' or 'for the benefit of.' But it can carry more freight than that— it also can frequently mean 'in place of.'[17] Probably both are in play here. Jesus is saying that in the pouring out of His blood He is both their representative and their substitute.

Some pages back I alluded to Jesus' words in verses 19-20 as describing the gifts of Jesus. However, I thought it necessary to drag you through a number of details to clarify and expand on matters in the text. But now, backing away as it were and looking at Jesus' words, what are the gifts they suggest? I find it hard to escape the 'signs' themselves, the bread and the wine, the eating and the drinking. Do these speak of the *sustenance* of Jesus? As if to imply that just as bread and wine sustain and refresh us bodily, so Jesus the (soon to be) crucified Lord will never cease to sustain us in every way required. The supreme gift comes in the *sacrifice* of Jesus. When Jesus says, 'This is my body,' He is essentially saying, 'This is myself,' and in the blood 'poured out' He says He is giving His life poured out in death. When we are at the Lord's table, shouldn't those simple NT statements come back to haunt us in a good way—'Who gave *himself* for our sins' (Gal. 1:4); 'who gave *himself* for us' (Tit. 2:14); and '… the Son of God who loved me and gave *himself* for me'? (Gal. 2:20; emphases mine).

Thirdly, Luke gives us a glimpse of **double problems** on that night (vv. 21-23, 24-30), the first is betrayal, the second pride.

Luke's arrangement is striking: Jesus goes right from the word over the cup to 'But, look, the hand of the one betraying me is with me on the table' (v. 21).[18] Jesus follows this stark note

---

17. See NIDNTTE, 4:553-55, and the extensive evidence cited in Daniel B. Wallace, *Greek Grammar Beyond the Basics* (Grand Rapids: Zondervan, 1996), pp. 383-89.

18. Matthew (26:20-25) and Mark (14:18-21) both place the betrayal announcement before the 'Lord's Supper.' But Luke follows his own arrangement. Cf. Bock: 'Perhaps Luke treated the meal first and then turned to all matters discussed at the meal in order to give the meal a prominent position and to present the final remarks as a unit, as a final testament' (*Luke 9:51-24:53*, BECNT [Grand Rapids: Baker, 1996], p. 1734).

with an explanation that seems packed with both profound theology and earnest appeal: 'Because the Son of Man indeed is going in line with what has been ordained, but woe to that man through whom he is betrayed' (v. 22). Note what Jesus holds together. He assumes that divine appointment does not cancel human accountability. And yet His 'woe' may be both threat and appeal. Several years ago, I had a lawnmower that I placed on the street in front of our house for the city trash collectors to pick up. I had used it for eight or nine years, its days were numbered, and I didn't want to go to the expense of having it repaired. My 'message' to the city was: This is trash; take it away. But there was something else. Sometimes people would drive through neighborhoods on 'trash days' and pick up potential 'treasures' that residents had put out on the street—getting to them before the city trucks came by. Might be a mechanically inclined fellow who liked to fiddle with small engines. He might see my mower, load it up in his pick-up truck, and know that, with his repairs, he could get several more years out of it. All of which was perfectly fine. Its presence on the street essentially said, You can have this if you want it. It was an invitation, a sort of appeal. And Jesus' 'woe' (v. 22b) may have included something like that, as if to say: Think, Judas, of the consequences of this—do you realize what it is to step into the outer darkness?

But Jesus' announcement is a shock to the disciples (v. 23). And it seems that Luke (and the other gospel writers) wanted readers to feel the shock as well. A lot of discussion went on behind the scenes before Ronald Reagan's speech at the Berlin Wall on June 12, 1987. People at the US State Department were nervous and disturbed over the line, 'Mr Gorbachev, tear down this wall!' It was, in their view, too provocative. But Reagan was insistent: 'Of course I will say it, I mean to provoke.'[19] That, I believe, is Luke's intent with the Judas episode. He wants to provoke, to shock. He wants to show us it is possible to be one who preached in Jesus' name, who in His name cast out demons, who healed the sick (cf. Luke 9:1-6), who saw for three-plus years perfect consistency in the life of the Son of God, that it is possible to be in Christ's

19. Peggy Noonan, *When Character Was King* (New York: Viking, 2001), p. 2.

intimate group—and to have no part in Him. Luke means to unsettle us. He wants to inject some horror and dread into us lest we too commit treachery against Jesus. He wants me to see that unless upheld by grace there is no depth to which I could not plunge and no vice which I could not practice and no treachery I am not capable of.

The second problem is pride (vv. 24-30). 'Now there was also a dispute that occurred among them about which of them was to be thought the greatest' (v. 24). It seems almost flippant and trivial right after the Judas-announcement.[20] Yet not surprising. Seating (or reclining) at table tended to be geared to relative status, so table arrangement at a festive Passover could have generated a bit of a melee.[21] Jesus tells them that they are not to operate on a status-driven political model (vv. 25-26a), but rather on a 'Jesus model.' The one who reclines at table is surely 'greater' than the one who is serving, but, Jesus says, 'I am among you as one who serves' (v. 27b).

Not long after Gerald Ford became the US president he took a vacation in Vail, Colorado, to do some skiing. One night while he and his family were eating dinner, one of their dogs had an accident, and one of the red-jacketed White House stewards hurried to wipe up the mess. But Ford shot out of his seat immediately, took the towel away from the steward, and cleaned the floor himself. 'No man,' he said, 'should have to clean up after another man's dog.'[22] He was the president who cleaned up dog messes! And that's a faint echo of the pattern Jesus leaves His disciples, 'I am among you as the one who serves.'

Jesus has still more to say regarding this pride problem. But He continues by first expressing His deep appreciation for their durable companionship: 'But you are those who have continued with me in my trials' (v. 28). This staggers us. There is simply no meanness in Jesus. Here are these sometimes bickering, sometimes dense-as-a-post disciples and Jesus is telling them how deeply grateful He is for their

20. For Luke's placement of this segment in contrast to Matthew and Mark, see Bock, pp. 1736-37.

21. Alfred Edersheim, *The Life and Times of Jesus the Messiah*, 2 vols. (reprint ed., Grand Rapids: Eerdmans, 1967), 2:492-93.

22. Paul F. Boller, Jr., *Presidential Anecdotes* (New York: Penguin, 1982), p. 333.

companionship. By His 'trials' He likely means all the assaults of the Tempter as well as the ridicule and opposition of men that He has faced, and in all of that, Jesus says, you have been 'with me.' How Jesus prized these men. He never rolled His eyes and let loose a heavy sigh when He thought of them.[23]

Jesus continues in verses 29-30, and I am convinced He still has the 'pride' problem in view and is answering it. After expressing His gratitude (v. 28), He goes on:

> And I confer on you—even as my Father has conferred on me—a kingdom, that you may eat and drink at my table in my kingdom, and you will sit on thrones judging the twelve tribes of Israel.[24]

Here Jesus grants gift (29), privilege (30a), and position (30b). Since all this is to be theirs, why do they need to keep jockeying to be the top dog in the present moment? Jesus gives all that they could long for, so why go on making such a ruckus over their status now? All this should set them free to be, like Jesus, 'one who serves' (v. 27b).

Finally, Luke sets before us the **double provisions** Jesus makes (vv. 31-34, 35-38), and the first provision is the one He makes *in our failures* (vv. 31-34).

Far from enjoying the thrones Jesus promises (v. 30) the apostles are about to be Satan's playthings (v. 31). Shades of Job 1–2. 'Satan has demanded you to sift like wheat.' The 'you,' as even some English translations footnote, is plural— all the apostles. Satan is going to pick them apart. But then in verse 32 Jesus comes back to address Peter directly—the 'you' is now singular: 'But I [emphatic] have prayed for you that your faith may not fail; and you, when you have turned back, strengthen your brothers.' Peter insists on his immovable devotion to share even prison or death with Jesus (v. 33), but Jesus goes on to predict his miserable failure (v. 34).

---

23. J. C. Ryle's comments on this text are well worth reading (*Expository Thoughts on the Gospels: St. Luke*, 2 vols. [New York: Baker & Taylor, 1858], 2:405).

24. The verbs in verse 29 can also be translated as 'covenant to give.' Verse 30b is fairly akin to Matthew 19:28. I take the 'judging' in the sense of 'ruling.' The verse seems to assume a future for Israel; some interpreters seem determined to flush that possibility down the hermeneutical stool.

What a marvelous word this is: 'But I have prayed for you.' Peter apparently didn't hear it at the time. But what a boon and a balm for all Jesus' falling disciples in the messes we make! 'We have an Advocate with the Father' (1 John 2:1). J. C. Ryle calls Jesus' intercession the *one great secret of a believer's perseverance in the faith:*

> The continued existence of grace in a believer's heart is a great standing miracle. His enemies are so mighty, and his strength is so small, the world is so full of snares, and his heart is so weak, that it seems at first sight impossible for him to reach heaven. The passage before us explains his safety. He has a mighty Friend at the right hand of God ….[25]

Dr John Kennedy of Dingwall once preached on this text at a communion season and appealed to 'every tempted, tempest-tossed soul in Caithness or elsewhere … to lay all its weight on this gracious Advocate—this glorious "I"—all its guilty yesterday, all its sinful today, all its unknown tomorrow!'[26] 'But I have prayed for you.' Yes, 'this glorious "I"!'

Jesus makes a second provision *for our service* (vv. 35-38). Jesus reminds the disciples of the time/s He sent them out on missions with absolutely no 'extras' (9:3; 10:4). He asks if they lacked anything on those occasions. 'Nothing,' they answer (v. 35b). But conditions are about to change: 'But now the one who has a money-bag, let him take it; likewise also a tote-bag; and the one who does not have (one), let him sell his cloak and buy a sword' (v. 36). Then verse 37 explains (note the initial 'For …') what is going to bring about this change in the conditions of their mission: there is a Scripture that must be fulfilled in His case, namely, 'he was numbered with the lawless ones' (Isa. 53:12). Jesus refers to the cross—that will change everything (v. 37). The disciples' response, as if they had only heard half of what He said, is: 'Lord, look! Here are two swords!' (v. 38a). Jesus' response may recognize that it's fruitless to pursue the discussion further and, depending on

25. Ryle, 2:411.

26. Cited in Malcolm Maclean, *The Lord's Supper* (Ross-shire: Christian Focus, 2009), p. 150.

how one translates His enigmatic words, He seems to say something like, 'Enough of this' (v. 38b).

Instead of leaking more ink over these two swords and over what is happening in this passage, let me just trace what I think is the main stream of Jesus' argument here. Jesus gets them to acknowledge that they lacked nothing when He sent them out on those previous forays. 'But now' (v. 36a) conditions will change. Now you will need money-bag, tote-bag, an extra pair of sandals, a sword—yes, be sure to get a sword. I think Jesus is describing how they will need to be equipped when they go out in post-Golgotha (and post-empty tomb) time. Is it too wild to think of missionary journeys in the book of Acts? From here on they will need to take the normal kinds of provisions needed for such travel—and wouldn't a sword be among such equipment? Might they not have to defend themselves against thugs who try to attack them, or, if you think that too un-Christian, what of attacks by wild animals? Conditions are going to change and your preparations must take account of that, Jesus seems to say. But isn't there still a certain *logic* implied in Jesus' words, even a certain assurance? If they lacked nothing before when He sent them out, is there not a suggestion that the same will be the case even under altered conditions? Indeed, by His very instructions informing them of what they will need, is He not in those very directions supplying them with what they require for their mission? Cannot Jesus always say to us, 'You did not lack anything, did you?' (v. 35). Jesus provides for them in their service.

Let us go back to verse 37. When Jesus cited what had been written He quoted from Isaiah 53:12, 'and he was numbered with the lawless ones.' The Hebrew text is traditionally translated, 'and he was numbered with the transgressors.' It may well be that the Hebrew verb carries a 'tolerative' or permissive sense and so should be read, 'he let himself be numbered with the transgressors.'[27] By including Jesus' quote from verse 12, Luke probably intends for us to think of all of that fourth 'servant song' (Isa. 52:13–53:12). What is easy

27. Alec Motyer, *The Prophecy of Isaiah* (Downers Grove, IL: InterVarsity, 1993), p. 443.

to miss is that Isaiah 53:11-12 are Yahweh's words about the suffering Servant, spoken in the first person ('my servant,' 'I will divide'). They express Yahweh's *sheer delight* in what the Servant is going to do, and part of that delight is in the fact that 'he let himself be numbered with the transgressors' (or, lawless ones). But the disciples do not hear Scripture; they are thinking about swords. They have picked up on Jesus' allusion in verse 36 to a sword as a part of their traveling equipment and transfix on that as though it is something to be obtained immediately. In any case, the upper room ends on a sad note: there's such a contrast between Yahweh's pleasure in His Servant who stands with transgressors (v. 37) and the disciples' delight that they can already produce two swords as part of their Disciple Defense Starter Kits.

20

The Lord's Prayer and Arrest
(Luke 22:39-53)

When I was in college, I served as 'student pastor' at a small village church in central Kansas. There was an older woman in that village who was a recluse, widely known for her filthy and unkempt home. She was not a church member, but I felt that I should visit her. She offered me a seat amid the clutter and there was a round table between our chairs. As I visited with her, I noticed a mouse on that table, nibbling away at a loaf of bread. But I didn't feel that I could mention it. (I was young and nicer then.) You are familiar with the expression 'an elephant in the room', something too obvious that no one mentions; only here it was not an elephant in the room but a mouse on the table. She was likely unaware of it and I was too wishy-washy to mention it. Sometimes there are items we simply choose to ignore.

It would be nice to do that with our passage—to skate right on by a major difficulty. However, most English versions either have a footnote at verses 43-44 or place them in brackets. So it's obvious there is some problem with these verses and, though it's a technicality, we must not try to ignore it.

Some of the earlier and better Greek manuscripts do not have verses 43-44, and so some scholars doubt they are part of the original text. However, there are a number of other manuscripts that have them. If one went by manuscript evidence alone, a slight edge would probably go toward omitting the verses.

However, they reflect Luke's vocabulary and interests, and one can understand why some would have preferred to omit the verses—they make Jesus appear too unbearably human and that may have been too unnerving. Then too the structure of verses 40-46 suggests the originality of these verses since verse 43 appears as the very hinge of the passage.[1] Hence I accept these verses as an original part of Luke's gospel and base the following exposition on that position.

Luke, as Calvin might say, studies brevity. His account of the 'prayer' and 'arrest' segments is significantly shorter than those in Matthew (26:36-56) and Mark (14:32-52). Luke is not writing any 'cookie-cutter' gospel—he has his own approach, interests, and touches. The theme of verses 39-46 is prayer (the verb in verses 40, 41, 44, 46; the noun in verse 45) and the primary note in verses 47-53 seems to be the control Jesus exercises.

The first matter Luke emphasizes is **the concern of Jesus** (vv. 40, 45-46). He and the disciples arrive at the Mount of Olives (Luke does not refer to 'Gethsemane' explicitly) and Jesus commands them to 'keep praying not to enter into temptation' (v. 40). If one 'enters into' a test or temptation, it can gain such a hold that will lead one to fall away (cf. 8:13). This command is part of Jesus' standard teaching (11:4).[2] Yet there is a particular urgency for such prayer in these moments, although Peter—and perhaps others (cf. Mark 14:31)—may not have felt the necessity (v. 33). But it is Jesus' premier concern—He hammers home the same command in verse 46, a verse that shows the disciples lost their opportunity for prayer.

---

1. Raymond Brown proposes this scheme:

   A Pray not to enter into temptation (22:40)
     B Jesus withdraws from the disciples, kneels and prays (22:41)
       C Prayer: "Father, if you will it …' (22:42)
         D Father's answer: angel from heaven appears (22:43)
       C' Prayer "in agony" with sweat like blood (22:44)
     B' Rising from prayer He came to His disciples (22:45)
   A' Pray not to enter into temptation (22:46)

Dropping verses 43-44 would wreck what appears to be a very deliberate pattern. This is cited in David Garland, *Luke*, ZECNT (Grand Rapids: Zondervan, 2011), 880. On the whole, Garland's discussion is very helpful (pp. 881-84).

2. Matthew 6:13 is the fuller parallel: 'And do not lead us into temptation, but deliver us from the evil one.'

It's the sheer simplicity of it all that should impress us: 'Keep praying not to enter into temptation.' The way of protection, the way to stand, is by prayer. There is no training required for this, no series of classes to take, no need to develop greater 'coping skills.' Simply cry to God to keep you faithful in the coming circumstances. But of course if one does not recognize his dire danger, he's not going to take Jesus' word very seriously. The best attitude a Christian disciple can have is expressed in the third stanza of Robert Robinson's hymn ('Come, Thou Fount'):

> O to grace how great a debtor
>   daily I'm constrained to be;
> let that grace now, like a fetter,
>   bind my wand'ring heart to thee.
> Prone to wander—Lord, I feel it
>   —prone to leave the God I love;
> Here's my heart, O take and seal it,
>   seal it for thy courts above.

Secondly, Luke traces **the crisis of Jesus** in verses 41-44. If the disciples fail to pray, Jesus does not. Some believers, if given to honesty, may find themselves disappointed in Jesus when they read verse 42. Luke has noted Jesus' repeated announcements of His coming suffering (9:22-23; 13:33; 18:31-33; 22:15)—indeed, He seemed eager to accomplish it (12:49-50). But now, Jesus seems to draw back, He seems to waver—now that it seems near He is flinching. So we must take some time with His prayer.

'Father, if you are willing, take this cup away from me' (v. 42a). This 'cup' is the focus of Jesus' prayer. But what exactly is 'this cup'? It is not Jesus' destiny in some general way. Rather, the 'cup' image has its roots in the OT, where it appears as the cup of God's wrath and judgment upon human sin. Note, for instance, the following texts (all taken from NIV):

> But it is God who judges:
>   He brings one down, he exalts another.
> In the hand of the LORD is a cup,
>   full of foaming wine mixed with spices;
> he pours it out, and all the wicked of the earth
>   drink it down to its very dregs (Ps. 75:7-8).

> ... O Jerusalem,
> you who have drunk from the hand of the LORD
>   the cup of his wrath,
> you who have drained to its dregs
>   the goblet that makes men stagger
> ... 'See, I have taken out of your hand
>   the cup that made you stagger;
> from that cup, the goblet of my wrath,
>   you will never drink again.
> I will put it into the hand of your tormentors ...'
> (Isa. 51:17, 22, 23a).

> This is what the LORD, the God of Israel, said to me:
>   'Take from my hand this cup filled with the wine of my
> wrath and make all the nations to whom I send you
>   drink it' (Jer. 25:15; see through v. 29).

Jesus then does not quaver at death or suffering as such—He had long known and faced that, but He trembles before, now that it is near, the *kind* of suffering required, for He must 'drink' the cup of God's anger and wrath and judgment (and remember it is a proper, holy, right anger) upon human sin. The Son of God's love must drink the cup of God's wrath. Only One closest to the Father's heart could sense the horror of that—forsaken by the Father to be lost in the outer darkness. That is what was involved when 'Yahweh brought down upon him the guilt of us all' (Isa. 53:6b).

This, then, shows us the *rightness* of Jesus' request. This cringing—if we may call it that—this cringing at the prospect of absorbing God's wrath underscores the *righteousness* of Jesus and the perfection of His human nature. Jesus' request is not a blemish that mars His commitment to the work of the cross, as if He were not 'macho' enough here. Rather, His plea is the jewel of His character. For if you understand the contents of the 'cup,' then the desire to avoid it is part of His perfection. His hesitation is a godly one. There would be something wrong if He *didn't* flinch at this.[3] Look at the

---

3. 'For holiness incarnate to welcome the prospect would be unthinkable' (David Gooding, *According to Luke* [1987; reprint ed., Coleraine, N. Ireland: Myrtlefield Trust, 2013], p. 354).

prayers of the righteous in the Psalms (e.g., 6, 13, 30, 71, 88, 102). For them what is the ultimate, the one unbearable terror? To be cut off from the light of God's face, to be under some outpouring of His anger—and it is the passion of the godly man to be free of that; that is the one thing the godly man does *not* want. How then could Jesus be a perfectly righteous Savior if He did not abominate such a portion and plead to escape it?[4] His plea is not a blemish on His perfection but a sign of it.

And yet ... if we must insist on the rightness of Jesus' prayer in verse 42a, we must also recognize the *victory* in Jesus' prayer in verse 42b, where Jesus wraps His petition (42a) in His submission (42b). '"Thy will be done," was the cry of the conqueror.'[5]

We should pause here to note the deep irony about the 'cups' in this chapter. The cup in our Lord's Supper (see v. 20) is usually thought to be the equivalent of the third cup in the Jewish Passover celebration. It was called 'the cup of blessing.' Here in verse 42 Jesus prepared Himself to drink 'the cup of God's wrath.' He drinks the cup of wrath in order that He can offer us the cup of blessing. How solemn it is to think that the trembling and stainless soul of Jesus is to be cast into the outer darkness for me, who can barely muster mild disgust over my own sin.

Now in verses 43-44 Luke describes the *answer* to Jesus' prayer:

> Now an angel appeared to him from heaven strengthening him. And being in anguish he prayed all the more intensely; and his sweat became like clots of blood falling down on the ground.

---

4. If that cup is the cup of God's wrath against our sin, then in lonely Gethsemane you already see the lurid shadows of hell. If you understand what is behind Jesus' petition, then you must understand that Jesus literally went to the cross for the hell of it. So if you love Jesus, don't ever make jokes about hell. If you yourself ever claim that in some experience you 'went through hell,' you had better realize you are speaking metaphorically. For you haven't the least idea what hell is—but Jesus does. And since this 'cup' is unique, Gethsemane is unique. We can truthfully say that the believer has no Gethsemanes. To suggest that any of us does is almost blasphemous. Some of us may conceivably suffer more physical pain than Jesus did in His death. But none of God's people has ever drunk the Gethsemane cup. Only Jesus has a Gethsemane.

5. Gooding, p. 355.

Here was heaven's help in Jesus' trouble (v. 43), but note that the 'strengthening' did not bring relief from the trial but more anguish and increasing intensity in prayer, with severe physical manifestations (v. 44).[6] The trial did not cease but Jesus is fortified to go on walking through the trial. One cannot help but think of Hebrews 5:7.

One of the stories about Dr John 'Rabbi' Duncan is of how he went into the vestry of Rev. James Robertson one Sunday. Robertson had been preaching a sermon series on angels and Dr Duncan asked, 'Will you be so kind as to let me know when you are going to take up the case of my favorite angel?' 'But who is he, Doctor?,' the pastor probed. 'Ah! Guess that,' came the reply. 'But I can't tell you his name,' Dr Duncan went on. 'He is an *anonymous* angel, mine—guess him—eh?' Robertson gave up and Rabbi Duncan told him: 'It's the one who came down in Gethsemane, and "strengthened" my Lord to go through His agony for me, that He might get forward to the cross and finish my redemption there. I have an extraordinary love for that one ....'[7] Hard to argue with that.

Is there not an 'overflow' we can read off from Jesus' experience? No disputing that Jesus' anguish is unique to Him. But isn't the pattern of His experience something that recurs in the lives of His people? How often they find heaven's resources suddenly appear for earth's emergencies. And—as with Jesus—not to give them escape from those emergencies but rather endurance to ride them out. How often Christ's people are pressed hard and seem to be hanging on by their fingernails. It's like the scene in Interpreter's House in Bunyan's classic: fire burning against a wall and one standing in front pitching water on it to extinguish it, but it keeps burning higher and hotter. Go behind the wall and there's a man throwing oil on the fire. 'This is Christ,' says the Interpreter, 'who continually with the oil of His grace maintains the work already begun in the heart.' For Jesus, it's an angel; for us, oftentimes the risen Jesus Himself who imparts needed strength to stand the strain.

---

6. I assume Luke describes heavy, profuse sweating in verse 44b, not bloody sweat but sweat *like* (*hōsei*) clots of blood.

7. David Brown, *The Life of Rabbi Duncan* (1872; reprint ed., Glasgow: Free Presbyterian, 1986), pp. 463-64.

We have been treading on holy ground here. In one sense, it seems like all of redemptive history is the story of two gardens: there was the rebellion of the creature in Eden, and there was the submission of the Son in Gethsemane. It took Gethsemane to overcome Eden.

The third segment of this text emphasizes **the control of Jesus** (vv. 47-53). Here it seems like all the 'wrong stuff' is happening in the garden. We commonly speak of this section as the 'arrest' of Jesus, but there is really no arrest until verse 54. What we see rather is Jesus confronting treachery (vv. 47-48), stifling violence (vv. 49-51), and exposing cowardice (vv. 52-53). In this chaos it is Jesus who is in control.

Jesus was not surprised to see Judas at the head of the crowd (see vv. 21-23). His response to Judas highlights both the hypocrisy ('with a kiss,' emphatic, v. 48) and the heinousness ('the Son of Man,' cf. Dan. 7:13-14) of his deed. Actually, Luke does not specifically say if Judas actually kissed Jesus.[8] Could it be that he simply couldn't bring himself to record it? Yet for all his treachery Judas, ironically, is a servant of truth, for 'No one in the church would have created a story in which one of Jesus' own disciples betrayed him.'[9] If the early church wanted to put the most persuasive face on Jesus' story, one of the last things they would want to do would be to tell how one of His most intimate circle betrayed Him. But here it is. It's as if the NT writers only cared to tell the truth, whether it damaged their appeal or not.

The disciples saw what was about to happen and so, even as they asked the question, they—or at least one of them—went into action (vv. 49-50a). John's gospel tells us it was Peter (John 18:10) but Luke does not specify. Probably the blow went for the head, the high priest's servant ducked, and only lost an ear—the right one (as Luke and John note). Donald Miller points out what is easily passed over:

> There was both bravery and loyalty in Peter's act. He had sworn to go to death with Jesus (22:33), and here he showed his willingness to make good on his vow. To take on an armed

8. Darrell L. Bock, *Luke 9:51-24:53*, BECNT (Grand Rapids: Baker, 1996), p. 1769.

9. Robert H. Stein, *Luke*, NAC (Nashville: Broadman, 1992), p. 560.

mob singlehanded is no sign of cowardice. But Peter's act was not one of faith.[10]

Jesus' reaction to His disciples (v. 51) is difficult to translate; it could mean something like, 'That's enough of this,' or perhaps, 'Let them have their way.' In any case, He squelches the defense. Obviously He is not stirring up any armed uprising.

Luke has a fascinating touch here. His is the only gospel that tells us that Jesus healed the fellow's ear (v. 51b): 'he touched the ear (and) healed him.' Matthew, Mark, and John all tell about severing the ear but they all go on immediately to other concerns—and just leave the ear dangling there! Only Luke tells of the healing. One wonders what impression that touch of power and compassion may have made on the high priest's slave? At any rate, it seems to me that this is one of those touches that must be historical—who would ever think to invent such a detail at such a moment?

Then Jesus exposes the cowardice of the religious leaders. For a mob there were certainly some high-class brass present. Luke specifies chief priests, temple guards, and elders. 'Have you come out as against a thug with swords and clubs?,' Jesus demands (v. 52b). He refers to how daily He was teaching in the temple complex and they made no move to grab Him. Every day, He was right there, a sitting duck as it were—they could have easily nabbed Him. But Jesus knows they were afraid of the people rioting in His defense (20:6, 19; cf. 21:37-38). Bluntly put, Jesus is exposing how gutless, what wimps, these Jewish leaders are. But more than that. He tells them, 'But this is your hour—and the authority of darkness' (v. 53b). That is a scary word. They are associated with and serving the dark power of the enemy. It should have shaken them.

During the American Revolution George Washington was constantly the object of plots to unseat him as commander

---

10. Donald G. Miller, *The Gospel According to Luke*, Layman's Bible Commentary (Richmond: John Knox, 1959), p. 157. I recall a lecture by Dr Miller to a group of Presbyterian pastors. He stated that he thought many preachers would have to apologize to Peter in glory for their sermons accusing him of cowardice. Peter (and likely other disciples) was willing to fight to defend his Lord, but what do you do when He *forbids* you to defend Him? This must have baffled and confused the disciples no end.

of the Continental army. Once, however, while he was in New Jersey, at New Brunswick, in late November 1776, Washington was handed a letter from General Charles Lee; it was addressed to Adjutant General Joseph Reed. Reed was in western New Jersey trying to rustle up more of the state's militia. Washington assumed the letter was army business and so opened it, only to discover that Lee and the here-to-fore trusted Reed were discussing Washington's 'fatal indecision of mind.' They were scheming against him behind his back. He could have exploded over this. But he did something far more effective: he simply forwarded the letter to Reed along with an apology for opening it.[11] Without any more remark on Washington's part, this would 'tell' Reed (and Lee) that all their shenanigans were known. In a sense it gave Washington a quiet control over it all. That is the impression I get from verses 47-53—the whole passage deals with how Jesus handles the various matters in the garden. Oh, He will be arrested all right (v. 54), but here in the garden He is in control. Jesus' sovereignty seems to squeak through the cracks of His humiliation.

---

11. Thomas Fleming, *Liberty! The American Revolution* (New York: Viking, 1997), pp. 209-10.

21

The Lord's Disciple—and Failure
(Luke 22:54-65)

Itry to help my wife by vacuuming the rugs and floors in line with our household cleaning regime. Recently, I had pulled almost everything off the living room rug to give it a thorough vacuuming. During that venture it occurred to me that the furniture in said room could be helpfully arranged in a different configuration. Hence I dragged the divan to a different position and three chairs likewise. The third time through she finally noticed it. Now this arrangement may prove temporary, but it demonstrates that furniture need not sit in the same old place in the same old way forever. And it's something like that with Gospel material. As noted before, Luke tends to go his own way. After the notice of Jesus' arrest (v. 54a), he turns our attention entirely on Peter and his denials (vv. 54b-62)—he does not intersperse the denials with the 'Jewish' trial as John does (ch. 18) nor does he place them after that trial as Matthew (ch. 26) and Mark (ch. 14) do; rather he tells us of Peter's failure first and then goes on to give a more concise version (vv. 66-71) of the Jewish trial than Matthew and Mark have.[1] Nothing wrong with that at all; he may have thought it would make for a more orderly, coherent, and perhaps simplified account (cf. 1:3).

---

1. On Luke's arrangement, see Robert H. Stein, *Luke*, NAC (Nashville: Broadman, 1992), pp. 563-64, 567. For a comprehensive view of the denials and Jewish trial that takes all four gospels into account, see Eckhard Schnabel, *Jesus in Jerusalem: The Last Days* (Grand Rapids: Eerdmans, 2018), pp. 232-66.

Luke then turns the focus on Peter and shows us **the sad failure of a disciple** (vv. 54-62). Peter sits among the group huddled round the courtyard fire. One of the servant girls eyeballs Peter, no doubt in her verdict: 'This fellow also was with him' (v. 56b). Peter's retort was, 'I do not know him, woman' (v. 57). It's all very close to the ban formulas uttered when someone was dismissed from the synagogue— 'We no longer know you,' that is, have nothing to do with you.[2] There could hardly be a stronger repudiation of Jesus. It was all down-hill from there. Luke's account gives one the impression of the *suddenness* of Peter's fall. Actually, it wasn't all that sudden, as Luke indicates when he says the second 'attack' came 'after a little while' (v. 58a) and the third 'after the interval of about an hour' (v. 59a). But the account is so compressed, eight and a half short verses, and the 'accusations' and denials come in such staccato-fashion that it seems like it was all so sudden.

It was a pathetic fall but a fall that landed amid the shreds of hope. For here Luke tells us something no other gospel does: 'And the Lord turned and looked at Peter' (v. 61a). Apparently Jesus was in a colonnade around the courtyard, or was being taken to another location—whatever, but He could turn and catch Peter's eye. What did Peter see in that look? Sadness? Disappointment? Grief? Compassion? Whatever it was, it was the beginning of Peter's recovery. Once Jesus had rescued Peter with the grip of His hand (Matt. 14:28-31), now He did it with the glance of His eye. No, not that Peter realized it at the time. Now he could only go out and 'burst into bitter tears' (v. 62). Grief and heartbreak and despair must have its way and time. But as he mourned and despaired, can we doubt that during that fateful week-end Peter must have replayed the moment of Jesus' look? And if he remembered Jesus 'rooster prophecy' (v. 61b), can't we assume that he may also have dredged up 'But I have prayed for you,' and 'when you have turned back, strengthen your brothers' (v. 32)?[3] I don't doubt that misery reigned but hope may have seeped through the cracks.

---

2. See Darrell L. Bock, *Luke 9:51-24:53*, BECNT (Grand Rapids: Baker, 1996), pp. 1783-84.

3. Cf. David Gooding, *According to Luke* (1987; reprint ed., Coleraine, N. Ireland: Myrtlefield Trust, 2013), p. 357: 'But now the darkness would never swallow him up

And the hope continues. For how many contemporary disciples find in Peter's story (in Peter's Jesus!) a paradigm of hope. Here is a Lord who looks on us in our failure, folly, and falseness and refuses to cast us into a landfill for miscarried disciples.[4] Yet along with the hope Peter's story urges on us a certain caution, a sanctified reticence to claim undeviating devotion. Sometimes we may pledge too much. It may be better if we do *not* sing 'My Jesus, I Love Thee.' Sometimes I cannot sing, 'Riches I heed not, nor man's empty praise' ('Be Thou My Vision') and tend to back away from 'I Surrender All.' It may be safer simply to settle for:

> O make me Thine forever,
> and should I fainting be,
> Lord, let me never, never,
> outlive my love to Thee.[5]

Luke also wants us to consider **the solid word of Jesus** (cf. 61b, 63-65). He draws attention to this overtly in verse 61. Significantly, Luke twice refers to Jesus as 'the Lord' in this verse. After Jesus' look, 'Peter remembered the word of the Lord' about Peter's denying Him three times before the rooster crowed. This refers to Jesus' prediction in verse 34— and here it has clearly and precisely come to pass. Jesus, the true prophet.

But Luke makes the same point in verses 63-65 (which is why I have retained these verses with the 'Peter section'). One could say the overt suffering inflicted on Jesus begins here. Whether the 'men' (v. 63) holding Jesus are the same leaders as in verse 52 or their toadies, they 'began mocking' Him, beating Him, then they blindfold Him and tell Him they're

---

completely: the link between Christ and him had been maintained, and Peter's faith in the truth of the word of Christ was actually at this moment stronger than ever. He had proved Christ's word to be true. And if Christ had been right about the denial, right too even about the detail of the cock crowing, he would be right in regard to the rest of his prophecy (see 22:31-32): Peter would turn again and strengthen his brethren. The memory of that assured statement saved Peter from ruinous despair.'

4. For a first-rate treatment of Peter within the gospels and beyond, see Edward Donnelly, *Peter: Eyewitness of His Majesty* (Edinburgh: Banner of Truth, 1998). For a story of a twentieth-century 'Peter,' see Faith Cook's sketch of Wang Ming-Dao in *Singing in the Fire* (Edinburgh: Banner of Truth, 1995), pp. 19-32.

5. From 'O Sacred Head, Now Wounded.'

going to play the 'Prophecy Game': someone will hit Him and He must identify the culprit (v. 64). It could well be that Luke intends 'blaspheming' (v. 65) to be taken literally and not simply as 'insulting.' In any case, they are doing what men with incurably sick hearts (cf. Jer. 17:9) love to do: inflict cruelty on the helpless.

Yet it's all ironic. Even as they treat Him as a phony prophet, in their very actions Jesus' prophecy is being fulfilled. One can scarcely read verses 63-65 without recalling Jesus' alert to the disciples in 18:32-33, which begins with: 'For they will hand him over to the gentiles and he will be mocked and insulted and spit upon ....' Here, verse 63, He is being mocked.[6] There will be more of this mockery (23:11, 36) and all else, but already Jesus' prediction is beginning to come true. Jesus' word is clearly coming to pass and yet, unlike in verse 61, Luke does not draw special attention to it; he expects the reader to remember forecasts like 18:32-33.

Sometimes things are like that; something momentous occurs and yet little special attention may be paid to it. Like an instance in American baseball. In 1952 the Brooklyn Dodgers and Cincinnati Reds were playing each other. Cincinnati's first baseman was Ted Kluszewski. 'Klu' was built a bit like a Sherman tank; he had massive arms, fully visible when he cut the sleeves out of his uniform shirt. Brooklyn's Jackie Robinson was batting and laced a line-drive single to right field, out beyond first base. Cal Abrams was Cincinnati's right fielder; he knew Robinson always rounded first base a good bit when he got a hit. So Abrams fielded Robinson's hit on one bounce and hustled a throw into Kluszewski at first base—they could get Robinson 'out' before he could safely get back to base. They could; but didn't. 'Klu' was looking down at the base (to make sure Robinson had legally touched it) and so didn't see Abrams' throw coming at him. It hit him square in the chest. It didn't even faze him.[7] What happened? Apparently, Klu picked up the ball, threw it to the pitcher and

---

6. 'He will be handed over to the gentiles and he will be mocked' (18:32) does not require that all the mocking would be done by gentiles—it can well include that done by Jewish underlings, as here.

7. Gene Fehler, *More Tales from Baseball's Golden Age* (Champaign, IL: Sports Publishing, 2002), p. 3.

the game continued. Fairly momentous or remarkable—and yet not much made of it.

That seems to be Luke's pattern here. He is low-key. Jesus' prediction is beginning to be fulfilled, yet he doesn't ring any bells. We are supposed to be alert enough to recognize it. But whether it involves the particulars of the denial of Peter or the beginning of the mockery of Jesus, he wants us to see how sure and solid Jesus' word is.

Is that critical? Seems so. It implies that if Jesus' word about denials and sufferings is true, then His assurance that 'on the third day he will rise' (18:33) is also spot on. Indeed, it should give you solid hope about everything Jesus says, whether it's 'the one coming to me I will never ever cast out' (John 6:37) or 'my sheep … will never ever perish' (John 10:27-28), or 'I am coming again and will take you to myself' (John 14:3). The solid word of Jesus is the pillow on which we rest.

22

The Lord's Trial and Innocence
(Luke 22:66–23:25)

Having to serve on jury duty is very educational. One learns—had one not known—that people lie. And sometimes our legal apparatus goes terribly amok. A few years ago a jury in Louisville, Kentucky, had deliberated for almost nine hours over two days in a murder trial before convicting the defendant of murder. They had been unable to reach a verdict, so they flipped a coin, and the defendant lost! And Luke's record of Jesus' trial(s) shows that malice, disrespect, and injustice can easily be houseguests in the sanctuaries of law. As previously noted, Luke's treatment of the 'Jewish' trial is significantly briefer than those of Matthew (26:57-68) and Mark (14:53-65), and his coverage of the 'Roman' trial lacks much of the drama and detail that John's account (18:28-19:16) supplies.[1] So Luke summarizes and selects in order to place the emphasis where he wants it, and his two major concerns are the identity of Jesus (22:66-71) and the innocence of Jesus (23:1-25).[2]

First, then, 22:66-71 focuses on **the identity of Jesus**. Come morning, the Jewish leadership carts Jesus off to their council

---

1. For a historical reconstruction of the 'Roman' trial correlating all four Gospels, see Eckhard Schnabel, *Jesus in Jerusalem: The Last Days* (Grand Rapids: Eerdmans, 2018), pp. 270-73.

2. The Fourth Gospel also underscores this latter theme (John 18:38; 19:4, 6).

chamber, perhaps to make official the deliberations from the previous night at the high priest's house (v. 54).[3] Their demand is, 'If you are the Messiah, tell us' (v. 67a). We will deal with verses 67b-68 later; but what was Jesus supposed to answer? What did *they* mean by 'Messiah'?

One often finds Psalms of Solomon 17:21-25 cited as an example of Jewish expectation, which speaks of Israel's king, the 'son of David,' who will rule Israel and overthrow their enemies. He's the king of David's line who will establish his righteous reign and settle Israel in their land (cf. v. 28).[4] However, according to Lynn Cohick, 'No single understanding of "Messiah" existed,' and she continues:

> The term 'Messiah' is found frequently in Second Temple Jewish literature, but without a commonly accepted meaning .... For most, the Messiah was a human endowed with extraordinary capabilities for leadership and holiness (Pss. Sol. 17:23-47), although some believed the Messiah was preexistent (4 Ezra 12:32; 13:26).[5]

And the separatists at Qumran apparently awaited two Messiahs, a royal one of David's line and a priestly one of Aaron's stock. And yet ... years ago, Edersheim surveyed the evidence available to him about the person of the Messiah. He said he could not claim that the synagogue taught the divine personality of the Messiah, but he did say that the cumulative evidence led him to the conviction

> that the Messiah expected was far above the conditions of the most exalted of God's servants, even His Angels; in short, so

---

3. Some raise a fuss because the gospel accounts of Jesus' trial do not mesh with the requirements set down in the Mishnah. On this matter, see ZIBBC, 1:291.

4. Interestingly, this king is also called 'Lord Messiah' (cf. Ps. Sol. 17:32); see J. H. Charlesworth, ed., *The Old Testament Pseudepigrapha*, 2 vols., 2:667n.

5. DJG, 2nd ed., 453-54. Something similar might be said for later rabbinic literature. According to Jacob Jocz, 'It must be remembered ... that the Rabbis have never worked out a consistent and systematic theory concerning the Messiah, his person, his coming, and his reign. Their ideas are confused, often contradictory and vague. On the whole, it may be said that Rabbinic notions connected with the coming of the Messiah show more signs of the play of imagination than of serious theological thinking' (*The Jewish People and Jesus Christ*, 3rd ed. [Grand Rapids: Baker, 1979], p. 283).

closely bordering on the Divine, that it was almost impossible to distinguish Him therefrom.[6]

My hunch is that Jesus' interrogators were wanting His assent to a 'Messiah' something like that.

However, they will not have to probe or dig. They receive a gift horse; there is a noose hanging there and Jesus puts His head through it. 'But from now on the Son of Man will be sitting at the right hand of the power of God' (v. 69). As if to say: take Daniel 7:13-14 ('the Son of Man') and combine it with Psalm 110:1 ('sitting at the right hand') and you have my portrait. The person from Daniel 7 and the posture from Psalm 110. But not the Son of Man 'coming to' God as in Daniel 7:13 but sitting (!) at His right hand, sharing in reigning and judging.

> They understood him to be claiming virtual equality with God, both in position and power, and they were delighted with the statement because to them it was the height of blasphemy and gave them ample grounds for having him executed. They just checked, however, to make sure that he was claiming to be the

---

6. Alfred Edersheim, *The Life and Times of Jesus the Messiah*, 2 vols. (reprint ed., Grand Rapids: Eerdmans, 1967), 1:179. Our concern here has been with the view of the Messiah in Jewish tradition. We must not forget, however, that there is a *biblical* (i.e., Old Testament) tradition about the messianic figure that does not hesitate to speak of his divine status, if not blatantly, at least clearly. It is hard to evade the import of Isaiah 9:6, when the child to come is called 'mighty God,' or when the messianic king of Isaiah 11 is called both the 'shoot' from Jesse (v. 1) but also the 'root' of Jesse (v. 10)—he is both the sprout from Jesse and the source of Jesse! Then in Isaiah 50:10 (in the 'footnote' to the third 'Servant song'), the prophet asks, 'Who among you fears Yahweh, obeying the voice of his servant?' Fearing Yahweh and obeying the Servant are placed in parallel, as if to ask whether the Servant is not on the same 'level' as Yahweh. There is Psalm 110:1, where David calls the messianic king at God's right hand, 'my Lord,' so that if he is David's son, as other texts affirm, he is also David's sovereign (see our discussion of Luke 20:41-44). The 'one like a son of man' in Daniel 7:13-14 is one whom all peoples, nations, and languages are to 'serve,' a verb used nine times in Daniel and always of 'serving' or paying reverence to deity or a purported deity (see my *The Message of Daniel*, p. 100). In Zechariah 13:7 Yahweh calls the messianic shepherd 'the man who stands next to me,' or 'my associate.' He is one 'who dwells side by side with the Lord, his equal' (Joyce Baldwin, *Haggai, Zechariah, Malachi*, TOTC [Downers Grove, IL: Inter-Varsity, 1972], p. 198). Then in Malachi 3:1 Yahweh speaks to the people of Judah and calls the Coming One 'the Lord (*adōn*) whom you are seeking' because they had been yammering for 'the God of justice' (2:17). These texts are merely a quick sampling but enough to indicate that the OT speaks of the deity of the Messiah either by assertion or by inference.

Son of God in the fullest possible sense of the term; and finding that he was, they concluded their investigation. Now they could get him executed. Ironically their execution of him would be but the first step in the process of translating their prisoner to his seat at the right hand of the power of God.[7]

They just checked—'*You*, then, are the Son of God?' (v. 70a) and received the response, '*You* [are the ones who] say that I am' (v. 70b). Clearly, verse 71 shows they take Jesus' words as an affirmation.

Scholars commonly take Jesus' response in verse 70 as an affirmation but a qualified one, as if He said something like: It is as you say, though I might have put it a bit differently. I am not convinced of that view—it seems to read a good bit of interpretive baggage into Jesus' words. I tend to think Joel Green is on the right track in taking Jesus' words affirmatively but also ironically. This fits with the way I translated above: '*You* [emphatic] are the ones who say that I am.' As if to say: You have just confessed it even if you don't believe it.[8]

But what is Luke's purpose in taking us through this interchange on the identity of Jesus? I doubt he merely wants to make us familiar with terms like Messiah, Son of Man, Son of God. I would wager it's more like a fellow who finds himself sliding off a roof and then his pants snag on a nail. Luke, I think, wants to snag you. The identity of Jesus is never just an academic matter. He wants to stop you, his reader, in your tracks and make you face Jesus' question again: 'But who do *you* say I am?' (9:20).

Secondly, Luke's major concern regarding the 'Roman' trial is to stress **the innocence of Jesus** (23:1-25). Luke hammers this home in the three-fold assessment of Pilate in verses 4, 14, and 22. The basic idea seems to be that there is 'no basis for a charge' (see v. 4), but it may be simpler and more telling to translate simply 'no guilt … no guilt … no guilt' as NASB does in these verses. That's Luke's point and he lets Pilate

---

7. David Gooding, *According to Luke* (1987; reprint ed., Coleraine, N. Ireland: Myrtlefield Trust, 2013), p. 358.

8. J. B. Green, *The Gospel of Luke*, NICNT (Grand Rapids: Eerdmans, 1997), p. 796; and Joseph A. Fitzmyer, *The Gospel According to Luke X-XXIV*, AB (Garden City, NY: Doubleday, 1985), p. 1463.

make it, including a little 'extra' in verse 15—'nothing worthy of death has been done by him.'

Death—that is the reason the Jewish leaders are here before Pilate, the prefect of Judea. They themselves do not have authority to execute Jesus.[9] So they bring Him before Pilate (v. 1).

Pontius Pilate's tenure as Rome's prefect in Judea ran from A.D. 26–36, though some recent research holds his duties may well have begun in A.D. 19. On either set of dates, to hold such an extended period of service in an area as volatile and touchy as Judea indicates that Pilate had to be several notches above a complete moron. In fact, recent studies have 'scrubbed up' Pilate's reputation somewhat, claiming that he was not necessarily the inflexible, Jew-hating rogue he has sometimes been depicted to be.[10] But today he is faced with Jesus—and with the Jewish leaders who are salivating for a crucifixion.

They state their initial charge against Jesus: 'we have found this fellow [emphatic position in the text—and derogatory in sense] misleading our nation' (v. 2a). I take the next two participial clauses as spelling out how Jesus has been disturbing or misleading their nation: 'opposing paying taxes to Caesar and claiming himself to be Messiah—a king' (v. 2b). They pitch their innuendos so as to suggest maximum danger to Roman dominance. They have twisted and turned the episode of 20:20-26 on its head to allege Jesus' seditious behavior in forbidding payment of taxes to Rome; and they make sure Pilate understands that 'Messiah' means a claim of kingship in the face of Caesar's. They have massaged the charges in order for Pilate to sense the potential threat to Rome.

Pilate asks Jesus, perhaps incredulously—'*You* are the king of the Jews?' Jesus' response is similar to that in 22:70:

---

9. A. N. Sherwin-White, *Roman Society and Roman Law in the New Testament* (Oxford: Clarendon, 1963), pp. 35-42.

10. On these matters, see David W. Chapman and Eckhard J. Schnabel, *The Trial and Crucifixion of Jesus: Texts and Commentary*, rev. ed. (Peabody, MA: Hendrickson, 2019), 158-59, pp. 196-98. For a balanced survey of Pilate and his career, see James R. Edwards, *The Gospel According to Luke*, PNTC (Grand Rapids: Eerdmans, 2015), pp. 663-66.

'*You* are saying it' (v. 3b). The pronoun is emphatic. Again, scholars dispute the exact sense. It is certainly not a denial. Jesus seems to be saying, 'You are the one saying that.' 'Jesus turns the question posed to him into an ironic affirmation about him—ironic because even though the question assesses Jesus' identity correctly, it is an identity not granted by those who ask it.'[11] It is fascinating that verse 3 contains the only words Jesus speaks in this whole segment (vv. 1-25). A mere two words in Greek: *su legeis*. So there is this relative silence of Jesus and there is also a seeming gap in the logic of Luke's account, for in verse 4 Pilate passes on his assessment to the Jewish leadership: 'I find no guilt in this man.' How could that conclusion follow merely from the brief exchange in verse 3? One senses a hiatus between verses 3 and 4. But I think this merely shows how selective Luke is in the way he tells his story. To be sure, it's likely that more was said than what Luke tells us in verse 3—something like the conversation in John 18:33-37 maybe. But Luke is not interested in Pilate's conversation with Jesus but in his verdict concerning Jesus (v. 4). So he gives the latter and omits the former even though it makes verse 4 seem abrupt. Each time, however, when Pilate announced Jesus' innocence, the Jews kept badgering him. Here, in verse 5, they assert he has been stirring up the people, 'beginning from Galilee to here.' When Pilate discovered the accused was from Galilee, from Herod's jurisdiction, he sent Him on to Herod who, conveniently, was in Jerusalem for the festival (vv. 6-7).

It is, then, second-opinion time (vv. 8-12). Pilate is not trying to 'dump' the case on Herod.[12] He is seeking advice and likely making a conciliatory political move (cf. v. 12). I will touch on Herod's hearing later, but, for the present, it turned out to be supportive of Pilate's assessment (v. 15). Herod's contemptuous attitude did not destroy his legal acumen.

Then it is time for a judicial summary (vv. 13-16), which Pilate addresses to the Jewish leaders. One could almost call it 'the case for Jesus.' First, he has made a thorough

---

11. Green, p. 801.

12. On this point, see Schnabel, *Jesus in Jerusalem*, p. 286; also David Garland, *Luke*, ZECNT (Grand Rapids: Zondervan, 2011), p. 905.

examination of Jesus in their presence (v. 14a). Second, his decided conclusion is that there is 'no guilt in this man of the things you keep on accusing [present tense—continuous] him of' (v. 14b). Third, Herod has supported his assessment (v. 15). And so, fourth, Pilate has determined to 'flog him and release him' (v. 16).[13] I may be wrong, but I think verse 16 is the first leak in Pilate's boat. My hunch is that his mention of flogging may have been intended to placate the Jews—if Jesus received some punishment, perhaps that would slake their appetite for vengeance. It is merely a tiny hint of compromise, but it augurs ill.

Pilate's intention to 'release' (*apoluō,* five times in verses 16-25) Jesus ignites his audience. 'Victorious voices' would be a proper rubric for verses 18-23. The whole mob cries out, 'Do away with this fellow, but release to us Barabbas' (v. 18). If Pilate is eager to 'release' someone, let it be Barabbas. Luke parenthetically explains that due to an uprising that occurred in the city and for murder Barabbas had been thrown in the slammer awaiting trial (v. 19). When Pilate called out his desire to release Jesus (v. 20), the crowd kept crying out (the imperfect tense here = continuing action), 'Crucify, crucify him.' For the third time in Luke's tally, Pilate announces Jesus' innocence and his own decision (v. 22). But he commits a fatal flaw. He begins his statement by asking, 'Why? What evil has he done?' (v. 22a). He is not simply announcing a judicial decision, he is debating with the accusers. And when he debates, he has already lost. 'But they kept pressing (the matter) with loud voices, demanding that he be crucified, and their voices carried the day' (v. 23). Voices—that's what did it. Case closed.

Remember, however, what Luke wants you to hear: not Pilate's concession but Pilate's thrice-repeated decision about Jesus' innocence (vv. 4, 14, 22). That is 'the gospel according to Pilate.' And believers of this 'gospel' know that the NT backs up Pilate big time. The apostles insist that Jesus' innocence in Pilate's dock was simply a part of the entire sinlessness of

---

13. The flogging in verse 16 is a less severe form than that before an execution, a sort of teach-him-a-lesson, sober-him-up sort of flogging. Still, it points to the injustice of Roman justice. If He is indeed innocent, by what right do you beat Him anyway?

Jesus' life and character (2 Cor. 5:21; Heb. 4:15; 1 Pet. 2:22; 1 John 3:5). The believer revels in this. Here is what we need, a lamb 'without blemish' (1 Pet. 1:19).

We need to go back over this passage and pick up some loose ends. One has the suspicion that, though Jesus seems mostly passive during these trials, He is, oddly enough, the judge. Hence it may be that Luke wants us to consider **the irony of Jesus** in this account.

First, Jesus places His Jewish interrogators under judgment in 22:67b-68. They are *the hardened and hopeless.* They demanded to know if He was the Messiah. 'If I tell you, you will never believe; and if I ask (questions), you will never answer.' It is useless, Jesus implies. If I tell you truth, you won't believe; you wouldn't even enter into a decent 'Q and A' session about it. You can't have the truth; you have already rejected the truth.

These Jewish leaders have had many 'soul brothers.' Arnold Dallimore tells of a skeptical clergyman dropping in on Lord Bolingbroke one day. 'You have caught me reading John Calvin,' Bolingbroke confessed. He went on: 'He was indeed a man of great parts, profound sense and vast learning; he handles the doctrines of grace in a very masterly manner.' After a sneering remark by his visitor about such doctrines, Bolingbroke insisted, 'These doctrines are certainly the doctrines of the Bible; and if I believe the Bible I must believe them.'[14] But, of course, he didn't. He was a famous infidel, who admired Whitefield, read Calvin, understood enough of the Bible and remained in unbelief. There are those for whom truth will make no difference.

Then Jesus comes before Herod Antipas (23:8-12) and both exposes and disappoints *the curious and frivolous.* Herod had long wanted to see Jesus—he'd heard so much about Him. He was hoping Jesus would do a little razzle-dazzle for him (v. 8b). It was not faith but fascination that drove Herod. He had plenty of time with Jesus—'he kept asking him (questions) with many words' (v. 9a, lit. trans.). But Jesus said nothing (v. 9b). This apparently aggravated Herod so

14. In Dallimore's *George Whitefield*, 2 vols. (Westchester, IL: Crossway, 1980), 2:268n.

much that he took the lead in mocking Jesus. To be sure, his troops joined in (v. 11), but the three participles in the Greek text in verse 11 (treating with contempt, ridiculing, placing a robe) are all *singular*, indicating Herod himself played head mocker. James Stalker has put it well:

> Such was Herod's estimate of Jesus. He put Him on the level of a new dancer or singer; he looked on His miracles as a species of conjuring or magic; and he expected from Him the same entertainment as he might have obtained from any wandering professor of magical arts.[15]

So Herod's verdict was: 'We did not think he counted' (Isa. 53:3d).

But don't think this frivolous attitude is always so blatant or erupts in such overt mockery. It may be quite subdued. For example, one can sense it in Benjamin Franklin's reply to Ezra Stiles, President of Yale, just a few weeks before Franklin died. Stiles had inquired about Franklin's religious faith and Ben responded:

> As to Jesus of Nazareth ... I have ... some doubts as to his Divinity, tho' it is a question I do not dogmatize upon, having never studied it, and think it needless to busy myself with it now, when I expect soon an opportunity of knowing the truth with less trouble. I see no harm, however, in its being believed, if that belief has the good consequence ... of making his doctrines more respected and better observed.[16]

It's a playful and humorous response. Which is just the trouble. His response is not as hostile as Herod's but just as dismissive. And, as Stalker has said, 'To such Christ will always be silent.'

Then in Pilate Jesus faces *the convinced yet compromised* (espec. 23:13-25). Not that he was convinced of Jesus' messiahship, but he was convinced of His innocence. Some of us can probably conjure more sympathy for Pilate than for

---

15. James Stalker, *The Trial and Death of Jesus Christ* (1894; reprint ed., Grand Rapids: Zondervan, 1970), p. 46.

16. Bruce L. Shelley, *Church History in Plain Language*, 4th ed. (Nashville: Thomas Nelson, 2013), p. 323.

the others. Not that Pilate was some sort of 'Mr Clean' or a 'swell guy,' but simply because we ourselves may know what it is to hold the truth yet face immense pressure to let go of it. And Pilate did.[17] The volume of the voices made his decision. His reward was calm in Jerusalem and temporary approval of the Jewish leadership. He traded conviction for a bowl of Jewish stew (cf. Gen. 25:29-34). And every Lord's Day is a day of infamy for Pilate, as thousands of Jesus' people stand to confess their faith and declare that He 'suffered under Pontius Pilate.'

---

17. One thinks of the Protestant Henry of Navarre, who became heir to the French throne and, after several years of war (1590-92), managed to nail down his power throughout most of France. Except where it mattered most—Paris, still controlled by the Catholic League. And so in 1593 Henry abandoned the Protestant faith and entered the Church of Rome (Nick Needham, *2,000 Years of Christ's Power*, 4 vols. [Fearn, Ross-shire: Christian Focus Publications, 2016], 3:343-46). His alleged explanation was: 'Paris is well worth a mass.'

23

The Lord's Death—and Victory
(Luke 23:26-49)

It was the first pastorate. I was doing some pastoral calling. I must've gotten the wrong house—he was not one of our church members. But he seemed glad to see me and invited me in. Probably about eighty, a retired lawyer, with the unlikely name of Smith. In course of conversation he told me of how he had once suggested to a minister that he preach on the words of Hosea 2:15, 'And make the Valley of Achor [trouble] a door of hope.' And, according to my new friend's report, the minister exclaimed, 'Oh, Smith, that's too big, that's too big!' Surely the reaction one should have coming on to Luke 23:26-49, a text that makes pygmies of all expositors.

Yet one must try. We begin, then, by noting that in his story of Jesus' death Luke sometimes follows his own preferences. No need to speculate about 'sources,' but verses 27-31, 34a, and 39-43 do not appear in other gospel accounts.[1] I think highlighting the key moments in Luke's story is the best way to cover most of the text.

First, we meet with **prophecy** (vv. 27-31). The guards commandeered Simon from Cyrene to carry the cross-piece for Jesus (v. 26). After this Jesus apparently recovered enough

---

1. This is simply basic. To see all twenty-three of Luke's distinctives, see Darrell L. Bock, *Luke 9:51-24:53*, BECNT (Grand Rapids: Baker, 1996), pp. 1837-38. For a helpful 'take' on the structure of the passage, see David E. Garland, *Luke*, ZECNT (Grand Rapids: Zondervan, 2011), p. 916.

strength to respond to the women who were 'mourning and lamenting over him' (v. 27b). These women were not disciples but were expressing sympathy for Jesus. Even if this grieving was partly customary, it could yet be genuine. Jesus turns and speaks to them:

> Daughters of Jerusalem, don't weep over me but weep over yourselves and over your children, because, look, days are coming when they will say, 'How happy the barren women and the wombs that have not given birth and the breasts that have not nursed.' Then they will begin to say to the mountains, 'Fall on us!', and to the hills, 'Cover us up!', because if they do these things when the wood is green, what can happen when it is dry? (vv. 28b-31).

These coming days are days of twisted blessings when barren, infertile, non-nursing women will be considered lucky because they are free of caring for infants and children in such severe conditions. And devastations will be so dire that people—a la Hosea 10:8—crave obliteration rather than to endure such ravages. In verse 31 Jesus may be identifying Himself with the 'green wood': 'If they do these things with the green wood, what can happen when it is dry?' That is, when conditions are truly ripe for the holocaust of judgment.

I think Jesus is prophesying of the conditions the Jews will endure forty years after His death, when the Romans will suppress the Jewish revolt of A.D. 66-70. Conditions will become beyond horrible for those besieged within Jerusalem. Josephus describes some of it. People were rabid for food; attacking one another, bursting into homes where they suspected there might be scraps. Catching and eating the 'most sordid' animals, even chewing belts and shoes and ripping leather off their shields to gnaw. Josephus also tells of Mary, daughter of Eleazar, from the Trans-jordan. She had come to Jerusalem which had proven no refuge. If she obtains any food, neighborhood thugs come to her house every day and cart it off. Finally she becomes so desperate that she kills her own infant son, roasts him, and consumes half of him before the hoodlums arrive to rob her that day.[2]

---

2. See Josephus, *Jewish War*, 6.3.3-4.

In such extremities, women who never knew motherhood were 'blessed.'

What was the purpose of Jesus' prophecy? Was He simply bent on being sensational or terrifying? No, the severity of His prediction was meant to awaken and lead to repentance. In 1943, during the world war, the morale of German troops fighting in the Crimea and facing massive Russian opposition plummeted. Quite a number were inflicting wounds on themselves so they could be flown out of the area for treatment. Such self-inflicted wounds always left powder burns and any soldier caught in this shenanigan would be court-martialed and shot. So here was Dr Peter Bamm, the head medical officer, very carefully examining the wound in a lad's hand. He touched the edges of the wound with a swab and saw it wasn't dirt. The lad was a peasant youth, barely eighteen, hadn't even begun to shave; he'd had a few weeks of training and was sent off to the front. Dr Bamm had no desire to send this terrified boy to the firing squad. He seized his scalpel and widened the wound. Made it worse than it was! But in so doing he destroyed the tell-tale evidence that it was self-inflicted.[3] His severity was in the service of mercy. That is surely Jesus' intent in His prophecy.

> He wished to thrust the impressions of the daughters of Jerusalem down from the region of feeling into a deeper place. They had given Him tears of emotion; He desired, besides these, tears of contrition.[4]

The second keynote is **simplicity** (vv. 32-34). There are two others, criminals, to be executed with Jesus (v. 32) — and they are, on either side of Him (v. 33b). When they come to 'Skull Place,' we read simply, 'There they crucified him' (v. 33a). So stark, so unadorned, so almost matter-of-fact. Such brevity 'should warn against overdramatizing and making a melodrama of Jesus' sufferings.'[5] I want to come back to this

---

3. Robert Leckie, *Delivered from Evil* (New York: Harper & Row, 1987), pp. 543-44.

4. James Stalker, *The Trial and Death of Jesus Christ* (1894; reprint ed., Grand Rapids: Zondervan, 1970), p. 94.

5. Robert Stein, *Luke,* NAC (Nashville: Broadman, 1992), p. 588.

point later, but presently we should try to appreciate what 'crucified' involved.

The soldiers in the execution squad were not likely 'Roman' in the geographic or ethnic sense; they were likely provincials recruited into Rome's service from the general area and could include Syrians, Samaritans, Idumeans and Judeans.[6] Crucifixions took place near the most crowded roads so that the most people could see them—Rome thought this led to maximal 'deterrent value.' The procedure was horrid but standard:

> The victim was stripped of all his clothing, which increased the public abasement. Not only does the victim suffer from excruciating pain, thirst, and the torment of insects burrowing into open wounds [which he could do nothing to prevent], but he must also endure the shame of jabs of spectators poking at his bodily parts and their mocking when he is unable to control his bodily functions.[7]

Soldiers assigned to 'execution detail' might add their own sadistic touches.

There are two notes that Luke adds to this report of the crucifixion itself. They are both in verse 34. The first is *intercession*: 'Father, forgive them, for they do not know what they are doing' (v. 34a).[8] Who are the 'them'? In the immediate context, it refers to the 'they' of verses 32 and 33, i.e., the soldiers of the execution detail. Immediately after Jesus' prayer, the text refers to what these soldiers are doing—dividing His clothes. It seems to me that this context decides the 'them.' I am aware that expositors appeal to Acts 3:17 and 1 Corinthians 2:8 to try to put elastic into Jesus' words and

---

6. Eckhard Schnabel, *Jesus in Jerusalem: The Last Days* (Grand Rapids: Eerdmans, 2018), p. 307.

7. Garland, 923. See also Schnabel, *Jesus in Jerusalem*, 314-16; anyone wanting to pursue all aspects of ancient and Roman crucifixion may consult David W. Chapman and Eckhard Schnabel, *The Trial and Crucifixion of Jesus: Texts and Commentary*, rev. ed. (Peabody, MA: Hendrickson, 2019), pp. 269-681. This tome will have far more than many readers are looking for, but it is a literary gold-mine of original texts, translations, and commentary on this topic.

8. Verse 34a is a disputed text; some very substantial textual witnesses do not have it, though others do. I think the evidence gives the edge for its inclusion as part of Luke's text. For details, see Bock, pp. 1867-68.

extend them more broadly. But here I take a minority opinion; I find it hard to get around David Gooding's contention:

> This prayer, uttered in the moment of fearful pain, on behalf of those who were causing the pain, has rightly moved the hearts of millions and become the ideal which has taught countless sufferers not to yield to blind retaliation, but to seek the good of even their enemies (see Matt. 5:43-48). It detracts nothing, however, from the glory of Christ's prayer to point out that it was prayed on behalf of the soldiers who in all truthfulness did not know what they were doing. False sentiment must not lead us to extend the scope of his prayer beyond his intention.[9]

But what remarkable words! It was par for such victims to spew out the most vicious venom they could think of on their executioners, to let go with blue streaks of vitriol. Not pleasant but understandable. Yet, as Peter writes, 'When he suffered, he made no threats' (1 Pet. 2:23, NIV). Can you imagine the impression this must have made on the centurion in charge (cf. v. 47)? These soldiers had never before had a victim pray for them. If Jesus speaks as a prophet to the daughters of Jerusalem (vv. 27-31), He also intercedes as a priest for the lackeys of Rome.

The second note Luke adds is one of *helplessness:* they divided up His clothes, casting lots to see who got what (v. 34b). Here Luke alludes to Psalm 22:18 (21:19 in LXX). The sufferer in the Psalm is describing a suffering that leads to death; he has said, 'They have pierced my hands and my feet' (v. 16) and then concludes his description in verse 18 with, 'They parcel out my garments among them, and over my clothing they cast lots.' That is a picture of total helplessness, for if they even have his clothing, he is utterly destitute and *completely in his enemies' power.* For those who conjure up the Psalm, the greater 'David' is clearly experiencing the suffering prophesied of Him.[10] Prayer (v. 34a) and prophecy (v. 34b) are bedfellows at the cross.

---

9. David Gooding, *According to Luke* (1987; reprint ed., Coleraine, N. Ireland: Myrtlefield Trust, 2013), p. 362.

10. There should be no dispute now that 'pierced' is the proper text in Psalm 22:16; see Conrad R. Gren, 'Piercing the Ambiguities of Psalm 22:16 and the

Let's come back now to our initial point. 'There they crucified him' (v. 33). I've always been impressed by the sheer simplicity of that statement. It's almost as if Luke wants to stress the bare fact, that there, in that place and at that time 'they crucified him.' But surely we must not get caught up in the mere factuality of the gospel? Surely the gospel is more than historical fact? Yes, but not less. Remember how Paul begins to summarize the gospel in 1 Corinthians 15:3f.: 'For I handed on to you as of first importance, what I also received—that Christ died for our sins according to the Scriptures ....' 'Christ died,' that is historical fact. But that is not 'gospel.' There must be an interpreted fact, a meaningful fact: 'Christ died *for our sins.*' But we must not forget that the meaningful fact is not meaningful unless the historical fact is historical. And there are those who deny such a fact, as Muslims who do not believe Jesus died on the cross, or ancient Gnostics who either said that Christ left the man Jesus at his crucifixion or said that Jesus was not a human being at all but only *seemed* to have a fleshly body, or modern 'gnostics' who tell us that whether Jesus died doesn't matter so much as having an intimate, personal relationship with him.[11] But facts matter. How can you dive into a pool and enjoy a swim unless there is, as a matter of fact, water in the pool? You dare not say that the only thing that matters is that you *believe* there's water in the pool, for if in fact there is no water in the pool, your faith, for all its confidence, will be splat. 'There they crucified him.' It's a grimy, gritty, blood-soaked, flesh-mangled, dirty historical fact. And there's no hope without it.

The **mockery** (vv. 35-39) provides Luke's third keynote. One constant item in all three bursts of mockery is the

---

Messiah's Mission,' *Journal of the Evangelical Theological Society* 48 (June 2005): 283-99. On how this Psalm may be taken of both historical David and 'dynastic David,' see my exposition in *Slogging Along in the Paths of Righteousness* (Ross-shire: Christian Focus, 2014), pp. 151-53.

11. For Islam, see Daniel Janosik, *The Guide to Answering Islam* (Cambridge, OH: Christian Publishing House, 2019), 165; on Docetism and Gnosticism, cf. *2,000 Years of Christ's Power*, 4 vols. (Fearn, Ross-shire: Christian Focus Publications, 2016), 1:70-71, 101-12, and on gnostic mentality in today's church, see Michael W. Philliber, *Gnostic Trends in the Local Church* (Eugene, OR: Resource, 2011), with a tragic literary example on page 51.

sneer that Jesus should 'save himself/yourself.' The same mantra comes from the rulers, the soldiers, and one of the criminals.

The irony about this mockery is that it is *true*. Listen to the Jewish rulers: 'He saved others' (v. 35). The stress is on 'others' since they are contrasting 'others' to 'himself.' But what a marvelous testimony! 'He *saved* others' — a testimony to Jesus' power. 'He saved *others*' — a testimony to Jesus' compassion. And any half-awake reader of Luke's gospel knows this testimony is on target: there was the demon-possessed man who wrecked a synagogue service (4:31-37); Simon's mother-in-law wracked with fever and restored to the kitchen crew (4:38-39); the leper Jesus didn't flinch to touch (5:12-16); the paralytic forgiven and healed with a house needing roof repair (5:17-26); a centurion's servant recovered by a mere word of Jesus (7:1-10), while a dead man is raised by the same (7:11-17); an uncontrollable demoniac made sane (8:26-39); a desperate woman healed and comforted and a dead daughter restored to life (8:40-56). Oh yes, 'he saved others.' They were perfectly right. He didn't merely sympathize with them or aid them in some piddly, superficial way — He saved them, delivered, rescued them from their trouble. 'He saved others' — there's a good bit of gospel in the Jewish rulers' testimony. Clean testimony can come from foul mouths.

Then the squad of soldiers mock Jesus about being 'the king of the Jews' (v. 37). Where did they get that idea? If from nowhere else, it was the official charge above Jesus' head: 'This is the king of the Jews' (v. 38). Yes, how true! Oh, He's more than the king of the *Jews*, but He *is* that, after all (cf. 19:37-40; 22:29-30). And how do we know that? Why, by the 'charge' Pilate ordered posted on Jesus' cross. Rome wouldn't lie to you, would she? Jewish leaders and Roman executioners join in mockery — and in declaring the truth about Jesus.

The irony here is startling. It's like hearing,

> I wouldn't offer a cigar or cigarette to anyone I admired or loved since I would be doing them a bad service. It is universally agreed that non-smokers live longer than smokers and during sickness have more resistance,

and then being told (truly) that Adolf Hitler said it.[12] Truth comes through surprising channels, even through the abuse of Jesus' enemies.

If in one sense the mockery is true, we must also say that the mockery is *wrong*, for the mockery is based on the false conception of the mockers about what a Messiah should be or do. A real Messiah, a real king, would save himself—he would by some slick trick extricate himself from such a predicament *and* get others out of their respective jams ('and us,' v. 39). They have their conception of what a Messiah should be like, and, if Jesus does not fit that conception, He is obviously bogus. No Messiah worth his salt would ever get hammered up on a Roman cross (cf. 1 Cor. 1:23-24). Preconceptions have a power that is hard to break.

In her autobiography Agatha Christie relates that she 'never had a definite place which was *my* room or where I retired specially to write.' This caused trouble for her when an interviewer would come and want to take a photo of her at work. He/she might say, 'Show me where you write your books.' Her response was, 'Oh, anywhere.' They couldn't grasp it. Surely she had a place where she always wrote, a desk where she sat, or some surrounding she found singularly conducive. Certainly some particular spot. No, anywhere there was a sturdy table, bedroom, dining room, where she could plunk her typewriter.[13] People could not conceive this nondescript way of being a writer of mysteries.

People still have this same problem with Jesus in our own day. They have their own expectations of what a decent Messiah will be and when Jesus does not meet these expectations disappointment pervades. He doesn't bring the kind of 'fulfillment' they were hoping for; He doesn't prevent a spouse from getting aggressive cancer; He allows a child to die in surgery, though she was the object of earnest and unrelenting prayer. Then cynicism perhaps—because that's what a Messiah should do, and Jesus didn't do it.

Fourthly, we see **victory** in the Lord's death. This appears especially in verses 40-43, the repentant 'thief' (unique to

---

12. John Toland, *Adolf Hitler* (New York: Ballantine, 1976), p. 741.

13. Agatha Christie, *An Autobiography* (New York: Bantam, 1977), p. 419.

Luke), but could take in the centurion (v. 47) as well. Oddly enough, this criminal's faith is a fulfillment of prophecy. I don't mean that Luke draws attention to this, but I can't help thinking of the fourth 'Servant song' and the clip in Isaiah 53:10, 'he shall see his seed.' Evangelical expositors tend to take the words as implying the suffering Servant's resurrection, but there's a sense in which Jesus 'saw his seed' while still on the cross. He saw this criminal defy the crowd and his context and place his faith in the One who was despised and rejected by men. Already in His suffering Jesus is victor.

Notice the miracle his faith demands. Some would likely say that his faith is perfectly explainable: the fellow is about to suffer and die; that's enough to make anyone soft and religious. But no, it's not. It didn't do that for his impenitent companion (v. 39). True, the considerations of verses 40-41 should have affected that man, but they didn't. In the supreme crisis of his life, on the edge of eternity, he wants no truck with Jesus. So the mere trauma of emotional upheaval does not explain the faith of this other criminal.

The man's faith is remarkable when one ponders what he assumes and confesses. He implies the wrongness and wickedness of Jesus' opponents. That is the upshot of his rebuke to his companion: 'Don't *you* fear God?' (v. 40), i.e., 'Don't you think you should stop aping these mockers (cf. v. 39) and their scorn?' He confesses the justice of God in their own case (v. 41a). He confesses the righteousness of Jesus—'But this man has done nothing out of place' (v. 41b). He assumes the kingship of Jesus—'when you come in your kingdom' (v. 42b). He assumes he has or can have a future beyond his coming death—there will still be an 'I' or 'me' to remember. And he assumes the care and saving power of Jesus—'remember me' (v. 42b).[14] It sort of defies explanation. Here is one who believes in a kingdom he cannot see, in a King wearing a crown of thorns (cf. Mark 15:17), whose throne is a cross, whose robe nakedness, whose glory a body shredded by Roman whips (cf. Mark 15:15), whose 'court' consists of

---

14. Was it a balm to Jesus' spirit to hear His personal name spoken (v. 42a) kindly and reverently in the midst of the prevalent abuse?

caustic blasphemers, and whose enemies had apparently conquered Him. Such faith must be a miracle worked by God (John 6:44). Isaac Watts has put it well:

> While all our hearts and all our songs
> join to admire the feast,
> each of us cries, with thankful tongue,
> 'Lord, why was I a guest?
>
> 'Why was I made to hear your voice,
> and enter while there's room,
> when thousands make a wretched choice,
> and rather starve than come?'[15]

Notice too the assurance his faith receives (v. 43). Jesus (even in His suffering) seems to delight for His people to be secure in their faith. Jesus speaks to him of something certain ('Truly I say to you'), of something immediate ('Today,' as opposed to the criminal's 'when you come'),[16] of something personal ('with me'), and of something wonderful ('in Paradise').[17] The most hopeless cases seem to receive the firmest assurance.

Even before His resurrection, then, even at His crucifixion, Jesus begins to enjoy His victory, for here already at the cross He is gathering His people, a criminal and perhaps even a centurion, for it is the latter who announces the justification of Jesus (v. 47).

Finally, Luke includes **mystery** in his account of Jesus' death (vv. 44-45). They might be called signs: a scary darkness (vv. 44-45a) and a torn veil (v. 45b). I would dub the darkness a *cosmic* sign and the veil a *cultic* (related to worship) sign. There is some dispute on the meaning of these signs, which, I guess, merits calling them mysteries.

---

15. 'How Sweet and Awesome Is the Place,' *Trinity Hymnal* (1990), No. 469, stanzas 2-3.

16. Not after some period of probation; he does not say he must endure a little purgatory first; cf. Philippians 1:23.

17. Cf. F. W. Danker, *Jesus and the New Age*, rev. ed. (Philadelphia: Fortress, 1988), p. 378: '"Paradise" (cf. 2 Cor. 12:3; Rev. 2:7) is a singularly appropriate word in the context. Its ordinary meaning is "garden" or "park" such as a king would have at his disposal .... The word appears frequently in Xenophon's descriptions of the royal properties located in Persia. To be with the king in his private gardens was an indication of singular status. In the intertestamental period the term was used of the realm reserved after death for the righteous.'

First, the darkness. 'Darkness came over the whole land' for about three hours. Luke explains: 'the sun failed.' This darkness could not have been an eclipse, for Passover took place at a full moon when an eclipse would be impossible, nor would an eclipse last nearly three hours. Seems like the darkness is supernatural. I suggest there are two ways to regard this darkness. It may be meant as a harbinger of judgment. One wonders if anyone remembered Amos 8:9 there at Skull Hill that day:

> And it shall be on that day, says the Lord Yahweh, that I shall make the sun go down at noon, and I shall bring darkness to the earth in light of day.

It's part of a judgment passage (Amos 8:4-14) against Israel. Does the darkness here mean to recall that in Amos with the implication that this darkness, like that, is a prelude to (more) judgment on Israel?

I would also suggest another possibility (not necessarily mutually exclusive of that just mentioned). As noted earlier, the darkness is a cosmic sign, one in the created order. It is not supposed to happen at mid-day. Should we then see in this darkness a reversal of creation (temporary as it is), as a deliberate undoing of the normal order of things, as if creation itself is acting in appropriate sympathy with Jesus in His suffering and therefore is an evidence of the silent compassion of heaven for the Son of God in His humiliation? Is this heaven's quiet answer to the cacophony of abuse heaped on the Crucified One?

Then there is the torn veil (v. 45b), just seven Greek words in Luke's account. This is the cultic sign. I agree with those who take the 'veil' or curtain (Gr.: *katapetasma*) as the one in front of the Most Holy Place in the temple.[18] This was actually a double curtain over 90 feet high. Both its bulk and its height mean it could not have been torn by any human hands.[19] Once again, God is at work. In verses 44-45a it was God's darkness, here in 45b it is God's destruction.

---

18. NIDNTTE, 2:639-40. Some may object, claiming that no one could know of this because only the priests would be aware of it. Anyone familiar with politics today knows the answer: leaks. Priests talk—especially about denture-dropping events.

19. Schnabel, *Jesus in Jerusalem,* pp. 334-35.

On the one hand the torn veil suggests *termination*. The temple is no longer the meeting place between God and His people. That function has come to an end. Is it more negative than that? Does it point to divine judgment? Does it signify the destruction of the temple itself in days to come (think A.D. 70)? Or is James Stalker closer the mark in suggesting that it 'betokened the desecration of the shrine and the exodus of the Deity from the temple whose day of opportunity and usefulness was over'?[20] The 'exodus of the Deity.' If that is it, then it may depict something akin to the 'Ichabod' process in Ezekiel 8–11, where the prophet tracks the departure of Yahweh's glory from the temple. Ralph Alexander summarizes it (references are to Ezekiel):

> The gradual departure of God's glory began in 9:3 and 10:4, when the glory of God left the Most Holy Place and moved to the temple's entrance. God's glory departs from the temple's threshold and assumes its place on the cherubim throne-chariot. Together they go to the temple's eastern gate (v. 19), from where they will finally depart (cf. 11:22-23).[21]

On the other hand, the torn veil signifies *inauguration*. One cannot help but think of Hebrews 10:19-22:

> Having therefore, brothers, boldness for entering the Most Holy Place by the blood of Jesus—a new and living way he inaugurated for us through the veil, that is, his flesh—and (having) a great high priest over the house of God, let us draw near with a true heart in full assurance of faith ….

It is no longer a matter of only the high priest on only one day a year entering that sacred precinct representing God's very presence, but Jesus has shattered the barriers and all of His own have free and open access to the Father. The One who was despised and rejected by men has caused us to be welcomed and received by God.

There is this double mystery in Jesus' death, the scary darkness and the torn veil. Neither of them can be explained

---

20. Stalker, p. 164.

21. Ralph H. Alexander, 'Ezekiel,' EBC, rev. ed., 13 vols. (Grand Rapids: Zondervan, 2010), 7:698.

by natural means. That means *God* was there in that raucous, stinking place; God showed up at Skull Hill.

There is nothing conventional about Jesus, not even in the moment of His death. Verse 46 says that Jesus used words from Psalm 31:5 ('Into your hand I commit my spirit'), the trusting words of a believing man, at the moment of death. But He spoke them 'with a loud voice' and then 'breathed his last.' The loud voice shows that Jesus did not die of utter exhaustion; rather He apparently still had quite a degree of strength or summoned it up from an inner reservoir. So when He 'expired' or 'breathed his last,' it was a decision of His will. He was not drained of life, but He handed His life over. 'No one takes it from me, but I lay it down of my own accord' (John 10:18, niv).

We can, therefore, say that we see Jesus in this text in all four of His 'offices.' Usually we think of three offices. We see Him as prophet, declaring the truth of God in verses 27-31; we see Him as priest in verse 34, interceding for His executioners; we see Him as king in the faith of Calvary's convert (v. 42).[22] And in verse 46, with the words of Psalm 31:5 on His lips, we see Him in His 'office' of believer. The prophet had long ago depicted the messianic Servant this way, as the believer who is defiantly sure of God's help (Isa. 50:7-9). What could be better but that in our hour of death we could follow Jesus in this 'office'?

---

22. See J. C. Ryle, *Expository Thoughts on the Gospels: St. Luke*, 2 vols. (New York: Baker & Taylor, 1858), 2:463.

24

The Lord's Resurrection—and Perplexity
(Luke 23:50–24:12)

Some friends are on a trip. They will be traveling through your area on their way. Could they drop in for a visit? Of course. Then the flurry. The ironing board must be stashed back in the closet. The bed must be made. The guest bathroom quickly cleaned, the kitchen counter cleared of old mail, decorative pillows (those curses inflicted by modern decorators) back in place on the divan and chairs. Everything must be 'touched up.' Something that Luke refuses to do. He doesn't 'clean up' his story. He leaves it all as it was—with followers of Jesus who don't remember His word and disciples who are skeptics and not about to believe some whacko report of a resurrection. Which is good reason to accept Luke's testimony about Jesus' resurrection. One might dub his testimony, 'From First Night to Third Day.' And we'll try to unpack that testimony.

First, in 23:50-56 Luke shows us **the moving prelude to Jesus' resurrection**. And we find that we are amid one of Luke's 'bookends' in this segment. For devoted women from Galilee and Joseph of Arimathea are here at the end of the gospel, just as Luke has Zechariah and Elizabeth, Mary, and Simeon and Anna at the beginning (chs. 1-2). There he had depicted a faithful remnant of Israel, and, now, here are other members of that remnant at the end of the story.

Let's go to verses 55-56 and consider these women first. They were 'northern' women; they had followed Jesus down from Galilee, and they followed Joseph (and, presumably, his helpers) to the tomb. Luke is explicit: 'they saw the tomb and how his body was placed' (v. 55b).[1] That means that no 'wrong tomb' theory will wash. That's a long-standing 'explanation' for the empty tomb—the women went to the wrong tomb and found it empty and so spread the resurrection story. No, they (not just one) saw the exact location. And note that they prepared spices and fragrances (v. 56; to alleviate the smell of body decomposition)—so they did not expect a resurrection. They were only dealing with a corpse. But they were there. Love drove them.

Let's come back to Joseph (vv. 50-54).[2] What can we make of him? Strange, isn't it, that he was a member of the council or Sanhedrin but had disagreed with its decision and action (vv. 50-51)? Was he perhaps absent from that convocation because it had been a hurry-up meeting? Who would think there would be a follower of Jesus in that assembly of iniquity? Which simply shows there are servants of Jesus in unexpected places. But he goes to Pilate and begs for the body of Jesus. Apparently because of his status he can get access to Pilate. Pilate, naturally, would have never granted Joseph's request unless he first had certified that Jesus was definitely dead (see Mark 15:44-45). He made sure it was Jesus' corpse that was being handed over to Joseph.

Though time was pressing (v. 54), Joseph gave Jesus a decent burial.[3] All this was at some risk to himself. If he had been a secret disciple (John 19:38), he now flies his colors.

---

1. Jesus' burial in a separate tomb by Himself is a crucial matter. 'Had his body been flung into a mass grave [which was frequently the case with crucifixion victims] along with other bodies, it would subsequently have been impossible to point to the empty tomb as clear evidence of the resurrection. As it was, Luke carefully indicates how and where the body was laid (see 23:53) and further emphasizes that the women who had followed Jesus from Galilee saw both the tomb and exactly how the body was laid in it (23:55)' (David Gooding, *According to Luke* [1987; reprint ed., Coleraine, N. Ireland: Myrtlefield Trust, 2013], pp. 366-67). F. Bovon (*A Commentary on the Gospel of Luke 19:28-24:53*, Hermeneia [Minneapolis: Fortress, 2012], p. 348) dismisses Luke's testimony with: 'It is probable that Jesus was buried in the pit reserved for those who were condemned to death. It is far from certain that such a place had been carved into the rock ....' In the end, why is the one 'probable' and the other 'far from certain,' except that Bovon says so?

2. The location of Arimathea is still a matter of guesswork.

3. On family burial customs, see ZIBBC, 1:495.

When he got Jesus' body at the cross, people then knew; when he carefully tended and buried Him, all was now out in the open. His commitment to Jesus was now clear, but his hope was not necessarily clear. Who knows what Joseph expected at this point, if anything? And yet with guts and courage he did what he could. What we see here may be a tenacity of devotion in an absence of hope. Are we putting too many words in Joseph's mouth if we imagine him saying, 'No, I can't see ahead right now, but I can give him a proper burial; I have a tomb he can have; I don't know what I think; but there is one thing I can do, and I am going to do it.'

It is likely true for both the women and Joseph that at this point there is not much depth of faith but there is a definite warmth of love. Maybe there's some spill-over here for Christians even in our far different situations. Could you sometimes be in such circumstances that you don't know what to make of Jesus but find that you can go on loving Him? Even when faith may be weak, love can be warm.

In 24:1-9 the primary emphasis is on **the solid basis for Jesus' resurrection**. The women came very early on that first day of the week to supplement Joseph's provisions and preparations (v. 1), but Jesus did not cooperate with them. Luke makes his point nicely: they 'found' the stone rolled away (v. 2), but they 'did not find' the body of the Lord Jesus (v. 3). What a marvelous disappointment! They are nonplussed (v. 4a) and encounter a couple of messengers who rebuke and critique them (v. 5b) and then stress the word of Jesus that they had neglected (vv. 6-7) but now can remember (v. 8). What was that word? Luke has already told us in 9:21-22 and 18:31-34. But their visitors rehearse it for their convenience:

> He is not here but has risen. Remember how he spoke to you while he was still in Galilee, saying, 'The Son of Man must be handed over into the hands of sinful men and be crucified and on the third day rise again' (vv. 6-7).

The two men assume that the women had heard this teaching. Verse 8 indicates they had. But, as 18:34 shows, what is said clearly can 'go right by' someone.

A nurse who worked in a pediatric clinic sent an anecdote in to *Reader's Digest*. She was up to the gills in a busy, crazy day at the clinic. She handed a young male patient a urine sample container and told him to fill it up in the restroom. He returned to the nurses' station a few minutes later with an empty cup. 'I didn't need this after all; there was a toilet in there.' One would think the procedure there was clear enough, but, well, it 'went right by' him. It simply didn't 'take.'

So heaven's messengers place the stress on the word these women missed. And we ourselves dare not miss this—the clearest, most cogent reason for believing Jesus' resurrection is *the word of Jesus* ('how he spoke to you,' v. 6). This may serve as a word of correction in our own day. We tend to be part of a 'touchy-feely' generation; we prize the experiential, and there can be a danger in that.

There is a hymn, not so popular now but favored some years back—'He Lives' by A. H. Ackley. It begins with

> I serve a risen Savior,
> He's in the world today;
> I know that He is living,
> whatever men may say ....

Then comes the refrain which closes with

> He lives, He lives,
> Salvation to impart!
> You ask me how I know He lives?
> He lives within my heart.

That last 'lives' comes on a high 'F' note with a 'hold' sign, which a songleader may have an audience almost uncomfortably extend until 'within my heart' brings welcome relief. There's nothing wrong with that in a sense; there is an experiential relation a Christian has with his/her risen Lord. But the emphasis is on the wrong syllable, we might say. The reason 'I know he lives' is not because of my subjective feelings but because of the word of Jesus. The basis for the resurrection is the word of your Savior, not the depth of your emotion. Your life is anchored by the word of Jesus not by the intensity of your feelings. This principle extends beyond the resurrection to one's whole approach to the Christian life. You must make a practice of leaning on the Lord's word, not on your emotional barometer. If I have assurance, for example, that I will be saved at the last, it is not because I have a level of inner peace about the matter, but because Jesus has said, 'I give (my sheep) eternal life, and they will never ever perish, and no one will rip them out of my hand' (John 10:28). For there are days when I don't have inner peace and times when my emotional stability may be shot, but Jesus' word has not changed. 'Remember how he spoke to you … .'

Thirdly, note **the strange testimony to Jesus' resurrection** in 24:10-12. Luke doesn't seem to be specifically collecting data to support the credibility of Jesus' resurrection, but these verses simply and naturally supply some of it.

First, note that women are the first and primary witnesses. They came back from the tomb and told the Eleven all that had happened there. Then in verse 10 Luke names some of the women: Mary Magdalene, Joanna, Mary of James (probably his mother). Their function here is remarkable in that 'most of Jesus' Jewish contemporaries held little esteem for the testimony of women.'[4] That's simply the way it was. If a writer, then, wanted to make the 'best possible case' for Jesus' resurrection to first-century readers/hearers, he would be well-advised to leave out this bit about women being the prime witnesses. After all, why put needless stumbling-blocks in the way of your message? Why mar your case?

Somewhere I have a copy of one of John Lawing's cartoons that used to run in *Christianity Today*. They ran under the rubric of 'What if …' and often did wild take-offs on possible biblical scenes. So here are two male disciples talking about Jesus' possible resurrection and the one, who is both provoked and derisive, says, 'If the Lord really did rise, he would not have appeared first to a couple of giddy females.' That may gall today's sensitivities, but it pretty well captures the first-century frame of mind. Which leads us to regard Luke's

---

4. Craig Keener, *A Commentary on the Gospel of Matthew* (Grand Rapids: Eerdmans, 1999), p. 698; see his additional notes there; also the 'Reflections' in ZIBBC, 1:188; and on Luke's text, James R. Edwards, *The Gospel According to Luke*, PNTC (Grand Rapids: Eerdmans, 2015), p. 712.

report as reliable. For if he were simply trying to 'con' us, he would have edited out the women. But if you have nothing to hide and simply plan to tell what happened—well, you just leave them there, front and center.

Then, according to verse 11, the Eleven were a hard-sell, non-gullible bunch. They thought the women were talking 'nonsense.' Sometimes one runs on to the claim that the disciples were so enamored with Jesus and wanted Him to be 'alive' and so invented such resurrection accounts. But the text will have none of that. The disciples would have none of the-wish-is-father-to-the-thought stuff. They were as skeptical as if they had passed through the Enlightenment in advance. And if you are simply wanting to make the most winsome case, this is usually not something you let out of the bag. It's hardly a commendation to say that Jesus' disciples wouldn't believe He had risen. Unless, once more, you are only concerned to pass on an accurate account of things. I've always been impressed by the statement in the First Gospel in Matthew 28:17, when, after the resurrection, Jesus meets the disciples in Galilee. The text says, 'When they saw him, they worshiped, but some doubted.' When I have a writer who is candid enough to tell me that, I think I can trust him. So here with Luke, when he writes, 'They were not believing them.'

There is yet another piece in this strange testimony: the silent witness of the grave clothes (v. 12). Peter is probably skeptical as well (v. 11), but he nevertheless decides to check out the scene. He gets up and runs to the tomb and, when he peers in, he sees 'the grave wrappings by themselves.' He goes away 'wondering to himself about what had happened.' What was he wondering? He had two facts: (1) there was no body there, and (2) the body had not been stolen. Surely the latter occurred to him. Had thieves somehow pilfered the body, they would hardly have taken time to unwrap the corpse but would have carted off body and wrappings as well. Surely Peter could put that together and keep wondering. If there was no foul play, then what explains it all? Maybe the report of the women (vv. 5b-7)?

These three bits of 'evidence' that we've reviewed are matters that can easily be ignored. Sometimes we speed-read the text and don't think enough about what is really quite telling and is right in front of us. But we should. Sort of like Chaplain William McBryde, serving with the (I believe) Confederates in my country's War between the States. After one engagement, McBryde 'found bullet holes in his shoe, haversack, the back of his coat, the front of his vest, his sleeve, and his Bible—yet he was not wounded.'[5] Makes a fellow think, I would suppose! I imagine McBryde surveyed those bits of data and thought they were 'saying' something pretty significant. In the case of the resurrection account, these items are not likely to convince rank unbelievers. But it often bolsters the faith of the saints to see that there are marks of authenticity and reliability simply in the way the resurrection account is written and reported. There are reasons to believe Luke's account—the fingerprints of truthfulness are all over it.

But you may say, Does this resurrection-matter really matter at all? Should we get that stewed up over it? Well, let's admit that there are some matters that don't matter. Some years back Boris Becker suffered an upset at Wimbledon. The TV interviewer afterwards wanted to know 'what went wrong.' Becker's eyes grew wide in surprise: 'Wrong?,' he asked. 'Nothing has gone wrong. Nobody has died! I lost at tennis, right?'[6] But 1 Corinthians 15:17-18 says, 'And if Christ has not been raised, your faith is futile; you are still in your sins. Then those also who have fallen asleep in Christ have perished' (ESV). Unlike tennis, sounds like it matters.

5. James I. Robertson, Jr., *Soldiers Blue and Gray* (Columbia, SC: University of South Carolina, 1998), p. 180.

6. Richard Bewes, *Words that Circled the World* (Ross-shire: Christian Focus, 2002), p. 87.

25

The Lord's Appearance—and Joy
(Luke 24:13-35)

Sometimes the explanation is not complicated. Do you ever wonder (probably not, but don't be difficult) why so many Irish immigrants to the USA settled in Boston rather than New York? Seymour Morris claims the answer is simple: the boat fare was $6.50 cheaper.[1] One wonders if such is not the case with some Gospel material—like this passage that occurs only in Luke. Scholars make all sorts of complex proposals about Luke's 'sources.'[2] But one wonders if Luke might say, 'Oh, it's all quite simple: I talk to people; I ask questions; I take notes' (cf. 1:1-3). In any case, he gives us this delightful narrative of 'The Familiar Stranger,' who walks and talks with two crestfallen disciples on a seven-mile trek to Emmaus.[3] We just want to eavesdrop on the conversation, following the main movements of the text,[4] in order to pick up what Luke

---

1. Seymour Morris, Jr., *American History Revised* (New York: Broadway Books, 2010), pp. xv-xvi.

2. See the survey in D. L. Bock, *Luke 9:51-24:53*, BECNT (Grand Rapids: Baker, 1996), pp. 1904-06.

3. The location of Emmaus is elusive; see, e.g., Barry J. Beitzel, ed., *Lexham Geographic Commentary on the Gospels* (Bellingham, WA: Lexham, 2017), pp. 344-45, 522-23.

4. The narrative may have a 'chiastic' shape; see Joel B. Green, *The Gospel of Luke*, NICNT (Grand Rapids: Eerdmans, 1997), p. 842, or, for the same but not such a 'tight' structure, see David E. Garland, *Luke*, ZECNT (Grand Rapids: Zondervan, 2011), p. 949.

wants to teach us, namely, to know the person, work, and ways of a risen Savior.

The first segment of Luke's story involves **hearing the tragedy** (vv. 13-24). There was a vigorous, lively conversation going on between Cleopas (see v. 18) and his companion (another unnamed male disciple or perhaps Cleopas' wife?). They were talking about all that had happened in Jerusalem that weekend. They were 'talking and discussing' (v. 15), the latter verb (*suzēteō*) perhaps indicating 'disputing,' and at such a point 'Jesus himself came near' and joined them. He asks them about the matters they are 'batting around [*antiballō*] with one another' (v. 17). This is a lively interchange, a bit of arguing perhaps. But when Jesus, unrecognized (v. 16), inquired, 'they stood stock still' (v. 17b). Nothing but gloom.

Now we hear an extended speech (vv. 19-24), coming after Cleopas' amazement that anyone could be so 'out of the loop' (v. 18) and after Jesus' innocently naïve response ('What things?', v. 19a). So they tell Him. They confess Jesus as a mighty prophet in word and deed (v. 19b), relate His crucifixion, the guilt of the Jewish leaders (v. 20), and their own disappointed hope (v. 21). They were indeed shattered: 'But *we* were hoping that *he* was the one about to ransom Israel' (v. 21a). And rumors of His being alive did nothing to relieve their pain (vv. 22-24).

Think, however, how in one way these words must have heartened Jesus (time for rebuke later, v. 25), for they *are* confessing their faith, even in the 'down' note of verse 21 — and they are confessing this before a total stranger, which, conceivably, could have proven a bit dangerous for them. They are both sad and bold. Theirs was a shattered faith, much in the dark, and yet it must've been bracing to Jesus to hear it.

As a reader you know more than those two disciples do. As so often in biblical narrative, you have a reader's edge. You can see the irony in the whole scene, for you know *how near their true comfort was* (vv. 15-16). 'Jesus himself came near.' Jesus was there in their despair and heard it all, though they did not realize it. Could it be that way with Christ's people quite often? That in the darkness we don't see how close our comfort is? I am not proposing some flimsy optimism, but only saying there may be times when faith is beaten down and almost smashed, when faith walks in darkness without any light—and Christ has drawn near, but you do not see Him. Your darkness may be only an inch from the light.

The next section focuses on Jesus' **explaining the scriptures** (vv. 25-27). Now in our 'empathetic' age, we might expect Jesus to reply to their woebegone words with, 'I can understand how devastated and crushed you must feel.' Instead He comes back with, 'O foolish fellows and slow of heart to believe all that the prophets have spoken!' (v. 25). He takes them, then, to the source (Moses and all the prophets, v. 27a), underscores the necessity of Messiah's suffering (v. 26, and so going against the grain of most current Jewish expectation about the Messiah), and walks them through a process of biblical interpretation (v. 27). They could handle prophecies like Isaiah 9:7 and 11:4-5. But suffering? For the Messiah?

So Jesus took these two to the scriptures to show them that the Messiah *had* to suffer (v. 26). As if to say: We can't be selective, can we? We have to take in *all* the data about the Messiah in the scriptures, not only the texts of the Messiah's glory but those about His sufferings. We might wonder, then, what passages Jesus took them through. Verse 27 doesn't say. And we don't have the tapes. But I don't think a little imagination will lead us far astray.

Jesus may have begun with **Genesis 3:15**, the prophecy of the Victorious Man who will crush the serpent 'head-wise' (= totally) but the One who will first be crushed 'heel-wise.' What, Jesus may have asked, do you suppose that may involve—this promised saving figure being 'crushed heel-wise'? Doesn't that connote some degree of suffering? Right from the very first?

Have you thought (Jesus might continue) about **Leviticus 16** and the Day of Atonement ritual? Remember the two goats, the one whose blood is shed to cleanse the sanctuary, and then the live one. Remember how the high priest presses his hands down on the head of the live goat as he confesses Israel's iniquities over it and transfers them, puts them on to the head of the goat, so that when it wanders off into the wilderness, it is 'carrying away' Israel's sins? Do you think that's a picture of what Yahweh's Servant in Isaiah was to do? 'He shall carry the sins of many' (Isa. 53:12).

Might Jesus have paused at **Deuteronomy 18**, when Moses promised Israel that Yahweh would raise up a prophet 'like me' (v. 15)? Was the 'likeness' to Moses to be not only in covenantal stature (as mediator for a people) but in similar rejection, as Israel had rejected Moses in, for example, Exodus 2:13-14, 32:1, and Numbers 14:1-4? And what of the Servant of Yahweh in **Isaiah 49:4**? What about his saying, 'I have toiled in vain, for nothing and futility I have spent my strength'? That does not sound like a triumphant, victorious Messiah. Why would he likely be so disillusioned unless facing some terrible reverse?[5] And that same messianic Servant speaks in **Isaiah 50:6**: 'I gave my back to smiters and my cheeks to ones plucking out my beard; I did not hide my face from scorn and spit.' Did not something like this, Jesus may have asked, just happen in Jerusalem? He likely went on to **Isaiah 53**: 'But he was pierced through because of our rebellions, he was crushed because of our iniquities' (v. 5). Did He also take time to linger on verse 8—'Because of the rebellion of my people the blow came to him'? Perhaps long enough to point out that since this 'servant' suffered for the 'people,' therefore neither the people of Israel nor the remnant could be the Servant. He must be an individual.

Surely Jesus took them to **Zechariah 9:9-10**. Did He point out to them that the king is described as 'righteous and having been saved, afflicted and riding on a donkey' (v. 9, Heb.)? Would He ask, Why do you suppose the king had to be 'saved'? Isn't 'afflicted' an odd way to depict a king? Why would the king be 'afflicted'? Perhaps Jesus pointed out that in the very next verse 'his dominion shall be from sea to sea' (v. 10) and take the time to point out how the king's suffering experience and world-wide sway are held together in the same text!

Perhaps Jesus took them to that 'last things' passage in **Zechariah 12**, where Yahweh Himself says, 'And they shall

---

5. Though the Servant in Isaiah 49 is called 'Israel' (v. 3), he is a personal 'Israel' since his task is to restore corporate Israel/Jacob to God (v. 5). Moreover, the Servant figure in Isaiah is also a king, for the first 'Servant song' (Isa. 42:1-4) depicts his task as bringing forth 'justice to the nations,' the mission of a royal figure.

look to me, whom they have pierced through, and they shall mourn over him, as one mourning over an only child' (v. 10). Would Jesus stress the conundrum of Yahweh Himself being 'pierced,' apparently in the person of the 'him' over whom Israel will mourn? The text implies a mysterious identity between Yahweh and the Messiah and so a 'strange' combination of a divine yet suffering Messiah. Nor would Jesus pass by **Zechariah 13:7-9**, where the sword will strike the one Yahweh calls 'my Shepherd,' whom He also calls the 'man who stands next to me' as an equal associate. He is Yahweh's equal and yet he is smitten.

Would Jesus have really hammered at them like that? Why not? He must correct a gross misconception and get them to see that for the Messiah suffering *had* to precede glory (v. 26). Jesus so much as says to them: You are at sea because you don't know or believe *all* that the scriptures teach about the Messiah; and such knowledge and understanding could have relieved your difficulty and given you stability.

For our own benefit I think we should pay attention to Jesus' method here. At this point it was more crucial for these two disciples to *hear* Christ than to *see* Him. Jesus could have disclosed Himself (with an ungrammatical, 'It's me, fellows!'). But Jesus didn't give them a neat experience—He rubbed their noses in the scriptures. You must not merely get relief, you must *understand* Jesus, you must grasp what sort of Messiah He is, and you will not understand Jesus unless you go to the scriptures. Otherwise, you'll always be making Him something He's not. Here Jesus thought learning Christ was more urgent than eliminating sorrow. We usually prefer an instant solution, for Jesus to lift the sadness, clear up the perplexity, while more than that He wants us to *know Him*. So how will Jesus often relieve you? Not by some mystical experience but by dragging you into the scriptures.

The third movement in this story centers on **recognizing the Lord** (vv. 28-35). And let's admit that there are elements in the text that are beyond us. For example, Jesus' sudden disappearance when they recognized Him (v. 31). Jesus has a real body but in resurrection mode it may operate on a different principle. Verses 40-43 will stress the reality of His body; phantoms don't eat fish.

One can't help but admire the gracious and insistent hospitality of these two disciples ('They put much pressure on him, saying, "Remain with us because it's near evening,"' v. 29). Then, at the meal, strangely enough, the guest becomes the host (v. 30). Did Jesus just assume this role or did they invite Him to do so? We don't know what triggered the recognition. Perhaps the familiar manner in breaking and giving bread? Actually verse 31 simply ascribes it, via a 'divine passive' verb, to God-given sight. And then, a bit of reflection (v. 32) and they're off (v. 33). Back to Jerusalem! When they finally get back to the Eleven & Co., they receive more good news from them (v. 34). But then they get to tell their story, and the focus of their testimony was 'how he was known to them in the breaking of the bread' (v. 35b). That detail 'had clearly impressed them.'[6] They never forgot it. Whenever they recalled it together they likely said, 'Remember how it hit us when …?'

Is there some legitimate 'overflow' for us from this account? Granted, we are dealing here with a special resurrection revelation. Yet for all that what may prove encouraging for us is that Jesus revealed Himself to them in a very ordinary, mundane circumstance, a daily meal. He is not above that. If He is a risen, living Savior, He can meet His people where He chooses. And rather than some grand and glamorous occasion, it's more likely you will find Him in the most common circumstances.

I recall that around 1980 or so in the US some of our grocery stores would have a section of 'generic' products— jam, peanut butter, cocoa mix, whatever. They were all put up or packaged with plain black-and-white or yellow-and-black labels. On the label a sort of 'waiver' would be printed. Say you picked up strawberry preserves. The label on the jar would read something like: 'These preserves may have less whole fruit in them than name-brand products, but they are a good, medium-level product, suitable for everyday use.' I have always remembered exactly those last words. I don't mean it in some crass, commercial way, but there's a sense in

---

6. Leon Morris, *The Gospel According to St. Luke*, TNTC (Grand Rapids: Eerdmans, 1974), p. 341. The meal (v. 30) was *not* a Eucharist; see especially Garland, p. 955.

which our risen Savior is suitable for everyday use. This risen Savior ascended to reign at the Father's right hand, but since He is a living Savior He can still meet with His people in the most common, ordinary times, and sometimes He prefers a kitchen table.

26

Epilogue as Prologue
(Luke 24:36-53)

During the 1970s in my country was the heyday of 'Columbo' on TV (with re-runs even today). The series starred Peter Falk as Lt. Columbo of the Los Angeles Police Department. He would be in someone's home or business, in his rumbled trench-coat and with his ubiquitous cigar, interviewing someone in connection with a crime. He would turn to leave to the immense relief of the 'interrogatees' but at the last second turn back, raise his index finger, and say, 'Oh, just one more thing.' There was always 'just one more thing.' That's the way verses 36-43 strike me here in Luke 24. Verse 36 begins with 'Now while they were speaking, he himself stood among them'—and unnerved them. The two 'Emmaus' disciples had returned and were telling their story to the group of disciples, then Jesus appears. It had been a very full first day of the week, all sorts of things going on at the tomb (vv. 1-12), on the road to Emmaus (vv. 13-33a), with Simon Peter (v. 34), and now this! Everything seems to have happened in 'bang-bang' mode, and now Jesus sends them into overload. This isn't in the text, but one could almost imagine Jesus saying: I know it's been a very full day for all of you, but just one more thing.

That 'one more thing' (= vv. 36-43) was very important. And even though these verses are tied to the preceding accounts (as verse 36a shows), they also point forward as

233

we will try to argue. Clearly the other two segments of this text (vv. 44-49, 50-53) point forward to the apostles' ministry in post-resurrection time.[1] Our passage, then, is a sort of 'hinge' to Luke's Volume Two (= Acts); it's a conclusion to his Gospel but one that points forward to more to come; it's an epilogue that serves as a prologue. What matters does Luke want to stress about the disciples before he releases us from his gospel?

First, he wants us to understand **how crucial their assurance is** (vv. 36-43). We should not be surprised by the disciples' surprise, as Luke depicts it here (vv. 36-38). After all, it was so sudden—Jesus is standing there among them with His word of peace (v. 36). It scared the liver out of them (v. 37a). An unflappable rationalist might look at this and ask why the disciples were so shaken when they had already known that Jesus had risen. Well, they had had less than a day to integrate all these matters. Nor had they heard anyone knock (cf. John 20:19)—He was just there. Knee-jerk reaction chalks it up to being a spirit or ghost. Not that the disciples had a carefully worked-out system of ghostology; it was simply their immediate, terrified reaction.

But Jesus had not appeared to spike their blood pressure but to provide assurance (v. 38). And so He offered them evidence that 'it is I myself' (v. 39a). They must be convinced *that* Jesus rose, but they must also be convinced that the *same* Jesus arose as was crucified, and so He told them to look at His hands and feet (v. 39a; cf. John 20:25, 27), indeed, He made a point to show them (v. 40). And He wanted them to be sure that He was the *real* Jesus, the physical Jesus, not some 'walkabout from Hades,'[2] and so told them to 'feel' Him— feel His flesh, His bones, items always absent in mere spirits (v. 39b). They are scarcely able to take it all in (v. 41a), when

---

1. If we simply read on after verse 43, we might assume that 44-49 and 50-53 happened on that same day. But Luke does not say that. He ties verse 36 to that resurrection day ('While they were saying these things,' v. 36a), but verses 44 ('Now he said to them ...') and 50 ('And he led them out toward Bethany ...') are not explicitly tied to that first day of the week. Jesus likely said and did these things (especially the ascension!) on other occasions during his forty-day post-resurrection sojourn (Acts 1:3) with the apostles. Luke is compressing and summarizing in our text and not providing a full-blooded, explicit chronology.

2. David E. Garland, *Luke*, ZECNT (Grand Rapids: Zondervan, 2011), p. 966.

He asks for something to eat. They give Him a bit of broiled fish and He eats it right in front of them (vv. 42-43). They know spirits don't eat, let alone eat fish.

Why was this so important? Why did Jesus do this? Because if they are to proclaim Him, and even die for Him, they must be lock-down sure that the crucified Jesus is the same as the risen Jesus and have absolute assurance of His resurrection. Christianity is always like this—it deals in flesh and bones and fish and nail holes; it won't allow you to escape into spiritual ether. Biblical faith, resurrection faith, is terribly crass and earthy. And the apostles must be irrefutably convinced of it; otherwise, why preach and why die for it? So Jesus here seeks to ground them.

I remember Dr J. O. Buswell once telling the story about a fellow who lived in a boardinghouse (or some such domicile). He was outside with a sledgehammer whaling away at the foundation of the establishment. A reasonably rational passer-by attempted to caution him about his own irrationality; he was, after all, trying to destroy the very place where he lived. But the man, unfazed, replied: 'It doesn't matter—I live on the second floor.' But the New Testament will have no truck with 'second-floor' Christianity. It must begin with a solid and sure foundation, with unshakable confidence that 'he was raised on the third day according to the scriptures' (1 Cor. 15:4).

Secondly, in verses 44-49 Luke underscores **how clear their mission is**. Here Jesus gives His men a commission: as His witnesses they will be proclaiming repentance and forgiveness of sins in His name (vv. 47-48). Actually, however, He gives them and us a whole approach to gospel ministry.

Jesus mentions, first of all, what we might call *gospel preparation* (vv. 44-45). He notes the inevitable truthfulness of the scriptures, that 'all things written in the law of Moses and the prophets and the Psalms about me must be fulfilled' (v. 44). The 'must' (Gr.: *dei*) is a divine 'must'—there is no other way that it can be. And some of these things had already been fulfilled in Jesus' death and resurrection and there were other things (e.g., His coming consummating reign) that were yet to be fulfilled. Luke adds that Jesus also gave them the necessary provision for understanding the scriptures (v. 45).

Notice what Jesus actually says. He speaks of the things written about Him 'in the law of Moses and the prophets and the Psalms.' Did you notice the preposition 'in'? He is saying that there are passages and texts in all parts of what we call the Old Testament that speak about Him in some way. And, naturally, Jesus is right. There are lots of such passages. But remember the 'in.' Jesus is not saying that everything or every passage in the OT is about Him, though some contemporary expositors seem to read it that way. Sometimes one hears statements from the pulpit that 'The Old Testament is all about Jesus.' Well, yes, if that's meant in only a broad-brush sort of way. However, we shouldn't go beyond what Jesus actually says.[3]

But isn't there an inference oozing out of verses 44-45? Isn't this emphasis implying that if we are to be servants of Christ, we must immerse ourselves in the word of Christ? Even in, especially in (!), His Old Testament word. How could the apostles, how can we, be equipped (cf. 2 Tim. 3:17 in light of v. 16) if these scriptures are not the focus, indeed, the playground of the soul? How easy it is for a contemporary pastor to find that programs and administration and technology and fund-raising have come in and 'choked' the word.

As Jesus moves toward the apostles' task, He is careful to stress once more (see v. 26) a *gospel pattern* (v. 46). Verse 46 is not a complete statement in itself; it is connected to what follows. But it speaks of what even the apostles had to get seared into their minds: the scriptures say the Messiah was 'to suffer and to rise again on the third day.'[4] In that order. That is the pattern: suffering then glory (see 1 Pet. 1:11). This is something that Judaism by and large ignored. It thought

3. I think this passage is almost nonchalantly misused by some contemporary expositors who press for a thoroughly 'Christocentric' approach to OT exposition. For discussion, see my *The Word Became Fresh* (Ross-shire: Christian Focus, 2006), pp. 134-38.

4. Part of the gospel tradition Paul passes on is that 'he was raised on the third day according to the scriptures' (1 Cor. 15:4). The most satisfying treatment I have found of this 'third day' matter is, Martin Pickup, '"On the Third Day": The Time Frame of Jesus' Death and Resurrection,' *Journal of the Evangelical Theological Society* 56 (September 2013): pp. 511-42. Regarding the Messiah's resurrection itself, Psalm 16 is especially central in apostolic argumentation (Acts 2:24-31; 13:32-37); this, in my view, is very true to the OT text itself, see my *Slogging Along in the Paths of Righteousness* (Ross-shire: Christian Focus, 2014), pp. 61-66.

of a glorious, reigning, victorious Messiah. It had little place for a suffering Messiah. Yet OT passages repeatedly bear witness to His sufferings (see my brief survey of some of these in the previous chapter). By this selective emphasis Judaism let one aspect of biblical truth dominate and so distorted the whole truth.

Arnold Dallimore shared an important insight about George Whitefield in his fine biography of that man. He said that Whitefield's *Journals* led to a distorted view of his life in that they only cover matters until shortly after his twenty-sixth year. The *Journals* tell of an amazing ministry but are also marked by 'exaggerative tendencies' of youth. The material in the *Journals* was readily available, but getting information about Whitefield in his more mature and later years proved more difficult to come by. This led, Dallimore says, several authors to focus mostly on the *Journals* with the result that they depict 'Whitefield's youthful characteristics as features of his whole life.' What was omitted, then, was the man of later years, 'humbly apologetic for his earlier errors and marked by a true maturity.'[5] Therefore some writers gave a one-sided and perverted picture of Whitefield.

Jesus says the biblical texts will not allow that in His case. If not selectively interpreted, they report Messiah's suffering and glory—and in that order. Anything other is a distortion. And this 'messianic' pattern overflows into the lives of His people. Paul speaks of his passion 'to know him' (Phil. 3:10). And what does that involve? Next phrase: 'and the power of his resurrection.' Knowing Christ entails victory over sin's power and strength to triumph in even hard circumstances. Christ's power does that. But there's another 'and': 'and the fellowship of His sufferings.' Make no mistake: it is the *fellowship* of His sufferings—He is there with you in them. But there are sufferings: weakness and distress and illness and perplexity. 'Knowing Christ' involves knowing a whole Christ—both the suffering and the victory, both the weakness and the power. That is the gospel pattern, and we must hold it together.

---

5. Arnold A. Dallimore, *George Whitefield*, 2 vols. (Westchester, IL: Cornerstone, 1970), 1:7.

Then Jesus leads into *gospel proclamation*. Not only do the scriptures say the Messiah is to suffer and to rise on the third day, but the biblical program also includes 'repentance and forgiveness of sins to be preached in his name to all the nations' (v. 47). Their proclamation involves a demand — repentance. In the immediate 'Jerusalem' situation, this will require a complete reversal in the people's view of Jesus (cf. Acts 2:36-37; 3:13-15). But with the demand comes a gift — the forgiveness of sins (cf. Acts 3:19-21). But the recipients of this good news are not limited to Israel; it is for 'all the nations.'

We should pay special attention to this last item. The OT basis for it is especially Isaiah 49:5-6, a text that Simeon had in mind at the very beginning of Luke's gospel (2:30-32). In that text the Servant of Yahweh speaks, relating how Yahweh intended through Him to bring Israel back to Himself; then the Servant passes on Yahweh's very words to Him:

> It's too trivial — your being my servant
> to raise up the tribes of Jacob
> and to bring back the preserved ones of Israel;
> but I shall give you as a light for the nations,
> to be my salvation to the end of the earth (Isa. 49:6).

Yahweh is saying that His redemption plan is simply not grand enough. It must not be confined or restricted to Israel. So here in Isaiah 49:6 we see the extravagance of God, insisting that 'all the families of the ground' be blessed (Gen. 12:3) in His saving work. It is a statement of the opulence and promiscuity of grace overflowing Israel and flooding on to 'the nations.' This is where the majority of us come in, because most of us do not belong to ethnic Israel. But it will take the apostles half the book of Acts to get this program in workable form (cf. Acts 10). It took a little doing.

I remember another of those *Christianity Today* cartoons from years back. It's likely a take-off on Acts 10. Two women are walking along, and one of them is scowling and saying to the other, 'We had a pretty refined group in the Way until Peter started bringing in all the riff-raff.' Maybe so, but blessed be God, He said to His Servant, 'I will give you as a light to the riff-raff.' And so repentance and forgiveness of sins in Jesus are offered even to us.

Finally, Jesus promises His servants *gospel provision* in verse 49. They are not to go on this task on their own steam. The pronouns are emphatic: '*I* am going to send the promise of my Father upon you; but *you*, stay in the city till you are clothed with power from on high.' He is promising the sending of the Holy Spirit. Jesus does not issue a call and withhold the capacity to fulfill it. Rather, Jesus' Surrogate will equip, empower, and enable them to carry out the calling He is giving them.

So … their mission is clear (vv. 47-48); it is grounded in the word (vv. 44-46) and sustained by the Spirit (v. 49).

In the very last segment of his Gospel Luke shows **how joyful their worship is** (vv. 50-53). I think these verses are a parallel to Acts 1:9-11. His disciples are not disappointed in Jesus' separation from them, instead 'they returned to Jerusalem with great joy and were regularly in the temple praising God' (vv. 52b-53). There are several ideas we ought to notice in this section.

One is *certainty*. Jesus led them out near Bethany and 'having lifted up his hands he blessed them' (v. 50). We must not think that 'blessed' refers to religious rigamarole or some sort of pious abracadabra.[6] Think back to Numbers 6:22-27. Yahweh told Moses how Aaron and sons were to 'bless' the people of Israel. You remember how that benediction begins: 'Yahweh bless you and keep you' (Num. 6:24). But after that benediction Yahweh adds His own footnote, indicating the significance of that blessing: 'And they shall place my name upon the sons of Israel, and *I* [emphatic in Hebrew] will bless them' (Num. 6:27). The priests aren't just playing with words. Yahweh Himself goes into action with those words and makes them effective. Perhaps then even the verbal idea should be emphasized: I *will* bless them. When Jesus therefore 'blessed' the disciples does it not convey a certainty regarding their ministry in His name? If He speaks blessing, there *will be* blessing. It seems to me that with this 'blessing' Jesus is guaranteeing the ultimate success of their mission, that the process of His building His church is irreversible and sure.

---

6. The verb (*eulogeō*) is used of Jesus' blessing in verses 50 and 51, but is also used in verse 53, where I translated it as 'praising.' So Jesus 'blessed' the disciples (v. 50) and they in the temple are 'blessing' God (v. 53).

That is a superb assurance with which to go out to all the nations beginning from Jerusalem!

The second idea is *deity* (v. 52a): 'And when they had worshiped him, they returned to Jerusalem.' It appears that this took place after the moment of Jesus' ascension (v. 51). What matters is Luke's blatant assertion that these trenchantly monotheistic Jews believed in the deity of Jesus and showed that by 'worshiping him.' It is quite a note on which to end a gospel. These men had had a fair amount of time to consider in all kinds of circumstances the mystery of Jesus' person. And this is where they came out. I would hold that in this descriptive statement about the disciples' worship Luke is saying to his readers, 'And *you* should worship Him too!'

This verse suggests a matter of practical import. When folks are dealing with the Christian faith (or when we are trying to help them to do so), they shouldn't go puzzling out over 'advanced' matters, like 'What am I to make of the doctrine of the "Trinity"?' No. Start with Jesus. Let yourself mull over the enigma He places before you. Bury yourself in one of the four Gospels and try to figure Him out. There is an alluring mystery to His person that tempts you to 'put the pieces together.' Bruce Shelley's comment is very revealing:

> So far as I know, Islam has no Mohammedology and Buddhism has no Buddhology. The debate in the history of Christianity is a monument to the uniqueness of the One Christians call the Son of God.[7]

Exactly, but there is such a thing as Christology, and the disciples are at the heart of it here when 'they worshiped him.' When you come to that point and confess Jesus is divine and must be worshiped, then you go on and ask how that may affect how you are to view the God of the Bible. But don't worry about the Trinity at the outset. Start with Jesus — and see where you end up.

There's a third idea here; I almost hesitate to mention it because some might say it's just a part of the circumstantial background. But I find it striking: mixed in with the joy of

---

7. Bruce L. Shelley, *Church History in Plain Language*, 4th ed. (Nashville: Thomas Nelson, 2013), p. 117.

their worship is a note of *irony* (v. 53). They returned to Jerusalem with great joy 'and they were regularly in the temple praising God.' In the temple!

Of course in chapters 1–2 the temple is the place where one finds God's faithful remnant (Zechariah, Simeon, Anna, Joseph and Mary, and Jesus). But in 19:45-48 it is a lair of thugs and needs purged; it is the place the chief priests and scribes control (20:1), those who are the 'wicked tenants' (20:9-19); and it is the place destined to become rubble when God brings the 'days of vengeance' on Jerusalem (21:5-6). Sinister associations, horrid destiny; yet for all that, it is where the Jesus remnant gathers to worship. Seems like an ironic twist.

Allen Barra in his book, *The Last Coach*, tells of the time in the 1963 football season that Paul 'Bear' Bryant, the University of Alabama's legendary coach, suspended his star quarterback, Joe Namath. Namath was a superb player but something of a 'loose cannon' off the field, and even with two big games yet to play in the season Bryant felt he had no choice but to suspend Namath from the team. Certainly for the season, perhaps permanently. Bryant didn't relish doing this at all, but he felt integrity demanded it. Why have rules if they can be broken without consequences? Apparently, after the season was over Bryant told a sportswriter that he'd decided to let Namath back on the team. But, he told him, 'I haven't been able to reach him' (Do remember, no cell phones or internet at the time). Enter irony. Jimmy Smothers, the sportswriter in question, knew where Namath was. He had been staying in the basement of Bryant's home, thanks to the good offices of Mary Harmon, Bryant's wife. She had a soft spot for wayward Joe and had provided him with temporary digs in their basement. Right in the Bear's own home!

That's what strikes me about this last scene in Luke's Gospel. Right in the bastion of the enemies of Jesus, His disciples are beginning their mission to be His witnesses 'to the end of the earth' (Acts 1:8). A Savior who can engineer such 'twists' as this can never be vanquished. His kingdom cannot fail.

Subject Index

Scripture Index

Page numbers with the suffix 'n' (e.g. 165n) refer to verses found only in the footnotes. 'LXX' refers to the Septuagint. Pseudepigrapha are listed at the end.

Christian Focus Publications

Our mission statement —

STAYING FAITHFUL

In dependence upon God we seek to impact the world through literature faithful to His infallible Word, the Bible. Our aim is to ensure that the Lord Jesus Christ is presented as the only hope to obtain forgiveness of sin, live a useful life and look forward to heaven with Him.

Our books are published in four imprints:

CHRISTIAN
FOCUS

Popular works including biographies, commentaries, basic doctrine and Christian living.

CHRISTIAN
HERITAGE

Books representing some of the best material from the rich heritage of the church.

MENTOR

CF4•K

Books written at a level suitable for Bible College and seminary students, pastors, and other serious readers. The imprint includes commentaries, doctrinal studies, examination of current issues and church history.

Children's books for quality Bible teaching and for all age groups: Sunday school curriculum, puzzle and activity books; personal and family devotional titles, biographies and inspirational stories — because you are never too young to know Jesus!

Christian Focus Publications Ltd,
Geanies House, Fearn, Ross-shire,
IV20 1TW, Scotland, United Kingdom.
www.christianfocus.com
blog.christianfocus.com